PARADIGMS IN MODERN
COMPARATIVE LAW

This book uses the philosophy of Thomas Kuh   ..sion of
the development of European comparative law that will challenge and inspire
scholars in the field.

With the 'empathic' use of some ideas from Kuhn's theories on the
history of science – paradigm, paradigm-shift, puzzle-solving research and
incommensurability – the book rethinks the modern history of European
comparative law from the late nineteenth century to the modern day.

It argues that three major paradigms determine modern comparative law:

- historical and comparative jurisprudence,
- droit comparé, and
- post-World War II comparative law.

It concludes that contemporary methodological trends are not signs of a
paradigm-shift toward a postmodern and culturalist understanding of comparative law, but that the new approach spreads the idea of methodological plurality.

European Academy of Legal Theory Monograph Series: Volume 16

EUROPEAN ACADEMY OF LEGAL THEORY MONOGRAPH SERIES

General Editors
Professor Mark Van Hoecke
Professor François Ost

Titles in this Series

Moral Conflict and Legal Reasoning
Scott Veitch

The Harmonisation of European Private Law
Edited by Mark Van Hoecke & Francois Ost

On Law and Legal Reasoning
Fernando Atria

Law as Communication
Mark Van Hoecke

Legisprudence
Edited by Luc Wintgens

Epistemology and Methodology of Comparative Law
Edited by Mark van Hoecke

Making the Law Explicit.
The Normativity of Legal Argumentation
Matthias Klatt

The Policy of Law
A Legal Theoretical Framework
Mauro Zamboni

Methodologies of Legal Research
Which Kind of Method for What Kind of Discipline?
Edited by Mark van Hoecke

Objectivity in Law and Legal Reasoning
Edited by Jaakko Husa and Mark van Hoecke

An Introduction to Comparative Law Theory and Method
Geoffrey Samuel

The Tapestry of Reason
An Inquiry into the Nature of Coherence and its Role in Legal Argument
Amalia Amaya

Democracy and Ontology
Agonism between Political Liberalism, Foucault and Psychoanalysis
Irena Rosenthal

Global Constitutionalism and Its Challenges to Westphalian Constitutional Law
Martin Belov

Legal Validity: The Fabric of Justice
Maris Köpcke Tinturé

Paradigms in Modern European Comparative Law: A History
Balázs Fekete

Paradigms in Modern European Comparative Law

A History

Balázs Fekete

·HART·

OXFORD · LONDON · NEW YORK · NEW DELHI · SYDNEY

HART PUBLISHING

Bloomsbury Publishing Plc

Kemp House, Chawley Park, Cumnor Hill, Oxford, OX2 9PH, UK

1385 Broadway, New York, NY 10018, USA

29 Earlsfort Terrace, Dublin 2, Ireland

HART PUBLISHING, the Hart/Stag logo, BLOOMSBURY and the Diana logo are
trademarks of Bloomsbury Publishing Plc

First published in Great Britain 2021

First published in hardback, 2021

Paperback edition, 2022

A catalogue record for this book is available from the British Library.

Library of Congress Cataloging-in-Publication data

Names: Fekete, Balázs, 1980- author.

Title: Paradigms in modern European comparative law : a history / Balázs Fekete.

Description: Oxford, UK ; New York, NY : Hart Publishing, an imprint of Bloomsbury Publishing, 2021. |
Series: European academy of legal theory monograph series ; volume 16 |
Includes bibliographical references and index.

Identifiers: LCCN 2021002366 (print) | LCCN 2021002367 (ebook) |
ISBN 9781509946921 (hardback) | ISBN 9781509946969 (paperback) |
ISBN 9781509946945 (pdf) | ISBN 9781509946938 (Epub)

Subjects: LCSH: Comparative law—Europe. | Paradigms (Social sciences)—Europe. |
Kuhn, Thomas S. Structure of scientific revolutions—Influence.

Classification: LCC KJC147 .F45 2021 (print) | LCC KJC147 (ebook) | DDC 340/.2094—dc23

LC record available at https://lccn.loc.gov/2021002366

LC ebook record available at https://lccn.loc.gov/2021002367

ISBN: PB: 978-1-50994-696-9
          ePDF: 978-1-50994-694-5
          ePub: 978-1-50994-693-8

Typeset by Compuscript Ltd, Shannon

To find out more about our authors and books visit www.hartpublishing.co.uk. Here you will find extracts, author
information, details of forthcoming events and the option to sign up for our newsletters.

Foreword

S CHOLARS ARE OFTEN under the impression that their discipline started just a few decades ago, or at least that what happened previously was largely preparing the real start in a (relatively) recent past.

Introductory comparative law books typically mention the 1900 Paris Conference as the starting point of the discipline. However, nowadays, most publications of twentieth century are considered to represent outdated views on comparative law, most notably as to its methodology.

The analysis of Balázs Fekete offers an interesting overview of the history of the discipline, including the innovative approaches of the nineteenth century, (long) before the Paris Conference in 1900. Most importantly, the author puts the varying theories and approaches in context: What were their underlying assumptions? Why did they come into being at that particular time? Against which approaches did they react and why? What were the reasons for their success and demise? To what extent were they influential beyond their country or cultural borders?

As a framework for this analysis, Balázs Fekete uses the theory of Thomas Kuhn on paradigm shifts in sciences. Whether paradigm changes in the strong Kuhnian sense, and even in the light version Fekete proposes, actually apply to the history of comparative law may still be a matter of debate, but it is certainly true that the focus of research has shifted considerably over time, and so have the methods used. Fekete shows how this focus was based on certain assumptions, goals and expectations as to the possible result of the research; in other words, how a theoretical framework or paradigm was replaced by another paradigmatic framework by scholars of a next generation.

In my view, the main focus in the nineteenth century was the search for an 'empirical natural law', the law that all legal systems would have in common. During the twentieth century this shifted to building a taxonomy of legal systems and legal families, whereas the twenty-first century seems to focus more on methodology. However, Fekete's overview appears to demonstrate that those research focuses were only an important current rather than mainstream, and co-existed for some time next to others. In most cases, they were more like research programmes without actual results. They never succeeded in establishing an elaborated theoretical framework, which could have become the paradigm for the whole discipline or a coherent set of basic assumptions on which all theories would build.

This history of comparative law, as presented by Balázs Fekete, is limited in two ways. First, it is limited to Europe. Indeed, most authors from outside this continent were educated in Europe and/or were immigrants from Europe (especially in the US since the 1930s). The 'international debate' on comparative law has mainly, and for a long time exclusively, been a European debate.

Second, comparative law has mainly focused on private law, while other fields developed later under the heading of 'comparative law': (comparative) criminal law was overshadowed by (comparative) criminology, which uses social science methods; and comparative constitutional law developed mainly during the last few decades in the US and Canada, and has links with political science and its methods. Hence, the paradigmatic frameworks in those areas are quite different from the ones in comparative private law.

Comparative (private) law also has two levels: the underlying culture, on one hand, and the legal technique, the system of concepts, institutions, principles and rules as developed and or used in a specific legal order, on the other.

For private law, virtually all state legal systems in the world have imported the legal technique of either the common law, or the French or German law and legal doctrine; or some combination of two of them, and sometimes even elements of all three. Hence, at the technical level (concepts, vocabulary, basic rules and principles), virtually all legal systems have European roots. Of course, at the level of legal culture and underlying general culture, there are important differences, and the same concepts, rules and principles may be interpreted quite differently, while the legal vocabulary will largely be the same as in England, France and/or Germany. This is particularly important in view of the fact that comparative law has, at least since the end of the nineteenth century, focused on state law only, leaving the study of non-state legal systems to legal anthropology.

For those reasons, Balázs Fekete rightly limits in this book his historical overview to comparative private law in Europe.

It should be noted that quite a few approaches in the history of comparative law were influenced by the exact sciences. In the Middle Ages, legal scholarship developed as an argumentative discipline. The use of authoritative legal sources would support a strong argumentation. For centuries the concept of 'science' was not linked to empirical evidence but to authoritative sources and their correct interpretation. This applied to all disciplines, but this conception of 'science' fitted best with theology and legal scholarship (the main authorities being the texts of Justinian and their interpretation by the glossators and post-glossators). As from the sixteenth and seventeenth centuries, exact sciences developed and the conception of 'science' shifted from sources of authority to empirical evidence. From the nineteenth century, technological developments showed very clearly the success of the exact sciences and their empirical methods, and made them a model. As a result, the hierarchy of disciplines changed dramatically. While legal scholarship had been one of the leading scientific disciplines since the eleventh century, from the nineteenth century it has regularly been criticised as 'unscientific'. Many shifts in the approach to comparative legal research may be understood as attempts to render legal scholarship more 'scientific' by following the methods of the exact sciences.

In the nineteenth century, comparative legal research originated in an attempt to exceed the pure dogmatic approaches of national legal doctrine on one hand, and the pure speculative, metaphysical characteristics of 'natural law', on the other. Some scholars wanted to replace it by a search for a kind of 'empirical' natural law. Following physics, they hoped to find basic legal concepts, institutions, rules and principles common to all societies and legal systems. In practice, this proved to be an unrealistic ambition, even when it was limited later on to the current law of 'civilised societies', which meant the Western world.

In the twentieth century, many comparative scholars dreamt of their Legal Table of Mendeleev or some comparable taxonomy of legal systems. A lot of energy was invested in drafting the perfect taxonomy of legal systems, until the collapse of the 'socialist' regimes in Eastern Europe. Strangely enough, the disappearance of *political* regimes caused the disappearance of a *private* law taxonomy of legal systems, at least of the category 'socialist legal systems'. Moreover, globalisation has turned virtually all legal systems into mixed systems. This meant the end of the focus on 'legal families'.

Methodology never properly developed in comparative law because of a lack of theoretical frameworks and a lack of clear view on research design, together with a regular change of research goals, with different kinds of research questions, requiring other methods.

As from the end of the twentieth century, competitive research financing forced lawyers to adapt to a certain extent to criteria of scientific quality developed by the positive sciences. The first one was generalisability, which almost by definition excluded purely national doctrinal research. Comparative legal research was welcomed as a way out of this problem. However, in practice, this research was often limited to a juxtaposition of legal rules and cases, without clear research questions or methods. It made comparative law more attractive for legal scholars generally, but at the same time it strengthened the need for a clear methodology.

Not only legal scholarship, but the whole of humanities and social sciences have, in the course of the last two centuries, been influenced by the natural sciences and been orientated towards a more empirical and quantitative approach. These social science methods have increasingly entered legal research, including comparative legal research. Economic analysis of law, more present in the US than in Europe, has entered legal research, including comparative legal research. Quantitative methods are no longer an exception in comparative law, not only when carrying out an economic analysis. However, quantitative methods, clearly inspired by the positive sciences, are constantly competing with qualitative methods, which are better suited to the humanities and social sciences, including comparative law.

This uncomfortable position is partly caused by a narrow unitary view on science, which assumes that one should have one and the same methodology across all disciplines, together with a naive belief that everything could be counted and that all figures and statistics would correctly represent reality. Just comparing statistics from two countries already questions this view. Moreover, law is a way of structuring reality. It is a worldview, which cannot be counted. Sometimes quantitative analysis may be useful, but qualitative research remains at the core of any comparative legal research.

This direct and indirect influence of natural sciences on comparative legal scholarship is not the focus of Balázs Fekete's historical overview, but he regularly mentions elements and developments that illustrate it.

Indeed, the same historical development may be looked at from different points of view and offer different histories. What I consider to be the most attractive characteristic of Fekete's overview is that he discusses authors and scholarly debates that have almost or completely been forgotten, and puts them into the broad history of comparative law in context. History always offers illuminating insights.

Mark Van Hoecke
Ghent, 1 November 2020

Acknowledgements

S INCE THIS BOOK is the outcome of almost 20 years of – sometimes continuous, sometimes disrupted – research and study, manifested first in a Hungarian PhD thesis in 2009 and then in a monograph based on that dissertation, published in 2011, it is simply impossible to list each person who helped me and contributed to the refinement of certain parts. Therefore, I shall only mention those whose help or assistance was surely indispensable to the entirety of my work. I should start with two Hungarian professors, Zoltán Péteri and Csaba Varga, since without their help, inspiration and support I could have never started to study the history of comparative law. I am especially grateful to Zoltán Péteri, who, as my *doctor father*, rigorously commented on and criticised my doctoral work, and those discussions contributed to the formation of my own position to a great degree. In addition, as a friend of René David, Péteri's personal stories of some comparative law congresses, seminars and other events also inspired the development of my attitude towards positioning Europe as the focus when studying the modern history of comparative law.

As for chapter 1, I am more than grateful to James A Macrum, professor of philosophy, who was kind enough to find the time to read through my ideas on the applicability of Thomas Kuhn's theses to the interpretation of the history of modern comparative law. His comments greatly contributed to the refinement of this chapter.

Professor Vittoria Barsotti from Florence also supported the preparation of this book, as she gave me the opportunity to work in her department during the summer of 2018. This was a wonderful period, and enabled me to finalise two chapters.

I am convinced that without the help and support of Professor Mark Van Hoecke, this book would have never been published. His comments and insights helped me to refine the original manuscript at many points, and, personally speaking, these comments really inspired me to do my best. The help and encouragement of the editorial team at Hart Publishing – Rosemarie Mearns, Linda Staniford and Kate Whetter – and of my copyeditor, Catherine Minahan, were also indispensable to the success of my work. Therefore, I would like to express my gratitude for their supportive and kind attitude. In addition, the help of Veronika Czina, Bálint Gárdos and Paul Berett was also essential when I was working on the earlier versions of the manuscript.

Last but not least, I should give thanks for the generous support of the Bolyai János Research Scholarship, provided by the Hungarian Academy of Sciences, as this made the completion of this book possible between 2016 and 2019.

Balázs Fekete
Budapest
1 December 2020

Contents

Author's Note

The preparation of this manuscript was supported by the Bolyai János Research Scholarship provided by the Hungarian Academy of Sciences (2016–19).

Chapters 2, 3 and 4 are based on the relevant chapters published in my Hungarian monograph on the history of modern comparative law (B Fekete, *A modern jogösszehasonlítás paradigmái. Kísérlet a jogösszehasonlítás történetének új értelmezésére* (Budapest, Gondolat, 2011) 44–159).

A slightly different version of chapter 2 was published in *Rivista di diritti comparati* in 2018 (B Fekete, 'Interpreting the History of Modern Comparative Law: Beyond Descriptive Linearity. The Case of Historical-Comparative Jurisprudence' (2018) 2 *Rivista di diritti comparati* 76–108).

Some parts of chapter 5 were published in the *Maastricht Journal of European and Comparative Law* (B Fekete, 'Inconsistencies in the use of legal culture in comparative legal studies' (2018) 25 *Maastricht Journal of European and Comparative Law* 551–64).

Introduction: Scope and Subject

I. THE HISTORY OF COMPARATIVE LAW AND
A HISTORY OF COMPARATIVE LAW

NO SINGLE HISTORY of comparative law has ever been written. This is not surprising, since comparative law has never been an obvious part of modern legal scholarship. Compared to such traditional fields of legal scholarship as private law or criminal law, comparative law has always been a blurred subject and dubious discipline since its birth. Its independent scholarly nature, its subject-matter, its methodology, its function(s) and its goals have always been doubted from various angles, and well-founded criticism has been formulated many times.[1] Thus, a constant uncertainty has certainly characterised various comparative law initiatives and their reception in the broader legal academia.

Nevertheless, there has also been a continuous scholarly interest with respect to the history of both the application of comparative methods in legal scholarship as such, and the specific history of comparative law thinking. A great number of scholarly works have been published on these issues, and the various manuals of comparative law – from the earliest to the latest – have also devoted some sections or chapters to the history of the discipline.[2] Undeniably, these all

---

[1] Günther Frankenberg submits that comparative law as a discipline has been suffering from 'inferiority syndrome', and therefore it has been considered as the 'Cinderella of legal sciences' (this term goes back to a point made by Harold Coke Gutteridge from the late 1940s). For details, see G Frankenberg, *Comparative Law as Critique* (Cheltenham, Edward Elgar, 2016) 3–5.

[2] Some examples of general accounts of this history include: J Husa, *A New Introduction to Comparative Law* (Oxford, Hart Publishing, 2015) 6–15; Frankenberg, *Comparative Law as Critique* (n 1) 37–76; V Varano and V Barsotti, *La tradizione guiridica occidentale* (Torino, G Giappichelli, 2014) 1–6; Z Péteri, 'Paradigmaváltás a jogösszehasonlításban?' in K Raffai (ed), *Placet experiri. Ünnepi tanulmányok Bánrévy Gábor tiszteletére* (Budapest, Print Trade, 2004) 228–38; K Zweigert and H Kötz, *An Introduction to Comparative Law* (Oxford, Oxford University Press, 1998) 48–61; LJ Constantinesco, *Traité de droit comparé I. Introduction au droit comparé* (Paris, LGJD, 1972) 50–161; M Ancel, 'Les grands étapes de la recherche comparative au XXe siècle' in K Zweigert and HJ Puttfarken (eds), *Rechtsvergleichung* (Darmstadt, Wissenschaftliche Buchgesellschaft, 1978) 350–60; HC Gutteridge, *Comparative Law* (Cambridge, Cambridge University Press, 1949) 11–22; W Hug, 'The History of Comparative Law' (1932) 45 *Harvard Law Review* 1027–70. Some examples of specific accounts include: I Schwenzer, 'Development of Comparative Law in Germany, Switzerland and Austria' in M Reimann and R Zimmermann (eds), *The Oxford Handbook of Comparative Law* (Oxford, Oxford University Press, 2006) 69–106; JW Cairns, 'The Development of Comparative Law in Great Britain' in M Reimann and R Zimmermann (eds), *The Oxford Handbook of Comparative Law* (Oxford, Oxford University Press, 2006) 131–73; DJ Gerber, 'Sculpting the Agenda of Comparative Law: Ernst Rabel and the Facade of Language' in A Riles (ed), *Rethinking the Masters of Comparative Law* (Oxford, Hart Publishing, 2001) 190–208; I Szabó, 'Elemér Balogh et l'Académie internationale de droit comparé' in I Szabó-Z Péteri (ed), *Comparative Law –*

are valuable pieces of the mosaic of this history, but a comprehensive work has not been published so far. Again, the lack of a comprehensive work presenting a thorough history of comparative law is not surprising, since the previously mentioned uncertainties over the nature of comparative law as a scholarly discipline may make such an endeavour almost completely unrealistic or impossible.

Due to these problematic points, this book will not attempt to cover 'the' history of comparative law; its intention is to present only 'a' history of comparative law. This means that its scope is seriously limited by its very nature, so that it is far from claiming either a universal approach or an encyclopaedic attitude. Its goal is much more modest. By identifying some relevant tenets that are able to orientate a study on the modern history of comparative law, this book aims to present one possible reading of its history. This introduction seeks to explain those tenets that provide a final system of references for this work.

II. THE DOMINANCE OF DESCRIPTIVE LINEARITY

Although the various works dedicated to different parts of the pre-modern or modern history of comparative law thinking are rather diverse in nature, they all share one specific presumption. Regardless of their actual interest and scope (that may range from the presentation of some general comparative law developments to the discussion of the oeuvre of a specific author), they all imply an understanding of the history of ideas that is based on 'descriptive linearity'. Descriptive linearity, in this context, means that these authors all assume that the history of comparative law ideas is to be envisaged as a continuous and unbroken process of evolution, and they also consider this historical process almost entirely free of any external influences, whether these come from the general historical context or from other directions, such as social or cultural transformations. In addition, most of these works simply aim to present an event, a phase, or an author from the history of comparative law in a detailed way, but other motivations – for instance, a critical reflection or deconstruction – besides the claim of a detailed description and

Droit comparé. Selected Essays for the 10th International Congress of Comparative Law (Budapest, Akadémiai Kiadó, 1978) 11–22; E von Caemmerer-K Zweigert, 'Évolution et état actuel de la méthode du droit comparé en Allemagne' *Livre centenaire de Société de législation comparée II* (Paris, LGDJ, 1969) 267–81; M Ancel, 'La doctrine universaliste dans l'oeuvre de Lévy-Ullmann' in *L'oeuvre juridique de Lévy-Ullman* (Paris, Centre français de droit comparé, 1952) 181–202; M Ancel, 'Cent ans de droit comparé en France' in *Livre centenaire de Société de législation comparée* (Paris, LGDJ, 1969) 3–21; M Rheinstein, 'Comparative and Conflicts of Law in Germany' (1934–35) 2 *The University of Chicago Law Review* 232–39; S Basdevant-Bastid, 'L'Institut de droit comparé de Lyon' in *Introduction à l'étude du droit comparé – Recueil d'Études en l'honneur d'Édouard Lambert* (Paris, Sirey-LGDJ, 1938) 11–15; Sir F Pollock, 'Droit comparé: prolégomènes de son histoire' in *Congrés international de droit comparé. Tenu á Paris du 31 juillet au 4 aout 1900. Procés-verbaux et documents* (Paris, LGDJ, 1905) 248–61.

presentation, seem to be almost completely lacking from the toolkit of these authors.[3] Hence, the usual approach to a disciplinary history of comparative law has been characterised by both the strong, almost all-inclusive influence of a linear view of the history of ideas and by the focus on how a phenomenon emerged, rather than why.

Needless to say, this approach to historical studies had already been questioned from various directions from the 1970s. For instance, Michel Foucault argued for an understanding of the history of ideas that takes into account the various ruptures and inconsistencies that occur in the evolution of human knowledge and does not regard it as a continuous and coherent evolution. Further, he also advocated a critical reading of not only sources but also their previous interpretations.[4] Thomas Kuhn developed a specific theory of the development of scientific thinking that put the internal revolutionary moments of this process into focus and also refuted the idea of a linear evolution of ideas. Even though he refined his position with respect to his original approach many times, he would never have accepted the validity of any account of the history of scientific thinking that regards it as a linear process.[5] It therefore cannot be denied that our conventional – and still popular – understanding of history and the history of ideas has been seriously challenged in the last decades, and a reflective history of comparative law cannot disregard these challenges.[6] On the contrary, it must learn as much as possible from them.

III. COMPARATIVE LAW AS A DISCIPLINE AND THE APPLICATION OF COMPARATIVE METHODS IN LAW

Perhaps the most pertinent challenge, when studying comparative law thinking with a historical scope, is the definition of the subject itself, of comparative law as a distinct field of legal scholarship. Without starting such a study with a precise definition of what comparative law is, no scholarly enterprise can make sense, since the lack of such a definition would definitely impede any analytical study of historical facts and data. The definition of comparative law is certainly among the major challenges for comparative law scholarship as, for instance,

---

[3] As a rare exception see Frankenberg, *Comparative Law as Critique* (n 1) 37–76. (Frankenberg here provides a critical reading of the 20th-century comparative law scholarship by heavily criticising universalism and functionalism.)

[4] See M Foucault, *L'archéologie du savoir* (Paris, Gallimard, 1969) 9–28.

[5] For a contemporary discussion focusing on the entirety of Kuhn's oeuvre see JA Marcum, *Thomas Kuhn's Revolutions. A Historical and an Evolutionary Philosophy of Science?* (London, Bloomsbury, 2015).

[6] Similar claims were formulated by Adolfo Giuliani with respect to the state of comparative legal history. See A Giuliani, 'What is Comparative Legal History? Legal Historiography and the Revolt Against Formalism, 1930–60' in A Masferrer, KÅ Modéer, and O Moréteau (eds), *Comparative Legal History* (Cheltenham, Edward Elgar Publishing, 2019) 30–77, 65–67.

the excellent summary of these definitions by Léontin-Jean Constantinesco demonstrates.[7] It should not be ignored that the question of whether comparative law is a simple method of legal studies or a *sui generis* field of legal scholarship dominated comparative law debate during the inter-war period, and it had a certain influence thereafter too. The emergence of a commonly shared definition of comparative law still seems to be far from settled, though, even now.

However, this book submits that the nature of comparative law, for the purposes of this study, may be defined without getting lost in the maze of the decades-long, and sometimes monotonous, debates on this issue. One thought of René David should be borrowed as a starting point for this. In his classic work, David recommends a sophisticated approach to all those lawyers and legal scholars who have already subscribed to comparative law thinking, at least to a certain extent. Basically, David suggests making a distinction between those who apply some comparative methods when studying or discussing a specific legal problem in their own fields of interest, and those who regard comparative law as an autonomous scholarly field. In David's words:

> Pour la plupart le droit comparé ne sera sans doute qu'une méthode, la méthode comparative, pouvant servir aux fins variées qu'ils se proposent. Pour certains en revanche on peut bien concevoir que le droit comparé soit une véritable science, une branche autonome de la conaissance du droit ...[8]

That is, not all of those who ever adopt a comparative perspective in the history of legal scholarship should be considered as members of the comparative law scholarly community *stricto sensu*; rather, only those who have a broader interest – historical, theoretical, conceptual, or methodological – in comparative law than just the technical application of comparative methods may be considered 'real' comparatists. Needless to say, the number of scholars with such a general interest is much lower than those who occasionally rely on comparative methods during their professional work.

When defining its subject – comparative law as a scholarly enterprise – this book will rely on this insight from David. That is, it does not intend to draft an encyclopaedic history of the application of comparative methods in jurisprudence; rather, it will focus solely on the ideas of those legal scholars who devoted themselves to a comprehensive scholarly study of comparative law as such. They approached comparative law as a distinct field of legal scholarship, having historical, conceptual and methodological features that make it possible to distinguish it from other, more conventional and settled fields of legal scholarship. Therefore, this story will focus on the activities and achievements of these scholars and their communities, and not on the general history of the application of comparative methods in the legal academia.

---

[7] For a detailed discussion of various concepts of comparative law see Constantinesco, *Traité de droit comparé I* (n 2) 176–205.

[8] R David, *Les grands systèmes de droit contemporains* (Paris, Dalloz, 1982) 13.

IV. ANCIENT OR MODERN HISTORY OF COMPARATIVE LAW THINKING

Most disciplines of modern social sciences can in some way be traced back to antiquity. Forerunners of modern or post-modern concepts and understandings are easily found in Greek or Roman sources in most instances. This is also true for comparative law, since the earliest application of comparative methods in the field of legal thinking also goes back to certain Greek practices. The Greek *poleis* were already interested in studying the law of other city states, while Aristotle also relied on the comparative method when he prepared his well-known classification of Greek constitutions.[9] In sum, the application of comparative methods in order to better understand legal problems and phenomena has been a constant, ever since the earliest phases of legal history. Numerous other precursors can easily be found in the Middle Ages and early-modern period.

Unlike this fascinating line of predecessors, this book focuses on the modern history of comparative law thinking. That is, its scope is restricted to the study of the intellectual developments from the mid-eighteenth century to the second decade of the twenty-first century. Thus, it encompasses only about 270 years of the story of comparative law thinking that began with Greek city states' interest in the comparative study of their respective laws. This restrictive choice may be justified from various points of view. First of all, it has to be emphasised that those conditions that enabled the formation of real scholarly communities, and thereby stimulated the birth of scholarship in a modern sense, only took shape in the nineteenth century. The first scholarly journal having a comparative law character, the first scholarly associations uniting legal scholars with a comparative law interest and the first university positions dedicated to the comparative study of the law were only established in the mid-nineteenth century. The institutional framework that made regular communication and cooperation between comparative law scholars possible, and which was also indispensable for the emergence of modern scientific activities,[10] was set up relatively late as compared to the general development of legal scholarship that started with the birth of medieval law faculties in Italy in the late eleventh century. This slowly developing network of scholarly journals, associations and faculty positions from the mid-nineteenth century helped comparative law thinking to mature, meaning that the application of comparative methods in order to better understand the law or a legal phenomenon had the opportunity to become a specialised, institutionalised and communal scholarly activity, in spite of earlier particular, fragmented and at many times marginalised attempts. In sum, the modern story of comparative law offers excellent subject-matter for a systematic and monographic study.

---

[9] cf Hug, 'The History of Comparative Law' (n 2) 1029–34.
[10] See TS Kuhn, *The Structure of Scientific Revolutions* (Chicago, The University of Chicago Press, 1970).

Second, it should not be forgotten that, due to the communal and cooperative nature of modern comparative law activities, in which scholarly communication through journals, books and conferences has a prominent place, the sources of this story are much more accessible than those, with special regard to primary sources, of the earlier activities. Therefore, again, it seems to be a rational restriction to reduce the scope of this research to the modern history of comparative law. However, it does not mean at all that study of the previous phases of development is unnecessary; on the contrary, the precursors are highly relevant, as their discussion can contribute to the understanding of the inherent plurality of comparative law thinking.

V. COMPARATIVE LAW AND COMPARATIVE CONSTITUTIONAL LAW

As contemporary developments show, comparative constitutional law[11] has gradually become a popular and fashionable stream of comparative law research. It has been animated and boosted by US constitutional law scholars, and its rapid emergence is certainly not independent of those historical and political changes that started in the late 1980s. William Ewald, when discussing the latest developments in US comparative law thinking, argues that comparative constitutional law is to be regarded as a way of carrying out comparative legal research qualitatively different from the 'old-fashioned' approach dominated by scholars who were socialised into the European approach that came from the inter-war period. Compared to the conventional US comparative law scholarship from the 1960s to the 1980s – practised by such scholars as Rudolf Schlesinger, Max Rheinstein and John Merryman – comparative constitutional law is characterised by several new features. First, its horizon seems to be much broader, as it not only focuses on Europe but also deals with the constitutional systems of other continents and, therefore, has a distinctive global aspiration. Second, the emergence of comparative constitutional law also implied a methodological shift, as it broadened its research interest beyond the usual black-letter-law-orientated approach and also tried to incorporate empirical methods coming from political science. Third, as a sociological point, it should be mentioned that comparative constitutional law, as an academic movement, has been led by US-trained constitutional lawyers, and their academic activities were sometimes inspired not only by pure scholarly interest but also by specific advisory and consultative ambitions.[12] In sum, the flourishing of comparative constitutional law certainly means the increasingly intensive presence of a comparative law attitude that radically differs from the conventional one, with its strong European roots.[13]

---

[11] From the latest literature, see M Tushnet, *Advanced Introduction to Comparative Constitutional Law* (Cheltenham, Elgar, 2018); and M Tushnet (ed), *Comparative Constitutional Law* (Cheltenham, Elgar, 2017).

[12] For this comparison see W Ewald, 'Rats in Retrospect' in S Besson, L Heckendorn Urscheler and S Jubé (eds), *Comparing Comparative Law* (Geneva, Schulthess, 2017) 19–34.

[13] Ewald openly argues for this interpretation (ibid 28): 'The new comparative constitutionalism was in many ways entirely independent of the old comparative law: the various handbooks contain

Because of these characteristics, implying a radical difference from the theses of European comparative law, and the specific way of development boosted by the transformation of the historico-political context, related to the proliferation of political regimes founded on the principles of constitutional democracy all around the globe since the 1980s, this book will not discuss comparative constitutional law as such, although its story and expansion are undeniably remarkable and fascinating. However, at this stage, the integration of these developments into the frame of this book would definitely make the preservation of the original scope impossible. The emergence and expansion of comparative constitutional law is obviously an important issue for study, but it cannot fit into a research frame designed primarily for the study of the modern European history of comparative law thinking.

VI. A MEZZO PERSPECTIVE APPROACH

From a different perspective, the occasional study of the history of comparative law thinking can be classified around the macro and micro perspective axes. Some earlier authors tried to provide a general view of the development of comparative law thinking. Here, 'general' means that their works aimed at covering broader historical periods – for instance, from antiquity to modern times[14] or the entire modern period[15] – and discussed and analysed authors with various national and cultural backgrounds together. These macro perspective-inspired studies were therefore intended to provide a 'big picture' of certain phases of the development of comparative law, and necessarily turned to and analysed various national developments, and thereby had an international character. In contrast, some other important historical inquiries obviously required a micro perspective in their historiographical ambitions. These usually focused on one specific author, work or event in the history of comparative law, and discussed it in great detail, using primary and secondary sources.[16] In sum, the historiography of comparative law has predominantly looked for either broader views on major trends or micro analyses of certain relevant points of this history.

As compared to these precursors, the scope of this book is certainly different; it may even be considered unusual in the light of these previous works. Certain restrictions have already been pointed out in this introduction. First, it is not intended to cover the history of the entirety of the comparative law movement; rather, this book will focus on the works and ideas of those scholars who regarded comparative law as an autonomous field of legal scholarship.

---

scarcely a reference to the scholarship of Schlesinger, or Rheinstein, or Watson, or any of the other scholars of previous decades. There is a little sign of influence.'

[14] For instance Hug, 'The History of Comparative Law' (n 2).

[15] For instance Constantinesco, *Traité de droit comparé I* (n 2) 50–161.

[16] For instance Gerber, 'Sculpting the Agenda of Comparative Law: Ernst Rabel and the Facade of Language' (n 2).

Second, the time period covered by this book is also seriously limited, since it concentrates on the modern developments starting in the second half of the nineteenth century, so that ancient, medieval and early-modern developments in comparative law are almost completely omitted from the discussion. Third, the contemporary story of comparative constitutional law, as an autonomous discipline with a strong US background, is also absent from the book's scope, due to its qualitatively different nature. Finally, it does not aspire to prepare a complete international analysis, meaning that it mainly relies on sources accessible either in English or French. At some points – but not systematically – certain German or Italian sources are also discussed and cited.

As such, due to all these limitations on the book's scope, it is best to determine it as adopting a mezzo perspective. This means in particular that the research design sets up serious limits for the scholarly inquiry, so it will not attempt to paint a comprehensive, 'big picture' of the history of modern comparative law as such. It is satisfied with drafting the main trends and analysing the main authors related to the European comparative law movement; however, it also wants to offer more than a well-focused analysis of a development attached to a given moment in time or a given author.[17] It is hoped that the room delimited by the above parameters will be filled properly with the material from this enterprise.

All in all, this book invites the reader to consider a new narrative on the history of modern European comparative law. It certainly does not intend to replace the previous, sometimes fragmented readings on this topic, but it seeks to call into being a coherent alternative vision by developing a new framework – the Kuhnian approach – and by subscribing to a new point of view – the mezzo perspective. Needless to say, both the novelty and the perspective of this new narrative bring about many doubts and ambiguities, but it may also inspire its future readers to challenge these issues without rejecting the entire concept.[18] If this happens then our understanding of comparative law as a discipline will definitely become more refined, and it will also lead to the strengthening of our professional community.

---

[17] The ambition of this book is somewhat similar to that of Duncan Kennedy's seminal paper, 'Three Globalizations of Law and Legal Thought'. Although Kennedy applied a different periodisation (1850–1914, 1900–68, 1945–2000), and tried to reveal and deconstruct some general patterns of 'global' legal thinking, the idea that 'a conceptual vocabulary, organizational schemes, modes of thought, and characteristic arguments' can establish common modes of thought that transcend national boundaries certainly links this book to Kennedy's vision. In addition, in this work my aim – as is the case in Kennedy's argumentation – is that the narrative will be able to relate certain 'previously disparate' events, ideas and authors to one another, thereby providing a fresh outlook. See D Kennedy, 'Three Globalizations of Law and Legal Thought: 1850–2000' in DM Trubek and A Santos (eds), *The New Law and Economic Development. A Critical Appraisal* (Cambridge, Cambridge University Press, 2010) 19–73, 22 and 24.

[18] cf ibid 20.

1

The History of Comparative Law and Kuhn's Oeuvre

I. STUDYING SCIENCE AS A HISTORICAL PHENOMENON: SOME PRELIMINARIES

A. On the Necessity of an Elaborated Historical Approach

S CIENCE HAS A prominently universalistic image in the Western world, and this implies a predominantly ahistorical and decontextualised understanding too. As such, science may appear as a phenomenon with universal validity, detached from any external condition that human existence may confront. However, the study of any branch or domain of science – whether from the field of natural or human sciences – can never completely neglect the historical perspective, as the relevance and importance of various achievements can only be understood properly in their broader context, mostly in comparison with previous developments. Thus, when studying the outcomes of scientific or scholarly activities, a certain degree of historical discussion is always necessary.

As this book is devoted to the study of the modern history of comparative law, the presence of a historical outlook is self-evident. There is no need to estimate how many manuals that discuss the intellectual history of a given subfield within legal scholarship have already been published. However, when trying to understand the history of legal scholarship, the application of the historical method in a conscious and scholarly way should give rise to other, hitherto unrecognised preconditions and outcomes. This issue requires the legal scholar to leave the comfortable and well-known area of legal scholarship and turn to other scholarly perspectives. For instance, contemporary philosophy of science may be capable of providing a valuable contribution to the design of any research programme that intends to map the modern story of any special subfield of legal scholarship. The relevance of the philosophy of science for such a study is strengthened by the simple fact that most of the developments in this field have largely been inspired by a dialogue or dispute with the oeuvre of Thomas S Kuhn, who brought tradition, and thereby history, within the focus of his inquiries into the nature of science.[1]

[1] cf B Barnes, *TS Kuhn and Social Science* (London and Basingstoke, MacMillan, 1982) 9; and DA Hollinger, 'TS Kuhn's Theory of Science and its Implications for History' (1973) 78 *The American Historical Review* 370–93, 373–78.

Furthermore, the rather fragmented historiography of comparative legal studies – already mentioned in the Introduction – seems to be dominated by a so-called 'descriptive linearity' with respect to their attitude towards historical understanding. This means that scholarship considers the development of comparative law thinking as a linear process that starts from the pre-modern period and leads directly to modernity; in other words, from some archaic pre-modern precursors to modern scholarship. This is not too surprising, as legal history deeply embraced the concept of linearity when discussing the evolution of both a legal institution and an idea or school of legal thinking.[2] Furthermore, most research remains satisfied with the description, reportage and evaluation of certain historical events in this course of development – the publication of a book, the emergence of an idea, the main theses of a given scholar, the foundation of a new research institute, etc – but, in most cases,[3] it does not reflect on the significance of the findings from other, broader perspectives, but simply familiarises the readers with what happened at a given moment or period and what has been explained in the field of comparative law by various scholars.

A 'profitable use'[4] of some Kuhnian ideas may be capable of providing a qualitatively different reading of the modern story of comparative legal studies, as they may enable the research to overstep the seemingly inherent limitations in the approach of 'descriptive linearity'. However, this 'import'[5] obviously cannot be a simple and one-way intellectual transposition of Kuhn's approach and insights to the field of legal studies; it must also be a reflective and critical process. This attitude is even more necessary if one takes into account the several controversies that have gathered around his work during the last 50 years,[6] including the simple fact that even Kuhn was rather sceptical of the applicability of his theses to human or social sciences.[7] This introductory chapter must therefore be devoted to an in-depth and critical analysis of how and

---

[2] As a classic example, see Sir F Pollock and FW Maitland, *The History of English Law*, vols 1–2 (Cambridge, Cambridge University Press, 1968). From the contemporary literature, see S Hähnchen, *Rechtsgeschichte. Von der Römischen Antike bis zur Neuzeit* (Heidelberg, CF Müller, 2012).

[3] As for comparative law, the papers of Marc Ancel on the history of modern comparative law may be regarded as exceptions, since he had a strong analytical claim when discussing trends in modern comparative. See M Ancel, 'Les grands étapes de la recherche comparative au XXe siècle' in K Zweigert and HJ Puttfarken (eds), *Rechtsvergleichung* (Darmstadt, Wissenschaftliche Buchgesellschaft, 1978) 350–60.

[4] Barnes, *TS Kuhn and Social Science* (n 1) x.

[5] cf Hollinger, 'TS Kuhn's Theory of Science and its Implications for History' (n 1) 372.

[6] The 'first wave' of criticism, targeted on *The Structure* explicitly, emphasising the perceived irrationalism of Kuhn's theory and propelled by the school of Karl Popper, is summarised in I Lakatos and A Musgrave (eds), *Criticism and the Growth of Knowledge* (Cambridge, Cambridge University Press, 1970).

[7] See TS Kuhn, 'The Natural and the Human Sciences' in DR Hiley, J Bohman and R Shusterman (eds), *The Interpretive Turn: Philosophy, Science, Culture* (Ithaca, NY, Cornell University Press, 1991) 17–24.

to what extent Kuhn's theory can be applied to the historiography of modern comparative law.

B. On the Historical Character of Scientific Development

If one takes Kuhn's ideas as the starting point of an exploratory study, the need for a historical approach should not require further justification, as it is a necessary consequence of this attitude. Nonetheless, the specification of a broader historical outlook, creating a macro context, is still essential for finding a solid basis for the study itself. It is particularly necessary because the status of science as a historical phenomenon is still disputed, that is, whether it is an autonomous phenomenon, solely ruled by its internal laws and logic, or determined by the impact and influence of external factors; and whether it is a *sui generis* and exclusively self-reflective human enterprise, or serves other human interests too. Fortunately, certain insights from general modern historiography seem to be appropriate to provide us with a background by which the historical nature of science, as a collective human endeavour, may be clarified to the extent necessary for this study.

History was compared to a polyphonic choir by Fernand Braudel, who played a key role in establishing a new way of understanding history in general – as represented by the *Annales* school – during the second half of the twentieth century.[8] With this metaphor, Braudel wanted to highlight the complexity of history, and he also implied that a comprehensive understanding of history must take this into account to produce a nearly complete picture of the past. As for the main layers of history, Braudel made a distinction between so-called 'traditional history' (*l'histoire traditionelle*) and 'the new economic and social history' (*la nouvelle histoire économique and sociale*). 'Traditional history' means the course of events, while another differentiation has to be made between conjunctures and basic structures within 'the new history'. The level of conjunctures refers to the interlinked history of economies, societies, countries and cultures. Conversely, the level of basic structures encompasses the history of material and intellectual culture, itself being a necessary precondition for ordinary life. In other words, material and intellectual culture defines the borders of 'the possible and the impossible' with regard to human existence.[9]

In sum, the 'multi-storey' building of history is composed of these three main floors in Braudel's eyes, and these levels of history are not only qualitatively different, but their relationships with time – as the general framework of existence – also diverge. Primary history occurs in 'short time', animated by the chain of consequent historical events; the time dimension of conjunctures flows by the slower rhythm cycles of middle-range time; and, finally, the basic structures are rooted in the almost immovable *longue durée*.[10]

---

[8] Braudel elaborated this approach at the end of the 1950s. For details, see F Braudel, 'La longue durée' (1958) 13 *Annales. Economies, Sociétés, Civilisations* 725–53.

[9] See ibid 731.

[10] ibid 727.

Interestingly, Braudel initially puts science in the *longue dureé*, as he considered it as a component of the basic intellectual structure, defining people's world views; he even uses it as a good example of *longue dureé*.[11] However, good arguments may also be found to suggest that science be repositioned at the level of conjunctures, thereby refining Braudel's vision at this point. If, inspired by Kuhn, the intellectual history of science and scholarship is to be conceived of as being sequential – a chain of paradigm shifts in the broadest sense – and not linearly, it becomes a more dynamic course of development, one composed of cyclical changes,[12] unlike the classic approach based on the idea of a continuous and unbroken cumulative development of human knowledge.[13] Further, it is rather likely that Braudel had this classic idea in mind, as the first edition of Kuhn's breakthrough book on the structure of scientific revolutions was published a few years later than Braudel's seminal article on the nature of *longue durée*. In sum, if the history of science is to be regarded as a story of the upheavals of paradigm shifts and the subsequent calm periods of normal science (to use Kuhn's phrase) then its place in Braudel's overview of history should be at the level of conjunctures instead of at the level of *longue dureé*.

This position of the history of science clearly implies that the story of a scientific or scholarly subfield is affected by many other external factors originating from upper layers – the events – or lower layers – the *longue durée* – of history in general. However, as it is a distinct entity, science also possesses its own, *sui generis* history emerging from the internal – either linear or cyclical – development of scholarly theses. Therefore, the intellectual history of science may be envisaged as a historical process, having an individual character that is always preserved under the pressure of various external, and thereby independent, influences. Many external phenomena – which come either from the level of events or basic structures, or from other phenomena of a conjectural nature – may have an impact capable of exerting some influence on the formation of science as such, but science's individual and peculiar development, due to its unending internal refinement, always continues. In other words, science can never be regarded as a simple corollary to more comprehensive structures.[14] In conclusion, factors

[11] See ibid 732. (Braudel refers to the durability of the 'Aristotelian universe', and argues that only the ideas of Galilei, Descartes and Newton were capable of overstepping it.)

[12] For a detailed explanation of Kuhn's cyclical understanding of scientific development, see A Bird, 'Kuhn and the Historiography of Science' in WJ Devlin and A Bokulich (eds), *Kuhn's Structure of Scientific Revolutions. 50 Years On* (Heidelberg, Springer, 2015) 23–38; and Hollinger, 'TS Kuhn's Theory of Science and its Implications for History' (n 1) 373–78.

[13] For a summary with respect to Kuhn's theses, see Karl Popper's polemic article: K Popper, 'Normal Science and Its Dangers' in Lakatos and Musgrave (eds), *Criticism and the Growth of Knowledge* (n 6) 51–58, esp 56–57. For details, see K Popper, *The Logic of Scientific Discovery* (London, Unwin Hyman, 1990) 276–81.

[14] This is explicitly argued by, for instance, classical Marxism, defining the economy as the basis of any other phenomenon, including science.

outside science as such must always be studied and considered, in the most empathic way possible, but their impact should never be overstated, as this approach may degrade science to a simple and artificial reflection – a mirror – of outside, sometimes totally secondary, civilisational circumstances.

C. Choosing a Proper Starting Point – The Importance of the Definition of Science

A serious additional difficulty came up in this inquiry. When studying the story of a scientific area, not only have the regular uncertainties of these endeavours to be confronted – for instance the lack of sources, the biases stemming from retrospective research goals, and the unintentional underestimation or overestimation of certain points – but some preliminary problems have to be clarified too. A major problem is the definition of science or scholarship in the field of social and human sciences. A properly chosen definition may considerably facilitate the research; it is then possible to tame and conceptualise a phenomenon composed of an almost unlimited number of facts and rather unclear internal connections and relationships. In sum, a proper and operational starting definition seems to be more than necessary for such an enterprise.

It should also not be forgotten that any intellectual history applies prioritisation as a research tool and simplification in its analysis and reporting; therefore, it is simply unable to grasp the entirety of the course of development. So, a factually complete description of the evolution of a given field of study is a simply unattainable point, an illusory goal. It implies that an attempt to prepare the intellectual history of a certain academic field is, in fact, an attempt to reconstruct the facts of this story by relying on the previously chosen concept of science or scholarship. It can even be argued that the concept of science applied (in our case, as this discussion will be about a sub-field of legal scholarship with strong ties to both the social and the human sciences, it seems to be more appropriate to use the term 'scholarship' in the following) provides a starting point that re-creates the intellectual history of a field of scholarship according to its own specific premises.

Thus, the historiography of science and scholarship is characterised by both reflection and creativity, not only by mere factual description and 'data' analysis. However, this 'subjective' element by no means decreases the academic value of such studies, as the reader can always have access to other, sometimes fundamentally different, interpretations of the same story on the shelves of the libraries. In conclusion, the task of the history of scholarship – from the perspective of this book – is definitely not to produce an encyclopaedic summary of all the events, persons and facts, but to make an attempt to understand this story in a reflective and critical way, by relying on certain well-defined premises in a logical and coherent manner.

II. APPLYING KUHN'S LEGACY TO UNDERSTAND
THE HISTORY OF COMPARATIVE LEGAL STUDIES

A. The History of Science and Kuhn's Paradigm Shift

No research project aiming at preparing the story of a given field of scholarship can disregard the fact that the philosophical context of the history of science radically changed due to the impact of Thomas Kuhn's seminal *The Structure of Scientific Revolutions* and the follow-up discussion and refinement. Kuhn's ideas broke through the so-called logical-cumulative approach that previously had a decisive influence over the approach of the history of science in the post-World War II period. This line of thought, elaborated by such authoritative authors as, for instance, Karl Popper and Imre Lakatos, regarded the history of science as a linear and progressive process, aiming at the discovery of scientific truths.[15] In essence, it implied the idea of progress toward true scientific knowledge, and this was reflected by those statements that explained the entire history of science as a sum of subsequent verifications (classical empiricism) or falsifications (method-ological falsificationism). The central role of either verification or falsification in the history of science implied the existence and accessibility of a true knowl-edge of the things of the world. That is, this approach was predicated on each scientific problem's having an adequate explanation based on truth – even if a permanent, immutable truth is unattainable using scientific methods[16] – and the history of science as nothing other than a slow but continuous convergence towards these adequate explanations.[17]

In essence, Kuhn's subversive ideas can be grouped around two major insights. Interestingly, they both remained mostly unchanged during the further, decades-long and often very critical debates, although Kuhn was open in general to refine his theory at various points. Thus, these two insights look to be the core of his 'revolutionary' vision of the history of sciences.

First has to be listed the rejection of the linear development of science.[18] As Kuhn argued, this process – generally seen as a continuous and cumulative growth in which human scientific knowledge improves toward a more perfect state – actually has a rather fragmented and strongly interrupted character, broken up by revolutionary changes. These revolutionary changes are the famous

---

[15] For a summary see I Lakatos, 'Falsification and the Methodology of Scientific Research Programmes' in Lakatos and Musgrave (eds), *Criticism and the Growth of Knowledge* (n 6) 91–132. For an analytical discussion, see B Hansson, 'Recent Trends in the Philosophy of Science' in A Peczenik, L Lindahl and B van Roermund (eds), *Theory of Legal Science* (Dordrecht, D Reidel Publishing Company, 1984) 5–12, 6–7 and 12; AH de Wild, 'Progress in Legal Science' in *ARSP Beiheft 25* (Stuttgart, Franz Steiner Verlag, 1985) 119–21.

[16] Popper, *The Logic of Scientific Discovery* (n 13) 278.

[17] Popper, 'Normal Science and Its Dangers' (n 13) 56–57.

[18] cf I Lakatos, 'Falsification and the Methodology of Scientific Research Programmes' (n 15) 92–93. (Lakatos summarises it this way: 'Kuhn thinks otherwise. He too rejects the idea that science grows by accumulation of eternal truths.')

paradigm shifts – a central concept of Kuhn's vision – that lead to a transformation of how scientists consider their research problems. Thus, Kuhn asserts, while the research issues remain essentially the same, the ways in which scientists view and think about them change radically.[19] Hence, there is no longer any progress, in the conventional sense, in modern scientific development, as had been assumed and passionately argued for prior to Kuhn's work; it is only the understanding of scientific issues that changes successively.

In *The Structure*, Kuhn argued that the earlier and the later understandings of research issues should be considered incommensurable, meaning that their qualitatively different representations of the scientific world view make it impossible to compare them with each other in a meaningful way.[20] As a result, paradigm shifts not only bring a new way of thinking about research problems in a given field of study, but they also make inaccessible and invalidate earlier research outcomes that addressed the very same set of problems. Just think of the seeming incompatibility between Aristotelian and Newtonian physics, argues Kuhn. Although he refined this 'incommensurability thesis' at various points during the debates of the coming decades (for instance, he later accepted that 'translation' is possible between two different scientific world views divided by a paradigm shift),[21] the idea of – at least partially – the incompatibility of scientific approaches following each other in a non-linear manner still remained a relevant component of his vision with a strong explanatory value.

Second, Kuhn also introduced a communal vision of science. That is, he emphasised the importance of community in carrying out scientific activities. Prior to his oeuvre, the history of science prominently focused on the individual scientist, but the community dimension of science appeared to be disregarded. Conversely, Kuhn put into focus the existence of scientific communities and argued that, without the study of the functioning of these communities, the world of science could not properly be understood. This fundamentally different vision led Kuhn to explore the phenomenon of 'puzzle-solving research', covering the rich everyday activities of scientists when dealing with scientific problems.[22] Research does not lead to world-changing inventions and discoveries in the great majority of cases but to structured and meticulous everyday work, with some sub-parts of a given research issue performed according to the commonly shared research premises by the members of the scientific community.

This community-orientated approach led Kuhn to his most criticised, doubted and praised conceptual invention: the introduction of the term 'paradigm'. In its original form, as it was expounded in *The Structure*, the word

---

[19] TS Kuhn, *The Structure of Scientific Revolutions* (Chicago, IL, The University of Chicago Press, 1970) 111–35.

[20] ibid 148–50.

[21] For an outstanding analysis see JA Marcum, 'The Evolving Notion and Role of Kuhn's Incommensurability Thesis' in Devlin and Bokulich (eds), *Kuhn's Structure of Scientific Revolutions. 50 Years On* (n 11) 115–34.

[22] See Kuhn, *The Structure of Scientific Revolutions* (n 19) 36–42.

'paradigm' meant the sum of those research premises – in the broadest sense (for instance, including common beliefs) – resulting in a specific scientific world view that is shared by the members of a given scientific community.[23] Thus, the communality of scientific communities is grounded in and provided by their commonly shared ideas about their problems, their work, and their beliefs and aims. When a paradigm shift occurs, this means the transition from an earlier paradigm to a new one, and so the conceptual preconditions of scientific work and activities change qualitatively. The concept of paradigm has been seriously questioned (see, for instance, the compelling analysis by Margaret Masterman regarding the inconsistencies in Kuhn's approach[24]), but the idea behind this concept, that commonly shared ideas direct the work of scientists, still looks to be meaningful and applicable.

All in all, Kuhn definitely stimulated, and thereby enriched, thinking on the history of science by two major conclusions. First, he negated the linearity and cumulative nature of scientific development and, in place of this, offered an understanding that was much less coherent and occasional, demystifying science to some extent. Second, by focusing on the role of scientific communities and their convictions and beliefs as to how and why to carry out scientific activities, he encouraged the study of normality and conventionality in science, unlike the earlier approach that praised individual, and therefore exceptional, efforts.[25]

Kuhn's theses have provoked strong criticism over the last decades, mainly from academics in the philosophy of science. For instance, many critics asserted that Kuhn's work is of an irrational, subjective and relativist character, and they argued that, therefore, this approach can have no say with respect to the rational world of science. Natural scientists were also rather unwilling to embrace Kuhn's perspective, as it seemed to pose harsh questions on the reasons for researching the objective truth, and it might lead to their being deprived of the very essence of their activities. In addition, even historians of ideas approached this theory with great scepticism, as they regarded it as excessively dogmatic and artificial, and as unable to describe the reality of scientific life and development. In sum, Kuhn's work attracted criticism from various fields, and this may have given rise to doubts over the validity of his theses.[26] However, the most interesting point in this difficult process of reception was that his work is still the focus of academic interest, although one may have the impression that almost everything and its opposite has already been questioned.

Therefore – with this broad, at many points self-contradictory and even fuzzy process of intellectual reception – one preliminary question should

---

[23] ibid 23–25.

[24] See M Masterman, 'The Nature of Paradigm' in Lakatos and Musgrave (eds), *Criticism and the Growth of Knowledge* (n 6) 59–90.

[25] See S Shapin, 'Kuhn's Structure: A Moment in Modern Naturalism' in Devlin and Bokulich (eds), *Kuhn's Structure of Scientific Revolutions. 50 Years On* (n 11) 11–21.

[26] For a summary, see J Laki, *A tudomány természete. Thomas Kuhn és a tudomáyfilozófia történeti fordulata* (Budapest, Gondolat, 2006) 8.

obviously be discussed: are Kuhn's theses worth any attention, and are they able to contribute any new insights to the understanding of the intellectual history of a given segment of legal scholarship? A Hungarian expert in Kuhn's oeuvre, János Laki, answered this question from such an angle, which is also relevant for this research project. Laki explains that even though much criticism has been expressed thus far, one highly important and relevant point remains unchanged with respect to Kuhn's oeuvre. Kuhn had a qualitatively different view on science as a human phenomenon, and it diverged strongly from the already-existing canon of history of science when his work was published.[27] The novelty of this understanding shocked and seduced, at the same time, the philosophical study of science due to its highly unconventional spirit, and it is still a strong stimulus for such studies. This insight is evidenced by the fact that Kuhn's book is among those works of philosophy that were published worldwide, and also served as a constant reference point for further similar studies, although its theses had already been comprehensively criticised.[28]

This broad impact shows the 'must-read' nature of Kuhn's theses, and also indicates that they are worth taking into account in those fields where their impact was not as decisive as in the natural sciences. Legal scholarship may be a good example of that. The application of Kuhn's vision to the history of comparative legal studies may be an important contribution to the self-reflection of legal scholarship itself, since it may shed light on issues that would remain invisible to the conventional approaches animated by the claims of descriptive linearity.

As an unavoidable step, however, Kuhn's theory must be scrutinised, because the reply to whether it can be applied to the world of social sciences is far from obvious. It should never be forgotten that Kuhn developed his theory with the help of some branches of natural sciences, mostly physics and astronomy.

All in all, the major concepts applied by Kuhn's theory have to be discussed reflectively and critically. This is an inevitable preparatory step, as these concepts will be adjusted to the features of the specific subject-matter of this research: the history of modern comparative legal studies. Needless to say, the intellectual history of physics or comparative law cannot be studied using the same tools, since they are more than simply different.

B. The Very First Problem: How to Apply Kuhn's Findings to Legal Scholarship

A main counterargument against the study of the history of modern comparative legal studies by relying on Kuhn's vision must surely be that even Kuhn was

---

[27] ibid.

[28] Almost 1 million copies had been sold so far and it was also translated to many languages; see W Sharrock and R Read, *Kuhn. Philosopher of Scientific Revolution* (Cambridge, Polity, 2002) 1.

rather sceptical regarding the applicability of his theory, in a strict sense, to scholarly fields other than the natural sciences. It is certainly true that Kuhn only rarely dealt with the field of social and human sciences, but he was definitely conscious of the question of its relevance for these academic areas too. In a talk in 1989, inspired by Charles Taylor's insight into the role of interpretation in the formation of human sciences,[29] Kuhn expressed his uncertainty whether his conception of science could be relevant for understanding the history of human sciences. On the one hand, he argued that a basic difference between the two areas – natural and human sciences – had to be kept in mind in any case. If human or social sciences, following Taylor's vision, are about understanding certain phenomena of human existence but not about discovering the laws of nature, it makes no sense to speak about paradigms, since puzzle-solving research cannot be carried out due to the lack of proper subjects. In addition, human and social sciences are characterised by problem instability, unlike natural sciences, since their subject-matters – for instance society, politics or human behaviour – tend to change relatively quickly.[30]

On the other hand, however, Kuhn also argued that these differences did not exclude *ab ovo* the application of the concept of paradigm to these fields. Non-natural sciences are in a premature situation in general, it is argued by Kuhn, but there may be some special fields already advanced to a more mature state, based on a paradigm, and he explicitly mentioned economics and psychology as examples where the transition to carrying out puzzle-solving research had already begun.[31] Thus, even Kuhn did not reject the possibility that his theory might be applied to academic fields outside the world of natural sciences.

This insight into the possible applicability of Kuhn's theory can be strengthened if one considers the nature of human sciences not as a conceptual disadvantage but as a special feature that may inspire the transformation of the original theory in order to make it applicable. It can be argued, from a structuralist perspective, that the original theory – created by Kuhn to model the functioning of mature natural sciences – is based on four points. These are: (i) the basic theory core; (ii) a set of intended applications, (iii) a paradigmatic theory net; and (iv) a positive and negative heuristic.[32] Due to the above-mentioned differences between natural and human sciences – discovery *versus* understanding and the lack of problem stability – one may assert that human sciences lack the so-called basic theory core, since no such fundamental laws for social phenomena can be identified, unlike the subjects of natural sciences. Nevertheless, this does not at all mean that human or social sciences

---

[29] C Taylor, 'Interpretation and the Sciences of Man' (1971) 25 *The Review of Metaphysics* 3–51.
[30] Kuhn, 'The Natural and the Human Sciences' (n 7) 22–24.
[31] ibid 23.
[32] For details see M Sintonen, 'Pragmatic Metatheory for Legal Science' in Peczenik, Lindahl and van Roermund (eds), *Theory of Legal Science* (n 15) 39–52, 40–41. (Sintonen's argumentation is grounded in a structuralist theory notion developed by Sneed, Stegmüller and Balzer during the 1970s.)

lack theories in general, but it points out the different nature of theories embedded in these fields.[33] Even though the theories that provide conceptual bases for the different branches of social sciences do not deal with general fundamental laws in most cases, they are capable of being converted into axioms, thereby offering coherent and consensual patterns of exemplars for scholarly activities. That is, if one regards these social or human science theories less strictly, and this is justified by their different nature, the occasional existence of paradigms in some scholarly fields – based on these already axiomatised theories grounding many exemplars for research activities – cannot be denied as a generalist. This means that no universal answer exists as to whether or not Kuhn's theory can be applied in the world of social sciences, but it must be proved or rejected in the context of a given subfield instead.

Fortunately, the utility of Kuhn's approach has already been proved in at least one segment of legal scholarship. The applicability and use of this theory in legal dogmatics was a rather well-discussed topic in theoretical legal academia in the 1980s.[34] Although, naturally, many divergent positions came up in this intensive discussion, the great majority of scholars[35] welcomed the application of Kuhn's ideas, and proved that they could enrich our knowledge of the nature and history of legal dogmatics. Without going into too much detail, this broad discussion of the relationship between the theory of paradigms and legal dogmatics may be able to justify the application of Kuhn's theory in the field of legal scholarship, of course with the necessary adaptation.

C. Which Kuhn to Apply for This Study?

Kuhn's oeuvre is broad and contains numerous relatively unknown writings as compared to the renowned *The Structure of Scientific Revolutions*.[36] In addition, at many points, he also refined his theses that were first exposed in *The*

---

[33] See ibid 42–43.

[34] See, eg, J Uusitalo, 'Legal Dogmatics and the Concept of a Scientific Revolution' in Z Bankowski (ed), *Revolutions in Law and Legal Thought* (Aberdeen, Aberdeen University Press, 1991) 113–21; J Wróblewski, 'Paradigm of Legal Dogmatics and the Legal Sciences' in Z Ziembiński (ed), *Polish Contributions to the Theory and Philosophy of Law* (Amsterdam, Rodopi, 1987) 75–88; E Zuleta-Puceiro, 'Scientific Paradigms and the Growth of Legal Knowledge' in *ARSP Beiheft 25* (Stuttgart, Franz Steiner Verlag, 1985) 126–34; E Zuleta-Puceiro, 'Legal Dogmatics as a Scientific Paradigm' in Peczenik, Lindahl and van Roermund (eds), *Theory of Legal Science* (n 15) 13–24, 13–14; A Aarnio, 'Paradigms in Legal Dogamtics. Toward a Theory of Change and Progress in Legal Science' in Peczenik, Lindhal and van Roermund (eds), *Theory of Legal Science* (n 15) 24–38.

[35] Aart Hendrik de Wild may be regarded as the sole exception to this general enthusiasm toward Kuhn's work, as he explicitly took the side of Lakatos in the general debate over Kuhn's ideas. See de Wild, 'Progress in Legal Science' (n 15) 116–25.

[36] The one-sidedness of the assessments and interpretation of Kuhn is also emphasised by Sharrock and Read when they point out that 'hardly anyone' read his historical and philosophical pieces together; rather, commentators only focused on a given piece from a given aspect. As Kuhn's oeuvre is clearly multi-dimensional, this distortion may hinder its comprehensive evaluation. cf Sharrock and Read, *Kuhn. Philosopher of Scientific Revolution* (n 28) 22.

Structure in his later works: for instance, Kuhn introduced the concept of the professional matrix to answer the criticism centred on the uncertainties of the concept of paradigm;[37] he also proposed new interpretations of the famous incommensurability thesis.[38] On this basis, we may even argue that at least two 'Kuhns' exist from the aspect of the philosophy of science: the 'young one', who wrote the breakthrough *The Structure* and thereby challenged the entire Popperian tradition; and the 'late one', who tried to refine and consolidate his theses in response to intensive, decades-long discussion and criticism. An interesting question may be whether the position of the late Kuhn, who even refuted the term 'paradigm' (the cause of too many controversies) and tried to introduce new terms, such as 'lexicon',[39] can be regarded as coherent with his starting assumptions.

In this fuzzy and distorted context, the choice of a conceptual set for a research programme inspired by Kuhn's theory is certainly not the easiest task. It also requires some hard decisions. For instance, excellent arguments may be found to discredit and, therefore, give up the use of the term 'paradigm'.[40] However, taking into account the popularity of this term and its continued use, despite the many – well-known – contradictions, this decision cannot be justified properly. Similar difficulties may come up regarding the concepts of scientific community, puzzle-solving research, normal science and paradigm shift. In order to carve out a coherent conceptual framework and also benefit from the later criticism of the Kuhnian oeuvre, this study will preserve all these classic terms, grounded by the work of the already mentioned 'young Kuhn', but it will reflect on them critically – sometimes even by applying the points of the 'late Kuhn' – and refine them by adjusting them to the subject-matter of this study.

D. The Novelty of Kuhn's Work from the Perspective of Legal Scholarship

Having studied the history of certain fields of natural sciences,[41] Kuhn reached some breakthrough conclusions on the development of science. Kuhn's line of reasoning and conclusions paved the way for both a qualitatively new approach to scientific development and a new concept of science, as was demonstrated by the worldwide reception of his theses. It has already had an impact on the reconceptualisation of the history of the natural sciences; however, it can be

---

[37] See TS Kuhn, 'Postscript-1969' in Kuhn, *The Structure of Scientific Revolutions* (n 19) 174–210.

[38] See TS Kuhn, 'Commensurability, Comparability, Communicability' (1982) *PSA: Proceedings of the Biennial Meeting of the Philosophy of Science Association* 669–88.

[39] See TS Kuhn, 'The Road Since Structure' (1990) *PSA: Proceedings of the Biennial Meeting of the Philosophy of Science Association* 3–13.

[40] See the masterful analysis by Margaret Masterman on the several inconsistencies in Kuhn's use of this term, in Masterman, 'The Nature of Paradigm' (n 24) 59–90.

[41] See Kuhn, *The Structure of Scientific Revolutions* (n 19) 10–42.

argued convincingly that it may have a comparable impact on the understanding of social sciences too.[42]

In addition, it must be taken into account that the real scholarly value of the theory of paradigms established by Kuhn is not just related to the novelty of the findings and insights. It is even recognised by Kuhn that his findings cannot always be regarded as real innovations, as he acknowledges in his work at various points. Obviously, some points of this theory were already raised in earlier studies in the history of sciences, and some biographies also directed their readers' thinking toward similar conclusions.[43] The real scholarly value of Kuhn's work is that he was able to create a comprehensive and coherent theory from these fragments that was able to explain the entirety of the history of sciences.[44] That is, this quite abstract theory appears to be capable of providing us with answers to the intellectual history of sciences that may be in harmony with the state of the art in philosophy, with special regard to the seemingly increased role of critical analysis.[45]

E. Refining the Kuhnian Vocabulary: Science

For Kuhn, science is primarily a sociological phenomenon.[46] In his view, science is a genre of human activities carried out by a special human community, by scientists or scholars. That is, science, in Kuhn's eyes, cannot be simplified to individual human acts inspired by a distinct methodology addressing the questions of the world around us; it is an activity with a strong communal character. Science or scholarship is carried out and managed by specific communities and, as each distinct human community, these also have their unique group features that are able to delineate them from other groups and communities. The main point among these features is that the sole way to become a member of these special communities is to accept commonly shared commitments and premises and to act based on them in the future.[47] These shared premises – inter alia, patterns for problem-solving (exemplars), values or beliefs – establish the possibility of a rational discourse on the scientific problems thus considered.

---

[42] However, some rare exceptions can also be found. For instance, Hollinger, 'TS Kuhn's Theory of Science and its Implications for History' (n 1), or SS Wolin, 'Paradigms and Political Theories' in P King and BC Parekh (eds), *Politics and Experience. Essays Presented to Professor Michael Oakeshott on the Occasion of His Retirement* (Cambridge, Cambridge University Press, 1968) 125–52.

[43] See Kuhn, *The Structure of Scientific Revolutions* (n 19) v–vii (mentioning the inspiration coming from various scholars, with special regard to Ludwik Fleck).

[44] See Bird, 'Kuhn and the Historiography of Science' (n 12) esp 27–28.

[45] For a contemporary account of the critical approach, see R Felski, 'From Literary Theory to Critical Method' (2008) 1 *Profession* 108–16.

[46] See Barnes, *TS Kuhn and Social Science* (n 1); Shapin, 'Kuhn's Structure: A Moment in Modern Naturalism' (n 25) 11 (arguing that *The Structure* 'dismissed method in favor of social consensus or of inarticulable informal criteria, … it elevated practice over formal theory, the hand over the head and the community over the free and rational individual knower').

[47] Kuhn, 'Postscript-1969' (n 37) 175, 182–83, 187–89.

Another essential feature of scientific communities is the need for the existence and functioning of scientific institutions that make it possible for members of the community to communicate among themselves. These institutions are manifold, from academies through university departments to scholarly journals, but modern science cannot be envisaged without them. To put it simply, in the absence of this institutional framework, with its ability to disseminate scientific achievements and foster the scholarly discourse, the so-called puzzle-solving method that characterises normal science cannot take shape, nor can a paradigm shift occur, as without the help of this framework, no scientist can be informed of the paradigm-shaking achievements.[48]

Science, in sum, is a communal activity, centred around the study of various problems and having a scientific character in accordance with the standards set up by the scientific community. This study is carried out by both relying on common premises and using the various institutional communication channels. Especially relevant given the scope of this book is that this communal character implies that the intellectual history of a given field of science cannot simply be prepared by discussing and analysing the evolution of certain theories; in addition, special attention has to be drawn to the status of scientific communities and their institutional background. Furthermore, to define the precise scope of a given scientific specialism is not only the researcher's exclusive task, but it also has to be determined by analysing the structure of scientific communities and their activities. That is, available sources must speak in general instead of relying on pre-existing classifications and prior assessments, that is, not on the researcher's own preconceptions. An excessive attachment to the already-known facts of scientific history – the interpretation of which was formulated based on an implicit conceptualisation of science, in most cases – would be a threat, as it may seriously limit the scope of historical research.[49]

F. Refining the Kuhnian Vocabulary: Parallel Paradigms

The problem of the applicability of Kuhn's theses to the sphere of human or social sciences has already been raised in this discussion. At that point, it was argued that its inapplicability to these fields cannot generally be stated, since if one applies a 'light' version of Kuhn's theory – based on the recognition of the different nature of theories in human or social sciences – it may nevertheless be relevant. In sum, a careful analysis is needed before inviting or rejecting Kuhn's idea in the historiography of a given subfield of social sciences.

---

[48] ibid 177 (explicitly mentioning professional societies and journals as constitutive components of community membership).

[49] This requirement was also set forth by Braudel, as follows: '"Observateur" aussi détaché que possible, l'historien doit se condamner à une sorte de silence personel.' F Braudel, *L'identité de la France. Espace et histoire* (Paris, Flammarion, 1990) 10.

Besides this analytical difference of social or human science theories, many other substantive differences can be identified between natural and human or social sciences.[50] From the perspective of this study, one of these has to be discussed in detail. It is more than a commonplace that the various phenomena studied by the natural sciences can be examined objectively to a certain extent;[51] however, the nature of those phenomena that are studied by social or human sciences is very different. All of them have a strong relation to human existence, in the broadest sense, naturally, and therefore the natural science-like mechanical modelling of human action is simply impossible, and, therefore, undesirable.[52] In essence, this is due to the fact that the actions of human beings, because of their capacities and abilities, may deviate from the normal and usual – mechanical – outcome of a given situation any time, as is illustrated by the unprecedented turns of history.[53] Therefore, human acts should never be assessed in a pure mechanical or teleological way, that is, exclusively from one perspective; a more refined approach is needed when trying to understand human actions in a scholarly manner.[54] This position is strongly supported by the critical findings of twentieth-century philosophy, which exposed the unrealistic nature of naive or logical empiricism and submitted that any methodological homogeneity of natural and social scientific research must be considered an unrealistic claim.[55]

That is, the phenomena – for instance society, culture, politics or law – studied by the human and social sciences always imply the possibility of divergent interpretations, due to what may be called a 'human factor'. That is, they are necessarily multi-dimensional from the aspect of scholarly study. Many examples offer themselves from the history of social sciences to demonstrate that a social phenomenon can even be interpreted in opposite ways, and these interpretations have never been justified by experiments or laboratory investigations.[56]

---

[50] See, eg, W Windelband, *An Introduction to Philosophy* (London, T Fisher Unwin, 1921) 204–05 (submitting the famous distinction between nomothetic and idiographic sciences).

[51] For a detailed analysis, see FA von Hayek: *The Counter-Revolution of Science: Studies on the Abuse of Reason* (Indianapolis, IN, Liberty Press, 1979) 41–60.

[52] The invalidity of mechanical theories with respect to the understanding of life as a complex phenomenon is demonstrated by Henri Bergson when he introduces the concept of 'creative time'; see H Bergson, *L'évolution créatrice* (Paris, PUF, 1907) 12–24.

[53] For a discussion from the aspect of values, see R Rezsohazy, *Sociologie des valeurs* (Paris, Armand Colin, 2006) 30–35.

[54] cf Nietzsche's position, where he argues that scholarly research should 'regain and recreate' the personality of early Greek philosophers in order to get a 'natural' vision on their oeuvre ('the polyphony'); F Nietzsche, 'Philosophy During the Tragic Age of the Greeks' in F Nietzsche, *Early Greek Philosophy and Other Essays* (New York, Macmillan, 1911) 71–170, esp 74.

[55] See V Villa, 'Theories of Natural Sciences and Theories of Legal Science. Models and Analogies' in *ARSP Beiheft 25* (Stuttgart, Franz Steiner Verlag, 1985) 110–15.

[56] A good example to illustrate this may be the concept of democracy. Originally, it was approached by Aristotle as a dysfunctional form of state; the era of Enlightenment also expressed some concerns when Montesquieu argued the citizens' virtues are a necessary precondition for the proper functioning of democracy, while modern political science celebrated it as the universal form of modern political organisation.

In conclusion, because of the inherent multi-dimensionality of the subject-matters of social and human sciences, and therefore the impossibility of reaching an exclusively true and objective interpretation,[57] it should be accepted that the precise and timely differentiation of subsequent paradigms in social or human sciences is not manageable.[58] To adjust Kuhn's theory to this challenge, the best way is certainly to accept the possibility that paradigms in social or human sciences may coexist with each other. That is, scientific communities in the same field of scholarship may simultaneously work in various conceptual frameworks that diverge substantially but share all necessary components of scientific paradigms. This insight, if one takes all implications into account, does not decrease the explanatory value of Kuhn's theses but only shapes it to the characteristic features of social sciences.[59]

This argument may be strengthened from a different aspect too. As theories providing bases for the paradigms in these fields cannot be based on fundamental laws (which is a basic requirement in the natural sciences, but only on less coherent scholarly assumptions),[60] the field of social and human sciences is necessarily richer in competing theories and, by definition, in competing scientific communities organised around a specific theory and a conceptual network. This theoretical plurality can be well illustrated by the formation of modern legal scholarship.[61] This coexistence of different theories and hypotheses in the same fields of study implies that there is an extremely limited chance for the emergence of a great and all-inclusive paradigm in a certain discipline, for instance the paradigm of legal scholarship. Nevertheless, puzzle-solving academic activities may be concentrated on special, conceptually more limited fields with their own particular theoretical backgrounds and their specific, narrower research interests. Thus, the existence of parallel paradigms is not only justified from the aspect of the inherent multi-dimensionality of the issues studied, but is also confirmed by the much more fragmented nature of 'normal science' activities stemming from various divergent and specialised theories.

The recognition of the parallel existence of paradigms gives rise to the question how to make a differentiation between these parallel paradigms attached to various academic subfields and the so-called pre-paradigm period, which is also characterised by the multiplicity of scholarly views and the lack of a generally

---

[57] cf Taylor, 'Interpretation and the Sciences of Man' (n 29).

[58] On the contrary, Kuhn submits that the emergence of a new theory establishing a paradigm also leads to the 'destruction of a prior paradigm and a consequent conflict of between competing schools of scientific thought'. See, eg, Kuhn, *The Structure of Scientific Revolutions* (n 19) 96.

[59] This is explicitly submitted by some authors discussing the value of Kuhn's theory for social sciences and legal scholarship. See J Dalberg-Larsen, 'Change or Progress in Legal Science' in *ARSP Beiheft 25* (Stuttgart, Franz Steiner Verlag, 1985) 79–80; M Flodin, 'The Possibility of Revolution in Legal Science' in Bankowski (ed), *Revolutions in Law and Legal Thought* (n 34) 175–82 (arguing that the complexity of human existence and society makes impossible the 'paradigmatic unity' of these kinds of studies).

[60] See Sintonen, 'Pragmatic Metatheory for Legal Science' (n 32).

[61] See, eg, M Villey, *La formation de la pensée juridique moderne* (Paris, PUF, 2003).

approved vision of science or scholarship. It is true that, due to the existence of parallel paradigms, one cannot envisage a commonly shared and unified paradigm providing a solid and all-encompassing framework for the academic thinking of certain fields of social or human sciences; however, this situation is to be delimited from the pre-paradigm period due to one distinctive feature.

In the case of parallel paradigms, specific, limited or broader scientific communities that back each simultaneously existing paradigm can be identified, although more than one vision and way of thinking compete in the same field and era. These academic communities work according to the rules of normal academic activity, and aim at finding certain puzzles and mosaics within the frame of their paradigms; in addition, they carry out research in the network of modern academic institutions established to satisfy the needs of normal scientific work. However, this high level of organisation and communal character is almost completely absent from the pre-paradigm period, as it is predominantly propelled by individual initiatives and not supported by an efficient institutional backing.

Therefore, the concept of the pre-paradigm period and that of the existence of parallel paradigms – contrary to some artificial similarities as the lack of unity and the undeniable plurality of visions – are qualitatively different: the constitutive character of community and institutional background is missing from the features of the pre-paradigm period.

G. Refining the Kuhnian Vocabulary: Paradigm

It is illustrated by its reception that the greatest challenge for Kuhn was the proper definition of the concept of paradigm. The broad criticism of the first edition of *The Structure*, especially that by Margaret Masterman, dissecting Kuhn's concept(s) of paradigm and pointing out serious logical inconsistencies regarding the usage of this term, led Kuhn to refine and improve the concept. One of the outcomes of this refinement was the distinction between two main senses of paradigm in his 1969 'Postscript'.[62] He provided a broader and a narrower sense of the concept of paradigm, and the earlier one was termed a 'disciplinary matrix' in order to avoid confusion with the narrower meaning of the concept.

The concept of paradigm as interpreted in a broader sense, the so-called 'disciplinary matrix', has various components. It is composed of (i) 'symbolical generalizations', (ii) beliefs or 'metaphysical paradigms', (iii) values, and (iv) 'exemplars', that is, concrete problem solutions applied and thereby shared by the entire community.[63] A paradigm conceptualised in this way set forth

---

[62] Kuhn, 'Postscript-1969' (n 37) 190.
[63] ibid 182–87.

the common vision and academic goals of a scientific community, or, from a different angle, the inherent limits in the thinking of this academic community. Therefore, the term 'group commitment' applied by Kuhn seems to be apt for summarising the requirements of 'disciplinary matrices'. The narrower sense of paradigm, however, is centred on one component: the 'exemplars' applied by given scientific communities as examples or models in their research projects. In sum, the narrower understanding of paradigm is solely focused on the specific research methods as sets of exemplars applied in scholarly inquiry; it does not intend to analyse the beliefs, values and generalisations in the life and functioning of scientific communities.

Obviously, the differentiation between the 'disciplinary matrix' and the paradigm in a narrower sense has a strong explanatory potential if one tries to understand the nature of scientific communities, as the term 'disciplinary matrix' renders it possible to integrate non-exclusively academic factors, such as values, beliefs, etc, besides the scientific method of inquiry. However, from the perspective of a historical study like this one, with special regard to the characteristic feature of social sciences, that they all accommodate the so-called 'human factor' besides a simple mechanical approach, it also implies the danger of reductionism. Based on the concept of 'disciplinary matrix', the division of a 'scientific movement' into various 'schools', and subsequently to different 'approaches', etc, is certainly not a difficult task, as diverging points on a given line of thought can always be spotted easily due to the specificity of the subject studied. However, the final outcome of this process of reduction may be the complete loss of the essence of paradigm, namely, the understanding of science as a community and ordinary communal activity. Such a history of scientific thinking, one that is based on arbitrarily identified and selected factors and leads to a vision of the history of science as an interplay between many academic approaches, cannot be capable of reflecting this core insight pointed out by the invention of the concept of paradigm.

In order to avoid this manifest threat of reductionism, this research focuses on the shared application of comparative law methodology as the constitutive conceptual component of the academic communities studied, since this method and its various incarnations are to be regarded as decisive for the formation of the particular sets of 'exemplars' applied within these communities. The role of values will be presented only sporadically, if especially needed; while certain beliefs and 'symbolical generalizations' will not be discussed individually with respect the various paradigms of comparative law, they may have an occasional role when the details of the method are scrutinised. That is, although the narrower sense of paradigm will be considered as a methodological starting point for this book, some insights stemming from the concept of the 'disciplinary matrix' will also be relied on – though mostly in an illustrative way.

Concentrating on the application of the comparative method in legal scholarship gives rise to the question of the extent to which this approach differs from the traditional one, which puts forward the role of scientific methodology in the usual way of preparing the intellectual history of a given academic field.[64] A Kuhnian contextualisation of the concept of 'exemplar' may lead us to a suitable answer. This concept has a strong relationship with the entirety of Kuhn's theory, while the term 'scientific methodology' does not have that kind of specific connotation. Therefore, the community and institutional nature of science is implied in the concept of 'exemplar' too; and it points out that this research will not be devoted to a general examination of the development of a given method (the comparative one in this case) but will focus on the study of the institutionalised scientific communities relying on a common method, based on shared 'exemplars' that operationalise the scholarly use of comparative method.

To put it differently, the endorsement of the term 'exemplar' points out that the method, merged from various 'exemplars', plays a crucial role in the formation of scientific communities. That is, a paradigm may also be described as an institutionalised academic community sharing a strong preference for a specific method. In this sense, comparatists in legal scholarship are to be defined as the institutionalised community of those legal scholars, from the entirety of the legal scholars, who apply a particular configuration of the comparative method, and the precise application of this method is determined by the occasional constellation of many 'exemplars' like these: the preferences when selecting the legal orders compared; the material and timely scope of the comparison; the concept of law applied in the comparative study; and the relevance of non-legal elements during the comparison.

H. Refining the Kuhnian Vocabulary: Paradigm Shift

In essence, it is argued by Kuhn, the development of scientific thinking is not linear and, therefore, continuous and unbroken, but is disrupted by revolutionary changes, and these revolutions lead to qualitative and incommensurable scholarly transformations. The moment in the history of scientific thinking when a new conception of science (a new paradigm) becomes dominant in a given academic field is termed a 'paradigm shift'. The most important feature of a new paradigm, in this context, is that it no longer shares the basic theory core of the earlier paradigm. Its conceptual setting, stemming from a new theory, is different from the earlier paradigm, and this makes it possible to approach the scientific problems from a novel angle and using new methods.

Kuhn compares this occurrence to the change in world view, and this analogy implies that the phenomena studied by the given academic field remain the same, naturally, but scientists will have a substantially different view of them as compared to their perception in the frame of the earlier paradigm.[65]

[64] The best example of this approach as for comparative law: LJ Constantinesco, *Traité de droit comparé I. Introduction au droit comparé* (Paris, LGJD, 1972) 50–161.
[65] Kuhn, *The Structure of Scientific Revolutions* (n 19) 113–15.

As a consequence of the paradigm shift, the given field of study will be based on new principles and theses – 'exemplars' – envisaging a new theory, and, in parallel with this, even the most rudimentary generalisations and the methods applied change to a great extent.[66] Therefore, the impact of paradigm shift on the structure of scientific thinking may be understood as an extreme tectonic move that so fundamentally rearranges the 'symbolical map' of the given academic field – composed of principles, generalisations, methods and a unique vocabulary; in sum, a set of exemplars – that it becomes almost incomparable, or incommensurable, to its predecessor.

The process of paradigm shift is to be described by the terms of anomaly and crisis in Kuhn's framework. In general, the functioning of the already settled paradigm is compared to 'puzzle-solving' research by Kuhn, that is, scholars devoted to a given field of study try to improve the paradigm along with its premises and within the framework offered by the entirety of the paradigm. However, in some cases the scientists or scholars may face occurrences that cannot properly be explained within the frame of the existing paradigm. These occasional disturbances in scientific thinking are called anomalies. Under certain conditions, their study may give rise to crisis, and this, eventually, may lead to the appearance of new hypotheses and the consequent birth of new theories too. All these may make obvious the 'breakdown' of the usual form of puzzle-solving research activities, or, in other terms, the inadequacy of the normal way of academic problem-solving that was previously regarded as conventional,[67] and this deficient situation (if the constellation of other conditions also supports it)[68] may lead to the birth of a new paradigm with all the necessary consequences.

Obviously, as the model of paradigm shift in Kuhn's theory reflects the specificities of natural sciences, it should be adjusted to the nature of legal scholarship, which is also struggling with the 'human factor'. In this necessary refinement, the point that an anomaly cannot exclusively be reduced to the discovery of a new scientific phenomenon – as, for instance, the discovery of oxygen or x-rays – may play an important role, as neither legal scholarship nor comparative legal studies have ever worked with phenomena based on similar 'hard facts'. In essence, legal scholarship, as a part of general social sciences, examines and discusses human actions and various components of human society, and the discussion of these on a level similar to the general objectivity of natural sciences is simply impossible. No one can carve 'hard facts' out of the multiple dimensions of human and social life, which may be compared to x-rays or electricity, without

---

[66] ibid 77.

[67] ibid 69.

[68] It is pointed out by Kuhn that not every anomaly or crisis leads to paradigm shift. Paradigm shifts have many other preconditions too, and Kuhn does not attempt to prepare a comprehensive list of them. External factors may have a strong role in them, as, for instance, communication between the scholars or the nature of the crisis may be decisive. It may even happen that the scientists solve the anomaly within the frame of the existing paradigm or they simply ignore it and, with it, have nothing to do with it in the prevailing paradigm: ibid 82–83.

depriving them of their essence, the already mentioned 'human factor'.[69] As such, it is better to conceive of anomaly, in this context, as a qualitatively new problem or question that cannot be answered properly within the frame of the actual paradigm by applying the conventional 'exemplars'; hence, it may be capable of inducing strong structural tensions that challenge the bases of this paradigm. This continuously growing tension between the settled frame of a paradigm and the new problem horizons may be one of the main engines of evolution in legal scholarship.[70]

As a consequence, the Kuhnian concept of crisis also needs to be refined. The meaning of this term, owing to the lack of objective certainty characterising legal scholarship and the inherent interpretive plurality of the issues studied, has to be reformulated in a more lenient way too. One may declare a crisis in the evolution of legal scholarship if anomalies give rise to such a body of problems and questions that cannot properly be answered according to the conventionally and widely used exemplars, that is, within the paradigm, and this growing uncertainty in the application of the settled exemplars may stimulate the emergence of brand-new interpretations and generalisations that substantially differ from the earlier, canonised approach.

In addition, as has already been indicated, it seems to be more appropriate to accept the existence of parallel paradigms instead of competing (and therefore exclusive) ones, due to the inherent interpretive plurality of non-natural sciences. Hence, in this field, a paradigm shift cannot be understood as an inflow of completely new academic ideas that are able to reset the settled map of scholarship in substance.[71] In this context, paradigm shift should be comprehended as a serious shift in emphasis that directs the attention of a researcher from the settled exemplars to a group of novel ones coming to the forefront because of the crisis. The settled paradigm that dominated the work of researchers until the start of the crisis will probably not disappear entirely; it may still possess a secondary role in the future of academic life. In sum, it may be better argued that, among the parallel paradigms of a certain academic specialty, a dominant one may exist, probably regarded as the mainstream of scholarly thinking, but the earlier paradigm or paradigms may also have some impact too.[72]

---

[69] See Flodin 'The Possibility of Revolution in Legal Science' (n 59) or M Sintonen, 'Scientific and Conceptual Revolutions' in Bankowski (ed), *Revolutions in Law and Legal Thought* (n 34) 11–21.

[70] See Zuleta-Puceiro, 'Legal Dogmatics as a Scientific Paradigm' (n 34) 16–19.

[71] This is illustrated by the development of the incommensurability thesis toward a 'softer' and 'weaker' interpretation in Kuhn' oeuvre. For details see Marcum, 'The Evolving Notion and Role of Kuhn's Incommensurability Thesis' (n 21).

[72] A good example from the history of modern comparative law. The Italian Giorgio Del Vecchio argued for a linear reconstruction of legal evolution determined by a general human spirit with the help of the comparative method even in 1950. This position is clearly embedded in the universe of the first paradigm, the historical and comparative jurisprudence that had already been convincingly criticised during the 1900 Paris Congress. Thus, Del Vecchio kept the spirit of the first paradigm alive in a radically different age, following World War II, when a newer paradigm started to take shape, the third one. See G Del Vecchio, 'L'unité de l'esprit humain comme base de la comparaison juridique' (1950) 2 *Revue internationale de droit comparé* 686–91. For Del Vecchio's general

III. LESSONS FROM KUHN IN THE HISTORIOGRAPHY
OF LEGAL SCHOLARSHIP

The foregoing may put forward strong arguments that Kuhn's theses can fruit-fully be applied to help in the understanding of the history of legal scholarship if they are applied in an empathic way, and also ensuring that some inherent specificities of legal scholarship as a field of inquiry embedded in the broadest tradition of social or human sciences are taken into account. However, this is not to argue for or against the validity of Kuhn's oeuvre as such, but to make a 'profitable use' of these still inspiring ideas. The final judgment on the value of this enterprise must be given by the scientific community of legal and other scholars in the future. However, the earlier discussion put forward one certain point: with the help of Kuhn, the settled framework of descriptive linearity in legal historiography can be overstepped, as it can enrich it with a different vision and attitude; that is, new ways of understanding may be opened up if this is carried out in a consistent and coherent way.

account on the nature of comparative law, see G Del Vecchio, 'L'idée d'une science du droit universel comparé' (1910) 39 *Revue critique de législation et jurisprudence* 487–505.

2

Historical and Comparative Jurisprudence

I. INTRODUCTION: THE CENTURIES-LONG PRE-PARADIGM PERIOD AND THE RISE OF THE FIRST PARADIGM

THIS CHAPTER WILL demonstrate that the first paradigm of comparative law began to take shape in the second half of the nineteenth century. The eighteenth and early nineteenth centuries were characterised by fragmentary attempts to apply comparative methods for studying law, while this process was boosted by the emergence of positivism and evolutionism in general social scientific thinking. Furthermore, it was also strongly supported by the formation of certain national scholarly associations devoted to comparative legal studies. All in all, it is argued, this transformation had an impact that made possible the birth of the first real comparative law scholarly community.

II. PROLOGUE: THE MODERN PRECURSORS AND THE PRE-PARADIGM PERIOD

As was mentioned in the Introduction, a comparative approach to legal issues has been a tool of both legislation and legal thinking since antiquity.[1] Contrary to previous linear analyses of the history of comparative law (for instance, that of Hug), this book argues, however, that some Kuhnian ideas also offer a valid framework for enabling this story to be understood properly. The contribution of early-modern and modern precursors should be discussed before presenting the birth of the first paradigm in the history of modern comparative law, since their works should be considered as an immediate prelude to it. Needless to say, the distinction between those legal scholars who relied on the comparative method in some way from the Enlightenment onwards but carried out their scientific activities without subscribing to a paradigm, and those whose writings followed the concepts and procedures within the framework of the first paradigm has an essential relevance for our further discussion.

---

[1] For an impressive list of these early attempts, see W Hug, 'The History of Comparative Law' (1932) 45 *Harvard Law Review* 1027–70.

If the linear historiographical approach is applied, as was the case in most of the previous discussions of the history of comparative law, a substantial differentiation cannot really be made between the theses of early-modern or modern legal scholars with a strong comparative law interest – for instance, Leibniz or Vico – and those late nineteenth-century authors who worked in the frame of the first paradigm, the historical and comparative jurisprudence. However, when the Kuhnian lenses are applied, with special regard to the differentiation between the pre-paradigm period and the establishment of the first paradigm, a new view of this approximately 200-year period may take shape. Basically, it is argued that the concept of pre-paradigm is useful for gaining a more refined understanding of the sporadic seventeenth- to eighteenth- and early nineteenth-century attempts to use the comparative method in legal studies, and how it compares with the oeuvre of certain legal scholars from the last decades of the nineteenth century.

The distinction between the pre-paradigm period and the emergence of the first paradigm is definitely a crucial point in Kuhn's vision of the historiography of science. Kuhn emphasised that this distinction is obviously relative in nature, so it cannot be applied to the history of various fields of sciences in a rigid or a mechanistic way. In essence, the pre-paradigm period is characterised by a wide variety of heterogeneous scientific approaches to the problems studied and the absence of settled scientific communities. For these reasons, the scientific activities of this period are not determined by a broader general consensus on some fundamental problems and the ways of doing science, but they are essentially driven by particular individual understandings. In addition, scientific or scholarly communities could not really emerge, as the modern, institutional infrastructure for scientific activities – the network of institutes, departments, associations and journals facilitating the dissemination of research outcomes – had not yet been established.[2] As such, in general, the main impetuses behind scientific and scholarly research during this 'immature' period were predominantly individual scholarly ambition and the quest for intellectual fame; compared with the modern setting, a collegiate mentality and collaborative searches for fundamental truths were a long way off.

Kuhn's basic idea about making a distinction in the history of science between the forms of 'immature', on the one hand, and real, or mature science on the other was substantially refined by Margaret Masterman in her meticulous criticism of Kuhn's theory of paradigms. Even though her work addresses abstract and general questions, some points can also have some relevance for this study of the history of modern comparative law. In essence, Masterman argues that Kuhn's view of the pre-paradigm period in the general history of science is 'confused and incompletely analysed', and so it needs further elaboration.[3]

[2] TS Kuhn, *The Structure of Scientific Revolutions* (Chicago, IL, The University of Chicago Press, 1970) 13–21.

[3] M Masterman, 'The Nature of Paradigm' in I Lakatos and A Musgrave (eds), *Criticism and the Growth of Knowledge* (Cambridge, Cambridge University Press, 1970) 59–90, 73.

In place of Kuhn's broad idea, summarising all scientific activities prior to the emergence of the first paradigm under the term 'pre-paradigm period', Masterman suggests defining three distinct concepts, each representing different settings of such 'immature' scientific activities. These are the states of (i) non-paradigm science, (ii) multiple paradigm science, and (iii) dual paradigm science.

Although Masterman recommends regarding these early phases as consecutive steps in a general development toward science in modern terms, they can also be interpreted as analytical concepts, helping us to reconstruct some distinct moments or phases in the history of scientific or scholarly thinking. All three point out a specific historical configuration of early scientific activities, with respect to the specific role of general theories and evolving communities; from the prominence of individual activities to the formation of two or more dominant schools in a given subfield of science. From the perspective of the history of modern comparative law, the most promising of these terms is certainly non-paradigm science. This concept focuses on the individual – that is, not community-centred – and occasional nature of scientific thinking, and the clear differences in the conceptual frameworks applied by the authors to back their research activities, and it seems to be appropriate for determining and assessing the real value of these earlier modern initiatives of undertaking comparative legal research. Hence, when referring to pre-paradigm initiatives, this chapter always narrows its understanding according to Masterman's insights on the non-paradigm state of science, by putting a strong emphasis on the individual and autonomous nature of applying the comparative method.

When examining the seventeenth-, eighteenth- and early nineteenth-century applications of the comparative method in legal scholarship, the individual, heterogeneous and competitive nature of these attempts is striking. In addition, the diverse scholarly background to these studies is also apparent, since these precursors based their research on very different premises, from early experimentalism to Hegelian ideas. It can be argued that the comparative method was applied in wide variety of forms and with no, or at best partial, shared common understanding. Happily, with the help of the Kuhnian idea of the pre-paradigm period and by relying on Masterman's additions, the assessment of these important precursors becomes a much easier task. Even though they all differ considerably from one another, they fit perfectly into the phase that Masterman calls 'non-paradigm science'.

A. Seventeenth- and Eighteenth-century Examples of the Use of Comparative Methods

Michel Villey, the famous French historian of legal thinking, stressed that the spread of the idea of modern science, gradually replacing the earlier Aristotelian-Thomist world view, had a decisive impact on the evolution of modern legal thinking too.[4] This shift originated from the realisation that the previous deductive, speculative and metaphysical approach had to be replaced by an entirely new orientation, one that gives preference to the study of facts and their causal relationships.[5] This qualitative shift in scholarly interest also led to the appearance of initiatives in legal scholarship that intended to integrate the application of the comparative method with a novel conceptual frame, departing from the long-held tradition of legal scholarship focused on natural law. In addition, this new understating in the era's comparative legal studies was aimed at overcoming attempts to reserve the use of comparative method to concentrate essentially on the practical side of legal comparison.[6] Creating a valid scholarly use of comparative methods was therefore the sought-after prize for those upcoming authors who were motivated by these subversive new influences.

The legal thinking of Gottfried Wilhelm Leibniz has to be mentioned first: not only was he an outstanding thinker of his time, but he also serves as a good example of this new understanding of the application of comparative methods in legal scholarship. In the seventeenth and early eighteenth centuries, Leibniz was considered as a brilliant personality of scientific and philosophical thinking – 'an academy in itself', according to Frederick the Great – and his restless interests covered a wide range of sciences; besides studying the problems of geometry and mathematics, Leibniz also dealt with questions of theology, philosophy and legal scholarship,[7] where he addressed the issue of applying the comparative method in legal studies, since he saw it as necessary to improve the scholarly toolkit of legal studies. In general, when discussing the law from a conceptual perspective, he wanted to give a central role to the comparison of legal orders as they manifest and work in reality, and he believed that this might lead to the establishment of a fact and reality-orientated legal science. He therefore advocated studying the law with the help of analysing and comparing various concrete legal provisions, and not by lamenting about some principles or other empirically unfounded hypotheses that led back to various concepts of natural law.

His main thesis on comparative legal studies was published in *Nova methodus discendae docendaeque iurisprudentiae*, in 1667.[8] This work showed that Leibniz overtly opposed the era's dominant natural law orientation, and he did

---

[4] M Villey, *La formation de la pensée juridique moderne* (Paris, PUF, 2003) 493–97.

[5] See esp Lord Bacon, *Novum Organum* (New York, PF Collier and Son, 1902) 6, III (11), LXXVII (54), and II (108–09).

[6] See, eg, the case of the initiatives in Renaissance France that tried to systematise the many corpuses of customary law in order to facilitate the creation of general state laws. They implied a comparative approach, but their aim was absolutely practical. See Hug, 'The History of Comparative Law' (n 1) 1040–41.

[7] For a comprehensive discussion, see BC Look, 'Gottfried Wilhelm Leibniz' in EN Zalta (ed), *The Stanford Encyclopedia of Philosophy* (Spring 2020 edn) at https://plato.stanford.edu/archives/spr2020/entries/leibniz/. For the legal dimension of his oeuvre, see M Armgardt, 'Leibniz as Legal Scholar' (2014) 20 *Fundamina* 27–38.

[8] GF Leibniz, *Nova methodus discendae docendaeque iurisprudentiae* (Francofurti, Zunnerus, 1667). Available at https://digital.slub-dresden.de/werkansicht/dlf/60761/1/.

so from a methodological perspective. In general, he rejected the tools of both deduction and abstraction in legal scholarship, and he also doubted the exclusive role of the study of Roman law in Continental legal studies.[9] Instead of all these, he advocated analysing the existing legal orders, and also suggested that the focus should be on particular sources of law, not on general legal issues. This new scholarly orientation led him to recognise that legal scholarship has to focus on every existing legal order and every legal order that ever existed. As a result of this approach, modern legal scholarship can fulfil its task: building up the so-called *theatrum legal mundi* – a collection of all laws from all times[10] – that can help in revealing the general development of law.[11] Needless to say, this approach to legal phenomena foreshadowed some components of the later initiatives that resulted in the birth of the first paradigm, but due to its obvious innovation and its potential to question the ruling conventions of the era's legal scholarship, deeply rooted in the ideas of natural law and deductive methods, it could not have any practical impact on legal studies.

Montesquieu also followed the new methodological orientation set forth by Leibniz to a certain extent in his magnum opus, *L'esprit des lois*. Montesquieu tried to reconstruct the principles of natural law in this book; however, the methodology he applied differed radically from the one prevailing in his era, the mid-eighteenth century. It was without precedent among the natural law scholars of the time that he concentrated on a systematic study of existing and historical legal orders instead of speculating on abstract principles having a general validity.[12] Montesquieu was convinced that this quasi-empirical way of study could help in the revelation of principles embedded in the nature of things.[13]

In order to fulfil this task, Montesquieu intended to compare every piece of legal information he was able to collect during his inquiries, including specific legal provisions and various customary rules, and he also decided to base his conclusions on the outcome of this wide-ranging legal comparison. Therefore, *L'esprit* is a treasury of a wide variety of legal provisions and legal customs, and some of them had a rather exotic background.[14] However, as some later commentators pointed out, his way of undertaking comparative law research was not very sophisticated from a scholarly perspective, and this intuitive and

---

[9] L-J Constantinesco, *Traité de droit comparé I. Introduction au droit comparé* (Paris, LGJD, 1972) 63.

[10] See R Hirschl, *Comparative Matters. The Renaissance of Comparative Constitutional Law* (Oxford, Oxford University Press, 2014) Epilogue.

[11] In Leibniz's own words, 'conficemus aliquando theatrum legale et in omnibus materiis omnium gentium, locorum, temporum placita', cited by Hug, 'The History of Comparative Law' (n 1) 1046, fn 90.

[12] See Montesquieu, *L'esprit des lois* (1758) Préface.

[13] See CP Courtney, 'Montesquieu and Natural Law' in D Carrithers, MA Mosher and PA Rahe (eds), *Montesquieu's Science of Politics. Essays on the Spirit of Laws* (Lanham, MD, Rowmand and Littlefield, 2001) 41–69, 46.

[14] See, eg, Montesquieu's discussion on the meaning of the term 'liberty'. Here, for instance, he refers to the customs of ancient Greeks, Cappadocians and the medieval habitants of Muscovy in order to reveal the real meaning of this concept. Montesquieu, *L'esprit des lois* (1758) bk XI, ch II.

inconsistent approach led to his making many errors as well. For instance, in some cases he relied on his sources without any criticism; in others he compared the legal institutions of peoples very far from each other in both geographical and historical terms. Moreover, due to the manifest incomparability in all these cases, the results of his comparisons are rather doubtful.[15] However, despite all these deficiencies, the role of Montesquieu cannot be overestimated in the modern formation of comparative law, since his oeuvre directed scholarly attention towards the empirical study of social and political reality, and he gave a pre-eminent role to comparative legal studies in this inquiry.[16]

Giambattista Vico's ideas on the philosophical grounds of history, which had a decisive impact on the formation of modern Italian historical and philosophical thinking in the coming period, are also relevant to the formation of early-modern comparative law thinking. The link between Vico's work and comparative law is the high importance he attached to legal history in his scholarly discussion. In essence, Vico argued that the unity of human spirit can explain why history evolves through similar phases in the age of gods, that of heroes and that of peoples. This universal thesis can most properly be justified by a comparative study of the course of legal development, since the comparison of various laws is capable of uncovering the existence of those identical principles that boost this process of general evolution. The synthesis of these principles, in addition, may lead to the establishment of a universal legal order – *diritto universale* – that conforms to the requirements of the human spirit to the fullest extent.[17]

Stemming from this thesis, Vico forcefully denies any historical opportunities for legal transplantation or legal borrowing, since he assumes that, owing to the existence of common human legal consciousness that is deeply rooted in the unity of human spirit, the same legal institutions will take shape in each legal order. Thus, the idea of legal borrowing or transplantation is simply unfounded from the perspective of his scholarly approach. Law evolves among the particular peoples independently, and the identical provisions of law are the basis of the unity of human legal consciousness during the various phases of history. That is, law has to be considered as a simple manifestation of this unitary general human spirit. These conclusions anticipated the position of the historical school of law of the nineteenth century, which also denied the option of legal transplantation; however, this nineteenth-century school of thought reached this conclusion by supposing the existence of various peoples' individual spirits – *Volksgeist* – instead of praising a universal human spirit.[18]

---

[15] On the problems and deficiencies of the *L'Esprit*, see E Ehrlich, 'Montesquieu and Sociological Jurisprudence' (1915–16) 29 *Harvard Law Review* 596–600.

[16] Constantinesco, *Traité de droit comparé I* (n 9) 61.

[17] For a detailed discussion, see ibid 64–65.

[18] cf G Del Vecchio, 'La communicabilité du droit et les doctrines de G-B Vico' in *Introduction à l'étude du droit comparé. Recueil d'Études en l'honneur d'Édouard Lambert* (Paris, Sirey-LGDJ, 1938) 591–601, 592–93.

In conclusion, the Italian scholar mostly formed his ideas by studying the course of historical development, and he mostly applied the comparative law method to justify and illustrate these ideas. It should not be forgotten that his approach had a strong intellectual influence on the future development of Italian comparative legal scholarship; for instance, Emerico Amari, in his work published in 1857 – *Critica di une scienza delle legislation comparate* – relied on his theses, and Giorgio Del Vecchio, in the first half of the twentieth century, also used Vico's insights as a scholarly starting point. In addition, Sir Frederick Pollock even argued that some of Vico's points are to be regarded as the antecedents of Sir Henry Maine's theses.[19]

B. Early Nineteenth-century Precursors: End of the Pre-paradigm Period

The success and fame of the first modern European codifications – the French *Code civil* (1804) and the Austrian *Allgemeines bürgerliches Gesetzbuch* (1811) – in the first decades of the nineteenth century strictly focused the attention of Continental legal scholarship on national and codified laws. As such, scholarly interest in foreign legal orders was weakened to a great extent, and the compartmentalisation of European legal knowledge seems to have intensified in this age.[20] However, contrary to these unfavourable tendencies, the flourishing classic German philosophy of the era preserved the interest in investigating the historical and comparative aspects of law, albeit within some restricted scholarly circles.

In 1810, Anselm Feuerbach argued for an empirical approach to legal studies, starting from some Kantian principles, and he also emphasised that the scope of legal scholarship has to include all the legal orders, from both a geographical and a historical perspective. In essence, Feuerbach had twin aims. First, he wanted to establish the framework for general legal scholarship, and he offered a crucial role to both comparative methods and contextual analysis in this impressive endeavour. Second, he also wished to point out that his era's natural-law thinking was in clear contradiction to the reality of the historical past. In order to do so, Feuerbach discussed and analysed, for instance, the legal customs and life of Siberian, Chinese and Mongol groups, and those of some other fishing/hunting people and nomadic tribes. Due to the lack of valid sources, he relied many times on travellers' tales of their own adventures that had, in legal terms, little probative value; therefore, he was unable to realise entirely his very ambitious scholarly aim of establishing a general legal scholarship. Even so, his method

---

[19] Sir Frederick Pollock, 'History of Comparative Jurisprudence' (1903) 5 *Journal of the Society of Comparative Jurisprudence* 74–89, 84, fn 4.

[20] See Hug, 'The History of Comparative Law' (n 1) 1060; M Rheinstein, 'Comparative Law and Conflicts of Law in Germany' (1934–35) 2 *The University of Chicago Law Review* 232–39, 232–34.

and his conclusions were in some conformity with the later ideas embedded in the first paradigm. In conclusion, as Gustav Radbruch argues, Feuerbach's method is certainly an antecedent of legal sociology, as he tried to understand and explain the specificities of legal development in the context of social facts. Moreover, he also attempted to determine some typologies in the course of legal evolution, and so he also had an important role in developing the later orientation and toolkit of comparative legal studies.[21]

In order to oppose the dominance of the German historical school of jurisprudence that was largely built on Savigny's theses, Eduard Gans,[22] using a Hegelian basis, planned to elaborate a general legal history – *Universalrechtsgeschichte* – that would encompass every legal order, past and present. Gans' book, focusing on the historical evolution of inheritance law, was an attempt at formulating his general approach. In this book, he discussed the relevant rules of Roman, Hindi, Chinese, Jewish, Muslim and Greek laws. In conclusion, he argued that the legal orders at different phases of development should be regarded as various states of a general and linear legal evolution.[23] Although this book was heavily criticised, inter alia because of the arbitrary classification of facts, the deficiency of sources and the invalidity of his generalisations, its four volumes were also praised by later legal scholars.[24]

Besides the activities of these two German scholars, the first legal journals containing discussions and studies of foreign laws were published in this period. A student of Feuerbach, Mittermaier, and another German legal scholar called Zachariae founded the *Kritische Zeitschrift für Rechtswissenschaft und Gesetzgebung des Auslandes* in 1829.[25] This journal served as a model for the French *Revue étrangere de legislation*, started by Jean-Jaques Gaspard Foelix, who published its first issue in 1834.[26] Both publications were intended to cover the developments of foreign legislations, and also published critical studies about foreign acts and other legal provisions. In addition to the publication of these journals, the comparative orientation appeared in the era's legal education

[21] G Radbruch, 'Anselme Feuerbach, precurseur du droit comparé' in *Introduction á l'étude du droit comparé. Recueil d'Études en l'honneur d'Édouard Lambert* (Paris, Sirey-LGDJ, 1938) 284–91.

[22] For the discussion of Gans' philosophy, see W Breckman, 'Eduard Gans and the Crisis of Hegelianism' (2001) 62 *Journal of the History of Ideas* 543–64.

[23] Constantinesco, *Traité de droit comparé I* (n 9).

[24] Hug, 'The History of Comparative Law' (n 1) 1056.

[25] On the ambitions of the editors, see Von Zachariä, 'Ueber den Zweck dieser Zeitschrift' (1829) 1 *Kritische Zeitschrift für Rechtswissenschaft und Gesetzgebung des Auslandes* 1–27: '[S]o bedarf wohl der Plan der vorliegenden Zeitschrift, der Versuch, dem Deutschen Publikum die Bekanntschaft mit den Rechten und den rechtswissenschaftliche Schriften des Auslandes zu erleichtern, ... 26.' This journal was published until 1856.

[26] This review existed until 1850. On the general French interest toward foreign law, see I Zajtay, 'Réflexions sur l'évolution du droit comparé' in H Bernstein and U Drobnig-Hein Kötz (eds), *Festschrift für Konrad Zweigert* (Tübingen, JCB Mohr, 1981) 595–602, 595. On some early minor French initiatives with special regard to the year 1833, see M Ancel, 'Cent ans de droit comparé en France' in *Livre centenaire de Société de législation comparée* (Paris, LGDJ, 1969) 3–21, 5.

too, since Eugène Lerminier, who focused on legal history earlier, was appointed as professor of comparative legal history in the *Collège de France* in 1830.[27]

These increasingly refined and delicate attempts, in theoretical terms, to include the comparative method within the scope of legal scholarship, and the rise – and fall – of some scholarly institutions, journals and professorial positions,[28] forecast the transformation of comparative law into a modern science, in a Kuhnian sense. Nonetheless, this promising process was also seriously hindered by the era's dominant school of legal thinking, legal positivism, which was bounded by the limits of national legal orders. However, the full-blown revolution that occurred in general social science thinking fundamentally changed this intellectual environment that had been rather indifferent to the issues of legal comparison.[29]

C. The Relevance of the Early-Modern Pre-paradigm Period

Why are these earlier, sometimes almost forgotten, authors relevant to the discussion of the modern European history of comparative law? First of all, their examples illustrate that Kuhn's idea of making a distinction between the pre-paradigm period, as refined by Masterman, and the rise of the first paradigm, if properly applied, results in a more refined picture of the modern history of comparative law. It seems obvious that these early-modern and modern authors worked within the circumstances of the pre-paradigm period. They already applied some form of comparative method in the course of developing their scholarly oeuvres, which also included a discussion of some legal issues, but they did so in quite divergent ways and in pursuit of different scholarly aims. In sum, a coherent application that would serve as a basis for establishing a paradigm cannot be detected.

In this period, the comparative method in legal scholarship had no uniform usage or broadly shared definition, as will be the case in the first and the subsequent paradigms. That is, these precursors did not subscribe to a coherent conceptual framework, and therefore *ad hoc* methodological choices and an occasional study of research problems dominated this period, without there being a convergence toward a possible consensual approach. These characteristics of performing scholarly activities fits perfectly into the concept of non-paradigm science, as elaborated by Masterman. In essence, it can be argued,

---

[27] The most relevant piece by Lerminier from this aspect was his *Introduction Général à l'Histoire du Droit* from 1829. On Lerminier's years in the Collège de France, see F Audren and G Navet, 'Note sur la carrière d'Eugène Lerminier au Collège de France (1831–1849)' (2001) 4 *Revue d'histoire des sciences humaines* 57–67.

[28] For an in-depth and meticulous discussion of the early history of comparative law institutions, see G Hamza, 'Az összehasonlító jogtudomány kibontakozásának útjai Európában' (1996) 38 *Állam- és Jogtudomány* 275–78.

[29] cf Pollock, 'History of Comparative Jurisprudence' (n 19) 79.

this early-modern and modern period in the history of comparative law justifies Kuhn's and, consequently, Masterman's statement that the general development of science is to be divided into two main phases: the preliminary history – the pre-paradigm period – and the 'real history' – the emergence of subsequent paradigms – and the real dividing line in this story is definitely the rise of the first paradigm, as this qualitatively transforms the general context of carrying out comparative law studies.

In addition, it has to be pointed out that all these precursors give good examples of a productive use of the comparative method in legal scholarship, but they also point out why it is impossible to conceptualise it as modern scholarship when the commonly-shared conceptual background and the scholarly community had not yet evolved. The use of the comparative method had a decisive role in the legal studies of all the previously mentioned precursors; however, there was no already-settled consensual and commonly shared set of scholarly principles and exemplars with which they could be in conformity; instead, it played its role according to individual and occasional preferences. It therefore seems more appropriate to consider their works as individual initiatives to apply various comparative methods in legal scholarship, rather than as the first appearances of an autonomous scholarly movement aiming at the creation of the first paradigm of comparative law. The claim of applying the comparative method in a proper scholarly manner was already manifested, but an institutionalised scholarly community, acting according to consensual and shared commitments and exemplars, had not yet taken shape.

III. GENERAL BACKGROUND: THE RISE OF POSITIVISM AND THE IDEA OF EVOLUTION

Continental European legal scholarship, originating from the mediaeval *ius commune* that was rooted in the wide reception of Roman law, seemed to be irreversibly disintegrating along national borders by the end of the eighteenth century. This was primarily due to the emergence of modern states and their efforts to centralise the formerly multifaceted legal orders.[30] For this reason, starting from the beginning of the nineteenth century, one can no longer refer to a united European legal scholarship. Instead, the major players of the European legal world became its national counterparts, which focused on analysing and developing their own legal orders. The attention of legal scholars was almost entirely in this direction, except for a few isolated attempts,[31] and the study of foreign laws lost its significance.

---

[30] cf M Weber, *Staatssoziologie* (Berlin, Duncker und Humblot, 1956); or N Davies, *Europe: A History* (New York, Harper, 1998) 577–674.

[31] cf Ancel, 'Cent ans de droit comparé en France' (n 26) 4; or Rheinstein, 'Comparative Law and Conflicts of Law in Germany' (n 20) 232–33.

However, following the first third of the nineteenth century, European scholarly thinking was affected by some fundamentally new impacts, which, by the middle of the century, led to a substantial transformation of the era's perception of scholarship dealing with political and social issues. This important change did not leave the previously national-legal-tradition-focused thinking of lawyers unaffected either.

These impacts are to be divided into two large groups. On the one hand, the general methodological transformation of the period's scientific thinking has to be pointed out; on the other, the idea of evolution, which had a great influence by the second half of the century, needs to be mentioned. This general methodological transformation of scientific thinking, and the wide penetration of the idea of evolution, had such a comprehensive impact on the thinking and intellectual atmosphere of the period that it could not leave legal scholarship unaffected either.

By formulating the theses of scientific positivism, Auguste Comte decisively contributed to the formation of modern scientific thinking in the social sciences. Inspired by the buoyant development of natural sciences in this period, Comte argued that social phenomena can be studied with the help of the methods of natural sciences. Hence, laws, having an objective character that affects social phenomena, can be reconstructed, and the laws of the world of physics offer suitable examples of such endeavours. As such, in Comte's eyes, research focusing on social phenomena should always be based on facts and not on *a priori* principles.[32] These insights show that Comte's ideal was research into social phenomena with a precision that can be compared to that of the natural sciences, and the simple fact that he gave the analysis and discussion of social phenomena the name 'social physics' (*physique sociale*) also reveals a lot about his thinking. In sum, due to the appearance of Comte's positivism, focusing on the method of induction, the application of methods rooted in natural sciences gained momentum in scholarly discussions of various socio-historical phenomena.

In addition, by the first third of the century, the comparative method had spread over a wider circle of natural sciences, among which the first such area was comparative anatomy, as Marc Ancel argues. This spread did not leave other areas of study unaffected either, mainly given that the inductive method required by positivist philosophy had created a favourable context for the wider application of the comparative method. The earliest attempts to do so first appeared in linguistics, literature and the history of religion, so making comparisons when analysing socio-historical phenomena became acceptable to an increasingly wide circle of scholars.[33]

---

[32] For details, see A Comte, *Discours sur l'esprit positif* (Paris, V Dalmon, 1844). For an analytical discussion and criticism, FA von Hayek, *The Counter-Revolution of Science: Studies on the Abuse of Reason* (Indianapolis, IN, Liberty Press, 1979) 253–55.

[33] In 1805, Cuvier's *Traité d'anatomie comparée* was published. In 1821, Raynouard's handbook *Grammaire comparé des langues de l'Europe latine* was published, and later writings in the area of

Hegel's philosophical system was of crucial importance to the development of the idea of historical evolution. According to Hegel, history is not merely blind evolution but a process based on certain principles that can be identified by philosophers. With the help of dialectics stemming from the triad of thesis-antithesis-synthesis, one may create a connection between the different steps of history, and this process can help in identifying the idea that determines history.[34] That is, there is always an idea that comes to life in history, and the step-by-step manifestation of this process is history itself. This approach paved the way to the step-by-step, development-orientated perception of legal development in legal scholarship, hence creating the possibility of reconstructing the general evolutionary lines of legal development itself.[35]

Hegel's doctrines strongly stimulated Continental academic thinking, while in the English-speaking world Darwin's theory of evolution had a profound impact. His idea of evolution made the application of the historical method accepted generally, by influencing the attitude of those nineteenth-century authors who were dissatisfied with the premises of the utilitarian-rationalist conceptual legal thinking that dominated the eighteenth century.[36] The idea of evolution could be used perfectly to establish legal scholarship with a more historical character, thus it gave more room for historic uniqueness as opposed to the universality of rationalism.

All in all, it can be argued that the spread of the idea of scientific positivism and the theory of evolution was the key contributor to the birth of the first paradigm of modern comparative law, in Kuhnian terms. These two notions, which are intertwined in many aspects,[37] endorsed methodological principles and philosophical aims that had a vital relevance for the emerging historical and comparative jurisprudence. Basically, by merging the idea of evolution with the need for comparison, the structural frame providing the basis for a paradigm was created.

It also needs to be highlighted that the strengthening and inner coherence of the theoretical frames alone would not have been sufficient for the development of the first paradigm of comparative law if that development had not

comparative literature also became more and more widespread. See, eg, Ancel, 'Cent ans de droit comparé en France' (n 26) 4.

[34] For the details, see GWF Hegel, *The Philosophy of History* (Kitchener, Batoche Books, 2001). For an analytical discussion and criticism, von Hayek, *The Counter-Revolution of Science* (n 32) 385–87.

[35] See E von Caemmerer and K Zweigert, 'Évolution et état actuel de la méthode du droit comparé en Allemagne' *Livre centenaire de Société de législation comparée II* (Paris, LGDJ, 1969) 267–81, 269–70.

[36] See Pollock, 'History of Comparative Jurisprudence' (n 19) 79; and Sir Frederick Pollock, 'English Opportunities in Historic and Comparative Jurisprudence' in Sir Frederick Pollock, *Oxford Lectures and Other Discourses* (London, Macmillan 1890) 42.

[37] von Hayek specifically raises awareness of and thoroughly analyses the fact that the seemingly distant theories of Comte and Hegel are very much connected in their presumptions. See in detail von Hayek, *The Counter-Revolution of Science* (n 32) 367–400.

been connected to the first wave of institutionalisation. It follows logically from Kuhn's concept of paradigm that one cannot suppose the existence of paradigms without institutional networks. Only academic institutions are capable of providing a structure and intellectual framework that supports the regular practice of scholarship in a given field of study (puzzle-solving research). If this institutional framework is missing then scientists are unable to share their results with each other and the wider audience, so 'normal science', as defined by Kuhn, cannot emerge.

Marc Ancel argues that 1869 was crucial in the process of the institutionalisation of modern comparative law, most probably because of a historical coincidence. This was the year when Henry James Sumner Maine was appointed Chair of *Historical and Comparative Jurisprudence* at the University of Oxford; when the *Société de législation comparée*, which later had a profound impact on the development of comparative law, was established in Paris; and when the journal *Revue de droit international et de législation comparée* first appeared in Belgium.[38] In 1872, the French society launched its own journal (*Bulletin Trimestriel de la Société de Legislation Comparée*), which was followed in 1878 by the German *Zeitschrift für vergleichende Rechtswissenschaft*, also dealing with legal problems from a comparative perspective.[39] The first professional society of the German language region, the *Gesellschaft für vergleichende Rechts- und Staatswissenschaft*, was founded in 1894, the same year as the *Internationale Vereinigung für Vergleichende Rechtswissenschaft und Volkswirtschaftlehre*[40] and the *Society of Comparative Legislation*[41] in Germany and England, respectively. These societies, their networks and their journals, combined with some law departments with a comparative law orientation, already provided fertile ground for scholarly research built upon regular communication between legal scholars with a comparative law interest, and thus led to the formation of a scientific community devoted to a comparative study of law.[42]

In the following, this paradigm will be discussed by presenting its two main streams, the English and the German schools of historical and evolutionary comparative law thinking. The differentiation between these two schools is justified by their linguistic and cultural uniqueness; however, it should also be borne in mind that a vast number of common presumptions connected them too.

---

[38] Ancel, 'Cent ans de droit comparé en France' (n 26) 6.

[39] I Zajtay, 'Réflexions sur l'évolution du droit comparé' (n 26) 596.

[40] See Rheinstein, 'Comparative Law and Conflicts of Law in Germany' (n 20) 234, fn 8. For details see H Wehberg, 'Internationale Vereinigung für Vergleichende Rechtswissenschaft und Volkwirtschaftslehre' in *Introduction á l'étude du droit comparé. Recueil d'Études en l'honneur d'Édouard Lambert* (Paris, Sirey-LGDJ, 1938) 664–68.

[41] See Z Péteri, 'A jogösszehasonlítás kezdetei az angol jogtudományban' (1975) 18 *Állam- és Jogtudomány* 393–414, 409, fn 57.

[42] On institutionalisation, see in detail Constantinesco, *Traité de droit comparé I* (n 9) 103–07.

IV. HISTORICAL AND COMPARATIVE JURISPRUDENCE –
THE EMERGENCE OF THE PARADIGM IN ENGLAND

A. The Fusion of the Historical and Comparative Methods in Maine's *Ancient Law*

It is no exaggeration to say that Sir Henry Sumner Maine's work marks one of the turning points of nineteenth-century English jurisprudence. Maine deliberately abandoned the previously dominant analytical approach – created by Austin and Bentham and based on a rationalist epistemology – and turned against the approach of eighteenth-century authors who manifestly neglected the historical dimension of legal phenomena.[43] In his magnum opus, *Ancient Law*, published in 1861 and soon to become popular all over the Continental Europe, Maine attempted to discover the general laws of legal development through examining the history of the various institutions of law. One may consider his efforts as ground-breaking, since he tried to analyse the phenomenon of law within the conditions of the given historical era, including its social, economic and ideological contexts. With this, Maine distanced himself from utilitarian-analytical thinking, which put legal principles at the centre of any study and applied the tools of logic to legal phenomena, without any interest in their contexts.[44]

Maine's view on legal scholarship, a novelty in his era, was formed as a result of several factors. First of all, the impact of natural science methods should be mentioned, as these methods opined that the discovery of objective, empirically-founded laws of nature was certainly possible. Maine, in accordance with the period's inclination towards positivism, firmly believed that one can find similar laws in human nature and in society as well,[45] and, as a consequence, legal history should also have its own evolutionary laws. As such, he wanted to make legal scholarship a real science, according to the current criteria of positivism, so he put the inductive method in the spotlight, instead of the previously dominant deductive and speculative approaches. His influencing model was geology, which, with regard to the questions of geomorphology, praised the idea of continuous and almost undetectable change, as opposed to those former concepts that regarded sudden and vast catastrophes as the reasons for geological variations.[46] It is apparent that this idea was the main inspiration for Maine's views on organic legal development, and he built up his theory of the levels of the development of law based on this analogy.

---

[43] About Maine's career in detail, see G Hamza, 'Sir Henry Maine et le droit comparé' (2005) 45 *Acta Antiqua* 193–206; Péteri, 'A jogösszehasonlítás kezdetei az angol jogtudományban' (n 41) 399.

[44] For the comprehensive critique of the utilitarian-analytical thinking, see J Bryce, 'The Methods of Legal Science' in J Bryce, *Studies in History and Jurisprudence*, vol II (Oxford, The Clarendon Press, 1901) 607–37.

[45] Sir Paul Vinogradoff, 'The Teaching of Sir Henry Sumner Maine' in *The Collected Papers of Paul Vinogradoff I* (New York, The Legal Classics Library, 1995) 173–89, 182.

[46] P Stein, *Legal Evolution* (Cambridge, Cambridge University Press, 1988) 88.

Besides his natural sciences-influenced thinking, based on external laws, Maine also drew ideas from the theses of the German historical school of jurisprudence. This conservative and romantic understanding, which argued passionately in favour of the historical and collective psychological character of law, clearly influenced Maine's work, especially in relation to the application of the historical method.[47] Both Maine and the historical school of jurisprudence shared the view that there were some distinct nations (superior or progressive ones) whose legal development followed its own unique path. Moreover, Maine also agreed with the scholars of the historical school that Roman law was the most important starting point of any legal research.[48] However, Maine abandoned the framework that Savigny had advocated, insofar as he expanded his research to include English, Greek and Hindu law (besides Roman law).[49] He also did not consider the national characteristics defining its legal development to be rigid and unchangeable.[50] To sum up, Maine incorporated the insights of the historical school in his theory but without its strictly national, that is to say German, bias. This may be one of the reasons behind the popularity of his theses abroad.

Another important element of Maine's scholarly attitude was his constant 'fight' against abstract and *a priori* theses. He agreed neither with contractual theories endorsing the idea of a natural state, nor with *a priori* constructions of natural law, because he thought that they were all founded on false assumptions. Among other things, they did not take into consideration the organic nature of social development, and he also believed that their picture of the so-called primitive human was fundamentally wrong. Besides these sceptical views, Maine heavily criticised the approaches of Jeremy Bentham and John Austin: first of all, he doubted the feasibility of utilitarianism; second, he considered Austin's concept of law, focusing on the central role of the sovereign, to lack any connection with history.[51]

These all shaped Maine's understanding of his historical and comparative method, by which he aimed to present the questions of legal development in a fundamentally new context, in his book, *Ancient Law*. The starting point of his theory was the differentiation between stationary and progressive societies.[52] He apparently needed this differentiation in order to avoid the mistakes stemming from the generalisation of the uniqueness of Western European social and legal development, which was especially striking compared to the societies in the colonies of the era, such as some parts of India. In light of this, Maine did not want to declare the laws of development that had determined Western

---

[47] Vinogradoff, 'The Teaching of Sir Henry Sumner Maine' (n 45) 180.
[48] Stein, *Legal Evolution* (n 46) 90.
[49] ibid 92.
[50] Vinogradoff, 'The Teaching of Sir Henry Sumner Maine' (n 45) 180.
[51] ibid 176–78.
[52] Sir Henry Sumner Maine, *Ancient Law. Its Connection with the Early History of Society and its Relation to Modern Ideas* (London, John Murray, 1908) 21.

legal development to be generally valid, as it was easily imaginable that a society outside Europe, due to the underdeveloped nature of its social relations, was unable to follow the Western path. Based on the previous differentiation, and through analysing the history of some legal institutions – fiction, equity and legislation – that harmonise legal development with social development, Maine concluded that developing societies necessarily move through the disintegration of traditional ties towards the development of individual relations determining the modern era. According to Maine, this process could be summarised, in legal terms, by the evolution from status to contract.[53]

With the help of this theory of 'legal evolution', a historical classification of legal systems also takes form. Based on his previous presumptions, an evolutionist way of legal development is to be reconstructed: cohabitation without provisions with a legal character[54] is followed by a state of society that is regulated by prompt individual decisions based on divine inspiration (the so called *themistes*);[55] then customary law, built on oligarchic bases, evolves;[56] and finally these customs are enacted in law, the rea of ancient codes.[57] This line of development was called the spontaneous development of law by Maine, who held that it occurs in all human communities. However, the differentiation between developing and stagnating societies takes on a real meaning at this point, as a further development from fiction, equity and legislation to contract is only a privilege for advancing or developing societies. It is evident that the previously described path of development provides an opportunity to place the legal systems of different periods and societies onto the different levels of legal development, and so it incorporates the possibility for a historical and development-based classification of legal systems too.

Ancient Law brought resounding success to its author, and some of the theses elaborated in the book, such as the strict formalism of ancient law, the connection between law and religion in the practice of ancient societies, and the role of procedural law in the earliest legal systems,[58] soon became core concepts of legal history and spread quickly. Obviously, this success and widespread reception was due to the fact that Maine's views could easily be fitted into the public thinking that already dealt intensively with the notion of scientism and the idea of biological evolution.[59]

To sum up, Maine's work opened up new prospects in English jurisprudence, and created an intellectual school in the meantime. In the following decades, this school, with Oxford University at its centre, continued to explore certain problems and develop the research method still further, inspired by the 'master'.

---

[53] ibid 151.
[54] ibid 110.
[55] ibid 3–6.
[56] ibid 8–12.
[57] ibid 12–18.
[58] For the listing of Maine's theses known as 'scientific commonplaces', see Stein, *Legal Evolution* (n 46) 98.
[59] ibid 99–100.

B. The Development of Historical and Comparative Jurisprudence

Sir Frederick Pollock, who took charge of Maine's department in 1883 and led it for 20 years, was a pioneer in improving Maine's findings. Besides his wide-ranging work on common law,[60] Pollock prepared commentaries to Maine's major writings; moreover, he studied the methodological problems and historical antecedents of comparative law in detail.[61]

To Pollock, historical and comparative jurisprudence relied on the same historical method that had previously been applied in natural and social sciences. To put it in a wider context, according to him, the historical method came from Darwin's theory of evolution, which Pollock understood as the historical, more precisely historical-evolutionary, interpretation of natural facts. Hence, it can logically be argued that the use of the historical method, in reality, means the application of the theory of evolution, through which the development of human societies can be explained from a general aspect.[62]

The most significant forerunners of applying the historical method in social sciences were Vico, Montesquieu, Burke and Savigny, but it was the 'master', Maine, who improved and refined the use of this method for the area of jurisprudence. For Pollock, the historical method itself became the newest and most important tool of the natural and the social sciences. The main advantage of this method is its inductive or facts-focused nature, which protects the researcher from the exaggerated, sometimes even surreal 'flow' of rational-deductive thinking. However, its deficiencies also come from its inductive nature, as the method is not able to provide answers to the final, abstract problems of philosophy. Due to these immanent barriers, the historical method can highlight where the competence of science ends and where the role of philosophy begins, and it can also show the point where pertinent philosophical questions can be raised.[63] Thus, the historical method, based on the idea of evolution, can accurately define the borders between science and philosophy, and consequently it defines the place of historical and comparative jurisprudence in the world of legal scholarship.

---

[60] Amongst others, Pollock dealt with the question of contracts and *torts*, the development of *common law* and participated in writing Maitland's comprehensive piece, *History of English Law*. See WS Holdsworth, *The Historians of Anglo-American Law* (New York, Columbia University Press, 1928) 94–98.

[61] See Pollock, 'History of Comparative Jurisprudence' (n 19); Sir Frederick Pollock, 'English Opportunities in Historic and Comparative Jurisprudence' in Sir Frederick Pollock, *Oxford Lectures and Other Discourses* (London, Macmillan 1890) 37–64; or Sir Frederick Pollock, 'Droit comparé: prolégoménes de son histoire' in *Congrés international de droit comparé. Tenu á Paris du 31 juillet au 4 aout 1900. Procés-verbaux et documents* (Paris, LGDJ, 1905) 248–61, 258–61.

[62] Pollock, 'English Opportunities' (n 61) 41.

[63] Pollock's words on this (ibid 42): 'It is a key to unlock ancient riddles, a solvent of apparent contradictions, and potent spell to exercise those phantoms of superstition, sheeted now in the garb of religion, now humanity, now (such is their audacity) of the free spirit of science itself, that do yet squeak and gibber in our streets. It is like the magic sword in Mr George Meredith's delightful tale, whose power was to sever thoughts.'

Furthermore, the results of Pollock's methodological research revealed that a strict separation of the historical and comparative methods was simply impossible, so legal scholarship has to be historical and comparative at the same time. Pollock based this conclusion on a quote from Maine and his opening remarks in *Village Communities*.[64] Through emphasising the inseparable nature of the historical and comparative methods, Pollock in reality declared the basic principle of the first paradigm of modern comparative law. The universality of his statement is further proved by the fact that, through referring to the work of Joseph Kohler,[65] Pollock stated that, from his perspective, it did not even matter whether one called this field of study historical and comparative jurisprudence or universal legal history (*Universale Rechtsgeschichte* or *Vergleichende Rechtswissenschaft*).[66]

With regard to specific research tasks and opportunities, Pollock thought that comparative jurisprudence had a huge potential for study; for instance, the historical analysis of English legal institutions and their comparison with Roman law, or the study of certain Indian laws. Besides theoretical aims, researching Indian law had practical uses as well, since getting to know Indian law was in the vital interest of the public administration of the British Empire. In his arguments, Pollock explained that he did not believe that India could be governed only through the rule of weapons; in order to establish a well-functioning public administration, knowledge of Indian legal orders was a must.[67]

Questions of methodology were also studied by Pollock's close friend, James Bryce, who usually dealt with political and public law issues, and who also shared the assumption about the unity of the historical and comparative methods. In his polemic piece about the methods of jurisprudence, which was also quite critical of Bentham and Austin, Bryce argues that the comparative method, as understood by Pollock, is nothing more than another 'face' of the historical method. With the help of the comparative method, the most important and general characteristics can be filtered from the legal historical facts collected through the historical method, so well-founded theoretical conclusions can be drawn this way.[68] In sum, both of them, Pollock and Bryce, conclude that jurisprudence cannot be imagined either without the historical or without comparative methods, since these complement and mutually help each other.

Sir Paul Vinogradoff, who emigrated from Russia, is to be considered the last representative of English historical and comparative jurisprudence. His work greatly contributed to the further development of the theoretical assumptions of the so-called Oxford school of comparative law, in that he incorporated the

---

[64] Pollock, 'History of Comparative Jurisprudence' (n 19) 75. For a detailed analysis, Péteri, 'A jogösszehasonlítás kezdetei az angol jogtudományban' (n 41) 404.

[65] Several versions exist when it comes to spelling Joseph Kohler's name. This study uses the version of the German National Library.

[66] Pollock, 'History of Comparative Jurisprudence' (n 19) 76.

[67] See in detail Pollock, 'English Opportunities' (n 61) 43–64.

[68] Bryce, 'The Methods of Legal Science' (n 44) 154–55.

results of the period's German social sciences, mainly Max Weber's points, into his works. His main work, which was planned to be his legacy in six volumes but remained unfinished due to his death, became the most compelling attempt to provide a summary and a well-structured explanation for historical and comparative jurisprudence, that is, for this paradigm.

Vinogradoff succeeded Pollock as head of the Historical and Comparative Jurisprudence Department in 1904, and in his inaugural lecture, besides praising Maine's work, he gave a detailed presentation of the theses of comparative jurisprudence. This was especially important, because it provided a structured and well-considered summary of those research principles, which had already, tacitly and many times intuitively, driven the works of his predecessors. He distinguished four fundamental principles: (i) the purpose of studying law cannot be restricted to the transfer of professional knowledge, law can also be a subject of scientific study; (ii) two distinct methods can be applied in legal research, the deductive and the inductive methods; (iii) in inductive research, law appears as a historical phenomenon; (iv) if research aims at discovering general laws then the historical method must also be comparative.[69] With the help of these four propositions, Vinogradoff organised the structural principles of the first paradigm of comparative jurisprudence into a logical system, thus largely contributing to the clarification of a previously fragmented and intuitive methodology, and thereby creating a stable framework for puzzle-solving research.

Another important methodological observation by Vinogradoff was the distinction between the analytical and synthetic study of law. This clarification is important, because the historical method was usually seen as the antithesis of the analytical method. Vinogradoff considered this a logical mistake, and argued that the antithesis of the analytical method was not the historical but the synthetic method.[70] In addition, the purpose of the synthetic method, as opposed to the analytical method solely focusing on law and legal provisions, was to examine the historical, social, economic and other factors influencing the development of law, and to understand law as a historical phenomenon in general. History can take a crucial role in this process, but other sources, such as statistical data – if available – can also be added to the research.

One of the most important benefits of the synthetic method is that it protects the researcher, who may frequently be enchanted by the attraction of a 'conceptual heaven', from drifting too far apart from social reality; moreover, it prevents the researcher from disregarding some factors, in the name of conceptual clarity and logic, without which the functioning of law is incomprehensible.[71] However, it should be emphasised that Vinogradoff, as opposed to the often categorical, or

---

[69] Vinogradoff, 'The Teaching of Sir Henry Sumner Maine' (n 45) 188–89.
[70] Sir Paul Vinogradoff, 'Methods of Jurisprudence' in Sir Paul Vinogradoff, *Custom and Right* (Union, New Jersey, The Lawbook Exchange, Ltd, 2000) 4.
[71] ibid 7–8.

sometimes even ironic opinions of his predecessors, did not discard the analytical method in its entirety, but instead recognised its relevance in conceptual legal thinking. He argued that the different national legal provisions accentuate the necessity for an analytical method. Furthermore, the comparative research of different national solutions opens the way to a synthetic research method, which looks for the causes of the differences between legal institutions in their contexts.[72] In this way, analytical research is an inherent step of legal study, but it can never become exclusive if one aims to find a general and comprehensive explanation.

In his main work,[73] Vinogradoff aimed to find a theoretical explanation for European legal development, starting from the work of his predecessors. In this late writing, he tried to provide a comprehensive, encyclopaedic summary of historical and comparative jurisprudence, as complementary to his predecessors' and colleagues' work. His views on legal development were framed by the differentiation of the historical types of legal development. In determining the historical types of law, Vinogradoff was inspired by the results of early German economic sociology; for example, in many writings he mentioned the impacts of the theories of Max Weber and Karl Bücher.[74] These historical types of the development of law were understood by Vinogradoff, similarly to the previously mentioned scholars, as ideal types, so he did not aim to consider them as exclusive patterns.

As for conceiving legal development based on historical types, Vinogradoff analysed the roots and theoretical problems of this approach in detail. He tracked their origins back to Aristotle and Montesquieu, but he also argued that their attempts at classification had lost their validity by then, because they had always started from the state when explaining law. However, law was not connected to the state in all historical periods; this had already been proved by Maine, and was why a new and valid attempt to create historical ideal types, in line with the requirements of the synthetic method, should be based on social arrangements, and not on a given political constellation of exercising public power. Vinogradoff agreed that law was closely tied to values, and he considered this feature as an important factor in creating the types, but he rejected both the 'idealistic monism' of Hegel and the 'economic monism' of Marx. These approaches did not fit in the synthetic method, as they were exclusive by putting only one factor of development at the centre of their argumentation. Further mistakes of Hegelian and Marxist theories were that, in some cases, they confused fact with idea and effect with cause, as was pointed out.[75]

---

[72] ibid 10–11.

[73] Sir Paul Vinogradoff, *Outlines of Historical Jurisprudence I–II* (London, Oxford University Press, 1920–22).

[74] Sir Paul Vinogradoff, *Outlines of Historical Jurisprudence I* (London, Oxford University Press, 1920–22) 156.

[75] See in detail Sir Paul Vinogradoff, 'Historical Types of International Law' in *The Collected Papers of Paul Vinogradoff II* (New York, The Legal Classics Library, 1995) 248–58.

Vinogradoff considered his method to be ideological, as he argued that the task of historical jurisprudence was monitoring the path of ever-changing legal ideas with the help of the facts of legal history. He used the expression 'ideological' primarily to emphasise the distance between his understanding of legal development and the chronological method. This task is facilitated by the fact that in human evolution some ideal developmental lines can be discovered.[76]

He differentiated between six historical types of law: (i) the law of totemistic societies; (ii) tribal law; (iii) the law of city-states; (iv) mediaeval law; (v) the law of individualism; and (vi) the law of collectivism. It has to be emphasised, at the very beginning, that this classification has no universal character as it is only relevant to the European development of law. Nor does this grouping require a chronological order, as some components of these settings may appear in different periods as well.[77]

It is apparent that Vinogradoff, similarly to Kohler, does not derive his arguments from the most radical version of evolutionism, according to which all human societies necessarily have to go through the same developmental stages, but he believes in a more 'relativist' version of the idea. This more 'relativist' understanding accepts that, in the process of general legal development determined by universal laws, unique phenomena and developmental lines in some ways different from others may exist.

Vinogradoff's work is essential from many angles. His methodological efforts made a large contribution to systematising and clarifying the methodology of historical and comparative jurisprudence. In Kuhnian terms, he managed to systematise the theses of the paradigm in an explicit way. It can be noted, however, that his work, which was very sophisticated both theoretically and historically, due to the spread of new ideas on legal comparison as elaborated by French authors, such as Lambert or Saleilles,[78] remained more-or-less unknown in the Western literature of comparative law. This is why Vinogradoff is mainly remembered today by academia as a legal historian.

V. FROM *ETHNOLOGISCHE JURISPRUDENZ* TO *VERGLEICHENDE RECHTSWISSENSCHAFT* – THE BIRTH OF A PARADIGM IN GERMANY

A. The Beginning: Ethnological Perspectives in the Legal Scholarship

In the nineteenth century, German legal thinking, in harmony with the general European scholarly atmosphere, was very much devoted to the dogmatic-positivist

---

[76] ibid 245.
[77] ibid.
[78] cf E Lambert, 'Conception générale et définition de la science du droit comparé, sa méthode, son histoire: le droit comparé et l'enseignement du droit' in *Congrés international de droit comparé. Tenu á Paris du 31 Juillet au 4 aout 1900. Procés-verbaux et documents* (Paris, LGDJ, 1905) 26–60; or R Saleilles, 'Conception et objet de la science du droit comparé' in *Congrés international de droit*

understanding of law. German lawyers accepted the boundaries of their national legal system as a given, and focused on its 'internal' problems.[79] Their efforts reached their peak in the pre-World War I decades, at the same time as the *Bürgerliches Gesetzbuch* was enacted and came into effect. However, despite all this, some authors still needed a 'broader perspective',[80] and this need, propelled by the rise of empirical and evolutionist methods in general scholarly thinking, led to the start of comparative legal studies and the formation of an academic community in the last three decades of the century.

These initiatives, which stretched beyond the dogmatic-positivist horizon of this period, started with a volume published at the beginning of the 1860s. In 1861, Bachofen's book on matriarchal legal systems was published, which, contrary to the dominant dogmatic trends, did not concentrate on Roman law alone, as did the influential 'Romanists' of the historical school of law, but also integrated the study of 'other' legal systems.[81]

The first comprehensive discussion of the research goals and methodology of the new approach was submitted by Albert Hermann Post, a lawyer and judge from Bremen.[82] The titles of Post's first writings[83] show that the aim of their author was to renew the methodology of jurisprudence, inspired by the new impetus provided by the rapid development of natural sciences. This need for renewal was propelled by Post's dissatisfaction with the legal thinking of his era, with special regard to methodological tenets: he considered the theses of both the natural law school and the historical school of law to be simply unfounded. From his perspective, a major shortcoming of the school of natural law was that scholars of this approach, in general, did not pay enough attention to studying the legal life of the different peoples of the world, so they failed to discover the reality of law. Moreover, he pointed out that the hypothesis of a general innate legal sense was absurd. Further, he criticised the historical school of law because this scholarly movement only dealt with the law of some peoples; it did not strive for more general research, and therefore only focused on written sources

comparé. Tenu á Paris du 31 Juillet au 4 aout 1900. Procés-verbaux et documents (Paris, LGDJ, 1905) 167–89.

[79] See in detail Rheinstein, 'Comparative Law and Conflicts of Law in Germany' (n 20) 232–38.

[80] ibid 233.

[81] JJ Bachofen, *Das Mutterrecht: eine Untersuchung über die Gynaikokratie der alten Welt nach ihrer religiösen und rechtlichen Natur* (Stuttgart, 1861). Gábor Hamza considers this writing the starting point of the school based on Kohler and Bernhöft; see Hamza, 'Sir Henry Maine' (n 43) 201–03.

[82] R Schott, 'Main Trends in German Ethnological Jurisprudence and Legal Ethnology' (1982) 14 *Journal of Legal Pluralism* 37–68, 38. It is interesting to note here that the first attempt to undertake empirical research on the legal life of tribes living in German colonies is also connected to Post. In 1893, Post developed a comprehensive questionnaire, which provided help in examining the legal systems of the tribal civilisations of the German colonies in Africa. See in detail A Lyall, 'Early German Legal Anthropology: Albert Hermann Post and his Questionnaire' (2008) 52 *Journal of African Law* 114–38.

[83] *Das Naturgesetz des Rechts. Einleitung in eine Philosophie des Rechts auf Grundlage der modernen empirischen Wissenschaft* (1867); *Einleitung in eine Naturwissenschaft des Rechts* (1872).

while neglecting others.[84] Due to these manifest deficiencies, a completely new jurisprudence had to be established, the preparation of which, according to Post, could largely be facilitated by the idea of empiricism and evolutionism; furthermore, the application of the comparative method must play a role.

In the creation of the methodology of this new jurisprudence, Post was largely inspired by three disciplines rapidly developing in the era: ethnology, biology and sociology. The universality of ethnology and its methodological outlook had a great effect on him, because these features could help to overcome the imperfections of the natural and historical schools of law that were already identified. The idea of evolution in biology – which preached the orderliness of development and had been considered broadly accepted since Lamarck[85] – could be integrated perfectly into a new, comprehensive account of legal development. Sociology, which had successfully applied the method of empirical research to the study of societies, had undoubtedly provided the most important pattern for methodological renewal in jurisprudence.[86]

Overall, Post's perception of scholarship was strongly shaped by the general scientific development of his era, and its most important goal was to lay down the foundations of a new empirically-grounded theoretical jurisprudence. This new way of thinking would accept the idea of evolution as a starting point, and would examine as many legal systems around the world as possible. An interesting aspect of his evolutionism is that even though Darwin's doctrine greatly influenced his attitude to legal development, Post never accepted the validity of the fight for survival – as the leading notion of social Darwinism – while he supported the unidirectional nature of evolutionary development.[87]

Besides Darwin's biological concept and the previously mentioned disciplines, Post's views on legal development were also influenced by the evolutionary theory of Adolf Bastian, an important ethnographer of his era. According to Bastian, due to the homogeneity of human nature, development takes place in the same way and goes through the same steps everywhere in the world (*Elementargedanke*); however, some differences can also be detected, which may be due to geographic, climatic or economic characteristics (*Völkergedanke*).[88] It follows logically from this approach that 'primitive people' show those early developmental levels from which the 'more civilised' Western peoples have

---

[84] R M Kiesow, 'Science naturelle et droit dans la deuxième moitié du XIXe siècle en Allemagne' in P Amselek (ed), *Théorie du droit et science* (Paris, PUF, 1994) 187–210, 193–94.

[85] For a detailed discussion of the idea of evolution at the first half of the 19th century, CC Gillispie, 'Lamarck and Darwin in the History of Science' (1958) 46 *American Scientist* 388–409, esp 392.

[86] Kiesow, 'Science naturelle et droit dans la deuxième moitié du XIXe siècle en Allemagne' (n 84) 200–03.

[87] ibid 208–09.

[88] P Koschaker, 'L'histoire de droit et le droit comparé surtout en Allemagne' in *Introduction á l'étude du droit comparé. Recueil d'Études en l'honneur d'Édouard Lambert* (Paris, Sirey-LGDJ, 1938) 274–83, 276–77.

already moved on. This insight is of great importance from the perspective of legal development, because the research of natural or 'non-civilised' peoples makes it possible to get to know episodes of Western legal history that could otherwise only be speculated about due to the lack of sources, argued Post.[89] Thus, research always has to focus on the similarities of legal development dominated by evolution, and differences, according to him, simply have to be disregarded.[90]

Post also examined the relation between legal philosophy and ethnology. In his view, ethnological research may point out that the phenomenon of law is inspired by a collective, and not individual, legal consciousness. The philosophical reason behind emphasising collective legal consciousness might have been the fact that, in relation to the general questions of consciousness, Post categorically rejected Schopenhauer's idealism, which separated world and consciousness and opposed them to each other. According to Post, the facts of the world surrounding us have a big impact on our consciousness,[91] which cannot be disregarded when analysing legal consciousness either. He argued that our perceptions of law are shaped predominantly by social conditions, so if these conditions change then our legal consciousness is also transformed: some of the previous elements disappear and are replaced by new ones. Consequently, all legal philosophies that only build on the given period's legal consciousness are unable to answer general – in a strict sense – questions of law, so their scope must always be limited in nature.[92] By recognising, ethnology must have a decisive role in laying the foundations of a new, general legal philosophy.[93] Thereby, in Post's eyes, the results of ethnology may form the basis of a new, general legal philosophy. However, Post did not intend to develop this new legal philosophy in detail; this would be undertaken by the key figure of this paradigm, Joseph Kohler, a decade later.

In 1878, Franz Bernhöft and Georg Cohn founded the already mentioned *Zeitschrift für vergleichende Rechtswissenchaft*, which went on to become the central forum of the German scholars sharing, at least partly, the previously detailed theoretical assumptions. The authors connected to the *Zeitschrift* formed the German scientific community, which approached legal problems in a new and original way, in a legal atmosphere that mainly focused on dogmatics and textual interpretation.

In his editorial in 1878, Bernhöft presented the main goals of comparative law (*vergleichende Rechtswissenschaft*). He argued that this field of study, which Post earlier called ethnological jurisprudence, has to examine the historical evolution of the institutions of different peoples and the appropriate development

---

[89] AH Post, 'Ethnological Jurisprudence' (1891) 2 *The Monist* 31–40, 34.
[90] Constantinesco, *Traité de droit comparé I* (n 9) 121.
[91] Kiesow, 'Science naturelle et droit' (n 84) 195.
[92] Post, 'Ethnological Jurisprudence' (n 89) 37.
[93] ibid 40.

of the general laws of evolution.[94] In accordance with Post's already-presented thoughts, Bernhöft stated that comparative law had to change its Roman- or German-centred orientation when identifying and discussing the general laws of legal development.[95]

Comparative law should significantly broaden the horizon of jurisprudence, the only barrier to which is that it should refrain from studying the law of peoples living under a certain legal and moral 'level', because these issues obviously belong to legal ethnology.[96] Moreover, he differentiated between ethnology and comparative law, as he thought that those nations where law was not yet objectivised and, therefore, not yet separated from the sphere of morality, which was a task for legal ethnology, again, could not be studied. When Joseph Kohler became the editor of the *Zeitschrift*, this methodological differentiation elaborated by Bernhöft was given up, and this marked the beginning of examining the peoples who were regarded as being at the bottom of legal development. This ambition has led to a historically universal comparative jurisprudence, which has started to build a closer and closer relation to general philosophical efforts.

B. Joseph Kohler's General Philosophy of Law

The main representative of the German school of historical and evolutionary comparative law, that is to say the first paradigm of comparative law, was definitely Kohler, who, besides his oeuvre in patent law, law of intellectual property, competition law, international law and legal philosophy, focused on issues of comparative law as well.[97] As an author of the *Zeitschrift für vergleichende Rechtswissenchaft*, during his almost four-decades-long career, he wrote more than 300 publications belonging to the area of comparative law. His writings cover most legal systems of historical and non-historical people, from Aztecan rights to the rights of Australian indigenous people.[98]

The purpose of his theoretical writings was to create a comprehensive legal philosophy based on a comparative understanding of the universal legal history of the world. In order to fulfil this ambition, he incorporated into his research the laws of both 'uncivilised' peoples and 'civilised' nations, since he argued that law is very much present in the ordinary life of 'less-developed' people,

---

[94] Constantinesco, *Traité de droit comparé I* (n 9) 105.

[95] R Schott, 'Main Trends in German Ethnological Jurisprudence and Legal Ethnology' (1982) 14 *Journal of Legal Pluralism* 37–68, 41.

[96] This standpoint was developed by Bernhöft in his editorial introduction. F Bernhöft, 'Über Zweck und Mittel der Vergleichenden Rechtswissenschaft' (1878) 1 *Zeitschrift für vergleichende Rechtswissenschaft* 1–37, as cited by Constantinesco, *Traité de droit comparé I* (n 9) 116–17.

[97] On Kohler's attitude, see R Pound, 'Scope and Purpose of Sociological Jurisprudence [continued]' (1911/12) 25 *Harvard Law Review* 140–68, 154–58; Schott, 'Main Trends' (n 95) 41–44. The complete list of writings on Kohler can be found in (1921–22) *Archiv für Rechts- und Wirtschaftsphilosophie* 12–13.

[98] Schott, 'Main Trends' (n 95) 42.

even if in ways that differ from the modern manifestations of law. This point, based on the theory of evolution, considered the laws of 'uncivilised' peoples to be equal to modern laws, and changed the previous editorial principles of Zeitschrift as developed by Bernhöft, and also stepped over the borders of the period's Eurocentric legal thinking.[99]

Hegel had a huge impact on the formation of Kohler's view of legal philosophy and philosophy in general. He embraced all the cardinal points of the Hegelian philosophy, to such an extent that Roscoe Pound considered him to be the leading figure of the so-called German new Hegelians,[100] while other contemporaries gave him the title 'Hegel revividus'.[101] However, it is important to highlight that this Hegelian influence did not mean that Kohler accepted all components of Hegel's theory without reservations. For instance, in relation to the development of history, he rejected Hegel's dialectic view of thesis-antithesis-synthesis outright, because he was convinced that such a sterile, logical approach towards history simply cannot be justified. As for history, Kohler refined Hegel's vision by accepting the concept of historical development; however, he did not think that the line of development could be determined with logical accuracy, because history consists of ad hoc and irrational events as well, which makes the path of development always uncertain. Thus, for Kohler, human history was a complex phenomenon, and this complexity justified the necessity of studying historical phenomena in detail, instead of explaining them in an abstract, philosophical way.[102] This eventual understanding of historical development, which is free from logical constraints, appears in Kohler's views on legal evolution.

However, the dominant Hegelian effect is also shown by the fact that Kohler never considered law to be an isolated entity; rather, he saw it as a phenomenon closely related to a given people's own culture.[103] This centrality of culture, associated with his views on historical development, is the key to Kohler's general legal theory. First of all, it follows from the cultural context that the ways in which law appears in reality may differ both in space and time. Therefore, law is a constantly changing phenomenon throughout history. On the other hand, the concept of culture may help in understanding the consistency of law as well, because the constant element in the historically changing concept of law is the purpose of law itself, which connects the manifold historical manifestations of law. The main task of law, according to Kohler, is to facilitate and support the creation of culture or, more precisely, so-called cultural development, which

---

[99] Constantinesco, Traité de droit comparé I (n 9) 113.

[100] Pound, 'Scope and Purpose of Sociological Jurisprudence [continued]' (n 97) 154–58.

[101] Z Péteri, 'A jogi kultúrák összehasonlításának előtörténetéhez' (2007) 48 Állam- és Jogtudomány 509–26, 515.

[102] J Kohler, Philosophy of Law (Boston, MA, The Boston Book Company, 1914) 28–31 and 49; LM Elison, 'Kohler's Philosophy of Law' (1961) 10 Journal of Public Law 409–25, 412–13.

[103] Kohler, Philosophy of Law (n 102) 4 and 58–61. For discussion, Péteri, 'A jogi kultúrák összehasonlításának előtörténetéhez' (n 101) 516–17.

aims at the most intense fulfilment of human capabilities and, thus, at securing human domination over nature.[104] Law can help in this process by creating a predictable system of relations, as opposed to the various eventualities driving human relations, by regulating human relationships and maintaining order. According to Kohler, the insecurities of our lives can be traced back to the often illogical factors of space, time, nature, chance, need and causality, and legal institutions are able to 'tame' these factors due to their ability to maintain and preserve order; in other words, by making the world more predictable around us. This predictability, the precise organisation of *ad hoc* elements of life by regulation, ensures that law plays an important role in fulfilling the conditions of cultural development.[105]

Thus, legal development is inseparable from the transformations of human culture, according to Kohler. In his view, in all cultures we can find 'legal postulates' that define the general setting of the legal system. Law is not only changing in a historical sense, but it is also developing within a given culture, always in in accordance with the expectations of that culture.[106] In Kohler's words, 'Thus every culture has its definite postulates of law, and it is the duty of society, from time to time, to shape the law according to these requirements.'[107] In this way, a legal provision is not given in itself, but society always has to aim at recognising the needs of law and shaping the actual rules accordingly.

This leads us to Kohler's critique of the legal theory of his era. In his view, legal theory, which neglected the cultural determination of law, could not yet pay enough attention to the sociological aspects of law-making, and therefore it simply overrated the role of the lawmaker in the process. It needs to be recognised that lawmakers are the 'products' of their era, so the culture of the period affects them as much as it affects simple citizens. Consequently, law cannot be understood solely as the will of the lawmaker; the individual legal provisions should be examined in a sociological frame, in their cultural context.[108]

In addition, Kohler considered law to be inseparable from human nature, so he considered the customs of the people in the beginning of their development to be law in the strict sense of the word. He thought that 'people cannot exist without law', though there can be cultures that are not yet familiar with courts or where there is no organised state in the strict sense, but this does not mean that they do not have law.[109] Law, to Kohler, or the idea of order is coded in our human existence and cannot be separated from it. However, it

---

[104] Kohler, *Philosophy of Law* (n 102) 58. For discussion, Péteri, 'A jogi kultúrák összehasonlításának előtörténetéhez' (n 101) 516–17.

[105] cf Kohler, *Philosophy of Law* (n 102) 28–31.

[106] Pound, 'Scope and Purpose of Sociological Jurisprudence [continued]' (n 97) 156–57.

[107] Kohler, *Philosophy of Law* (n 102) 4.

[108] Pound, 'Scope and Purpose of Sociological Jurisprudence [continued]' (n 97) 158. Here Pound cites Kohler's *Lehrbuch des bürgerlichen Rechts*, §38.

[109] Kohler's thoughts about this question are as follows (translated by Schott): 'Therefore there is no people without law: there are people without courts, there are people that lack a state organization … but … Man cannot be non-Man' (Schott, 'Main Trends' (n 95) 43).

has to be emphasised that a legal order, a distinct and historically determined phenomenon, always reaches its final shape due to the individual and community impulses that shape the given culture.[110] Thus, law is a phenomenon that emerges as a totality of culturally determined, very complicated and intensively interrelated effects. Its development is influenced by many impulses, so it can only be examined in very far-reaching studies, which simply cannot be imagined without applying the comparative method.

Another important thesis of Kohler is that the genius of humanity can be visible to the researchers through the specific spirits of peoples, and this makes it possible to realise that the legal development of humanity is influenced by the same civilisational effects. Humanity has always been striving for law, *Drang nach Recht*, since the first humans appeared on Earth.[111] As such, the specificity of the human spirit is its striving for progression, so legal development is also determined by the law of progression.[112] From the point of view of the evolutionist understanding of legal development, Kohler's opinion, stemming from the critique of the Hegelian idea of development, was that it was not necessary for legal development to happen similarly in all civilisations, because only the goals are fixed; the tools for achieving those goals may differ significantly. Consequently, the main methodological principle of comparative law is that it considers different national laws to be parts of the same human civilisation, and it searches for their relationship with the development of humanity.[113]

Human civilisation, which is united in its diversity, has had different levels, and civilisation itself is a developmental process from lower towards higher levels. Hence, for Kohler, the most severe mistake for a comparatist is to compare legal systems that are not on the same civilisational level; for example, when they compare the laws of a people who make marriages through buying and selling women with those of a society that already stands at the level of religious marriage.[114] Besides this mistake, a comparatist also has to be careful to examine the substantive correlations on every occasion, and through this to make more of a distinction between the important elements in legal development and other, secondary components.[115] The task of scholars is further hampered by the irregular path of legal development, which results in situations when a legal institution may not always appear in the same form in the case of a given people.[116]

---

[110] See in detail Elison, 'Kohler's Philosophy of Law' (n 102) 415–16.

[111] J Kohler, 'De la méthode du droit comparé' in *Congrés international de droit comparé. Tenu á Paris du 31 Juillet au 4 août 1900. Procés-verbaux et documents* (Paris, LGDJ, 1905) 227–30, 228.

[112] ibid 229.

[113] ibid 230.

[114] ibid 231. Pollock comes to the same conclusion when determining that only legal systems that are on the same civilisational level are worth comparing, taking into account their individual development. According to him, comparing Indian law and customs with modern English law would only lead to ridiculous and dangerous misunderstandings. Pollock, 'History of Comparative Jurisprudence' (n 19) 76.

[115] Kohler, 'De la méthode du droit comparé' (n 111) 231.

[116] ibid.

Kohler's intellectual efforts integrated comparative law into the framework of general legal theory and created a unique understanding of jurisprudence as such. However, his philosophy-orientated work was not continued after his death in 1918, because his successors, Leonhard Adam and Richard Thurnwald, gradually gave up their former universalist aims and directed their attention only towards uncivilised peoples.[117] In sum, the background of German legal ethnology changed radically too. Following World War I, the evolutionist thinking focusing on similarities, which had been created by Bastian and further developed by Post, was discarded, and it turned towards the theory of cultural circles (*Kulturkreise*), which emphasised the uniqueness of historical development. According to this approach, every civilisation is a unique historical phenomenon that develops individually and independently.[118] Moreover, legal development can be divided into typical and atypical elements, but the typical elements are not submitted to natural laws, so their significance can only be relative. These arguments change the former paradigm-creating presumptions fundamentally and mark the separation of German legal ethnology from comparative law.[119]

VI. THE FIRST PARADIGM OF MODERN COMPARATIVE LAW: A SUMMARY

One may convincingly argue, based on the earlier discussion, that the first paradigm of modern comparative law gradually emerged in the second half of the nineteenth century and improved according to its own presumptions with the help of its own, distinctive exemplars. One may therefore also point out that this four-decades-long intellectual development meets two crucial points of Kuhn's philosophy on paradigms. First of all, as compared to the earlier attempts to use a comparative method in legal scholarship – mostly fragmentary and individual initiatives discussed in the prologue to this chapter (section II) – during the first half of the nineteenth century, the methodological coherence of these English and German scholarly works, including their conceptual bases and working premises (generalisations in Kuhnian terms), is striking. For these reasons, the 1860s can definitely be regarded as marking the end of the pre-paradigm period and the birth of the first paradigm of modern comparative law; that is to say, the idea of 'normal science'[120] was established in comparative law thinking in these years. Second, it is also apparent that the work of these German and English scholars corresponds to what Kuhn calls puzzle-solving scientific activity.[121] In both cases, methodological and substantive questions, the discourse on legal

---

[117] Schott, 'Main Trends' (n 95) 47–52.
[118] Koschaker, 'L'histoire de droit et le droit comparé' (n 88) 277.
[119] ibid 280.
[120] cf Kuhn, *The Structure of Scientific Revolutions* (n 2) 23–35.
[121] ibid 35–42.

evolution and its details are to be regarded as products of mutual discussion and reflection.

The extent to which this 'normal' academic activity was based on the same scholarly premises shared by members of the comparative law academic community, at that time mostly scholars of the English and German-speaking world, is also remarkable. Obviously, this would have been impossible without the first wave of institutionalisation, the birth of a network of journals, academic associations and university departments. The 'institutions' provided wide opportunities to get to know one another's work and to reflect on it. Even though, obviously, there were relevant differences in the works of the English and German scholars, for personal and cultural reasons, they all started from the same set of presumptions (again, symbolic generalisations). For example, German authors most often strove to identify and understand general tendencies,[122] while the English interest in legal comparison was partly dominated by its focus on particularities and aimed at examining unique phenomena as a starting point.[123]

At the centre of these presumptions stood the insight that legal development, similarly to the previous biological understanding of evolution, is ruled by laws having a similar general validity to those of natural sciences, and these laws can be discovered through devoted scholarly work. Each scholar in the paradigm attempted to reveal these universal laws determining legal development and the consecutive stages of legal evolution. They intended to carry out this research plan by examining legal development with an empirical interest – in this context, this term meant an opposition to pure philosophical deduction and fictions, so that it implied a robust attention to the facts of legal history – and by comparing the legal systems of different periods and peoples. The step-by-step examination of legal evolution was especially relevant because one of the major hypotheses of the paradigm stated that legal development goes along the same path, so by studying the legal systems of 'uncivilised' peoples, early periods of the legal history of 'civilised' nations, which were not previously to be found in written sources, can be met.

Eventually, a paradigm-creating community, predominantly composed of English and German legal scholars, emerges in front of our eyes. They were not able to make fundamental changes to the dominant, basically legal-positivist and dogmatic legal scholarship of the period, but they still created a framework and achieved results that arguably created the first paradigm of comparative law, relying on stable methodological premises and research goals. The maturity of the paradigm is proved by the simple fact that when the paradigm shift occurred

---

[122] cf Schott, 'Main Trends' (n 95) 38.

[123] According to Vinogradoff, 'The necessity for revising the comparative method is one of the lines on which modern jurisprudence has to take up the thread of investigation. Inferences must be preceded by a careful study of individual cases, and in this study juridical analysis ought to receive more attention than has been the case hitherto. This side is very poorly represented in the books of anthropological jurisprudence'. Vinogradoff, *Outlines of Historical Jurisprudence I* (n 74) 149.

in the first decades of the twentieth century, the representatives of the new thinking set forth their qualitatively new starting points in relation to or in opposition
to these presumptions.[124]

In sum, in the nineteenth century, English and German scholars played the
leading role in the development of modern comparative law thinking and the
formation of the first real paradigm, while French legal scholarship did not
participate with such intensity in creating it, although a certain scholarly interest toward comparative legal history already existed in legal scholarship, as
the example of Lerminier demonstrated. However, the Parisian International
Congress of Comparative Law, held in 1900, would not only swiftly change the
general understanding of comparative law by triggering the first paradigm shift
in the history of comparative law, but the geographical focus of comparative
law studies in Europe would also be altered as France becomes the centre of this
new paradigm (*droit comparé*). Édouard Lambert and Raymond Saleilles set
forth such new insights into the nature and goals of comparative law as would
be incompatible in scholarly terms – that is to say incommensurable – with the
earlier, well-developed premises.

---

[124] Lambert, for instance, differentiates between the goals of the historical school and the new
thinking. See Lambert, 'Conception générale et définition' (n 68) 32. Rabel, within the framework of
systemic-dogmatic comparative law, sets fundamentally different goals for comparative law than the
previous ones. Rheinstein, 'Comparative Law and Conflicts of Law in Germany' (n 20) 246–47.

3

The Paradigm of Droit Comparé

I. *FIN-DE-SIÈCLE* ATMOSPHERE

T HE SCHOLARS WHO were working along the structural premises of the historic-evolutionist paradigm of comparative law did not manage to change the positivist and dogmatic view of law[1] that became dominant at the end of the nineteenth century. The rule of this way of legal thinking culminated at the beginning of the twentieth century.[2] By accepting the borders of modern states and their legal orders as a given, this approach aimed at further elaborating a systematic and logical study of national legal concepts. Due to the predominantly inward-looking nature of this research method, legal scholars (inspired by the various dogmatic-positivist theories) tried to keep a distance from both the broader historical aspects of legal questions and foreign legal developments.[3] Thus, in general, late nineteenth-century European legal scholarship was as compartmentalised as the political map of Europe in this period.

However, a distinct feature of *fin-de-siècle* intellectual life – in which legal scholarship was also embedded – was a growing internal tension, which was expressed through many intellectual and public debates. This apparent tension stemmed from the clash between the success of modern Europe's socio-political development and those traditions of thinking that heavily and fiercely questioned the real value of these achievements (such as, for instance, Marxism or Anarchism).[4] These economic, moral, political and social debates revealed a great many concerns that were felt across Europe and beyond.

---

[1] For an excellent sketch of this approach, see J Wróblewski, 'Paradigm of Legal Dogmatics and the Legal Sciences' in Z Ziembiński (ed), *Polish Contributions to the Theory and Philosophy of Law* (Amsterdam, Rodopi, 1987) 75–88.

[2] M Ancel, 'Cent ans de droit comparé en France' in *Livre centenaire de Société de législation comparée* (Paris, LGDJ, 1969) 3–21, 4 and 8.

[3] The German jurisprudence of the era was analysed in detail from this perspective in M Rheinstein, 'Comparative Law and Conflicts of Law in Germany' (1934–35) 2 *The University of Chicago Law Review* 232–39. Rheinstein points out that the works of Rudolf von Jhering, Josef Kohler and Georg Jellinek were important exceptions to the general attitude of indifference to critical perspectives and German law orientation. The reasons for this 'legal introspection', in Rheinstein's view, are to be found in the general atmosphere of Germany, dominated by the confidence stemming from the successful creation of the German Civil Code (*Bürgerliches Gesetzbuch* (BGB)).

[4] cf CE Schorske, 'Politics and the Psyche: Schnitzler and Hofmannsthal' in CE Schorske, *Fin-de-siècle Vienna* (New York, Vintage Books, 1981) 3–23.

Thus, in order to have an in-depth understanding of the development of late nineteenth-century comparative law thinking, this general cultural phenomenon is also worthy of brief discussion. Insights into the general intellectual atmosphere of the era may also bring us closer to a more appropriate understanding of the changes in the configuration of early twentieth-century comparative law thinking. This outlook seems to be capable of ensuring that legal scholarship is approached not as a completely original, self-dependent and independent intellectual phenomenon, hermetically separated from its broader context, but as an organic part of the period's culture. In addition, this wider horizon may offer such perspectives in which the unique features of the reconfiguration of comparative legal studies might be revealed more sharply than if we examined its own scholarly context in isolation.

At the turn of the century, it seemed that Europe had developed as far as it could within the existing political and legal orders. In line with this, the debates surrounding the possibilities and dilemmas of further development began immediately. The main impetus behind this discourse was usually doubt whether Europe, which had reached the peak of its socio-cultural development and acquired a leading position in international politics too, could give answers to the most recent problems, such as growing social tensions, the emergence of the working class as an organised political actor, the limits to the previously seemingly limitless technical development and the sudden boom in the development of scientific knowledge. Moreover, another important point of these debates was what kind of role the classical European intellectual heritage, which had dominated European thinking until the turn of century, could play in this quest for answers.

This inner tension – the clash between the classical and modern, more progressive world views – manifested itself in many attempts to rephrase existing cultural conventions laying down the bases of nineteenth-century European culture. In this vein, the achievements and the success of the Enlightenment, the virtue of civic humanism, the prominence of the nation state and the omnipotence of science, inter alia, were all questioned and approached critically.[5] To put it in a nutshell, in the decades of the turn of the century, those cultural, political and scientific axioms that were formerly believed to be unshakeable became debatable, and these lively debates and discourses provided such new intellectual impulses that constantly urged perceptive European thinkers to rethink their generally agreed-upon theses.[6]

As an illuminating example, the fast-growing popularity of the style of secessionism or *art nouveau* can be mentioned in the visual arts, that is, in the

---

[5] For a literary presentation and dramatised account of this doubtful atmosphere, see the excellent novel by Thomas Mann: *Der Zauberberg* (1924).

[6] A good example of this is the writing of the Spanish philosopher and writer, José Ortega y Gasset, from 1923, entitled *The Theme of Our Time*, in which he defines the major intellectual tasks of the post-war period: exceeding the 19th century's dominant theories, namely rationalism and

spectrum of material culture. Besides its artistic value, *art nouveau* – stretching across many fields of art and merging the need for everyday use with the exalted nature of artistic inspiration – also mirrored the above-mentioned internal tension within European culture, deeply rooted in insecurity and the pressure of path-finding. Secessionism or *art nouveau*, touched by a Japanese influence, embodied the wish to escape from rigid and predetermined academic-classicist confines into more lively and, thereby, unconventional designs. That is, the artistic movement of secessionism may also be considered as an expressive symbol of this era, animated as it was by powerful tensions.[7]

All in all, European *fin-de-siècle* culture – with special regard to public thinking and art – was motivated by an intellectual climate in which the need to update the old ways and find new paths vibrated continuously. This atmosphere stimulated the emergence of completely new artistic and scholarly ambitions, aiming at exceeding the former conventions, as happened, for example, in the case of *art nouveau* or secession, in the philosophy of Henri Bergson[8] – concentrating on the presence of the so-called *élan vital*, and thereby questioning the previous mechanistic, goal-orientated world explanations – or in the case of legal scholarship.

In this period, which was a really inspiring and fruitful time from the viewpoint of legal scholarship as well, legal sociology was born; the first aspirations of legal anthropology also appeared; legal realism took shape as a new outlook on law;[9] and the neo-Kantian legal theory emerged as a leading line of legal philosophy too.[10] In addition to these new developments in the field of legal scholarship, it should be noted that the emergence of the new paradigm of comparative law – passionately arguing for the reconfiguration of the earlier exemplars based on dominantly historical and evolutionist tenets – was a product of the turn of century. This new understanding of comparative legal studies identified such hypotheses, goals and research techniques as differed in their nature from those that were outlined by the historical-evolutionist paradigm that had dominated comparative legal studies up until that time.

---

relativism, and re-evaluating the phenomenon of life. See JOY Gasset, *Korunk feladata* (Budapest, ABC, 1944) 7–99, esp 58–59.

[7] See CE Schorske, 'Gustav Klimt: Painting and the Crisis of the Liberal Ego' in CE Schorske, *Fin-de-siécle Vienna* (n 4) 208–78.

[8] In his book, Henri Bergson aims at dissolving the one-sided nature of the rationalist world-explanations of the 19th century by using the concepts of life and intuition, and he tries to open up new perspectives of thinking at the same time. See H Bergson, *L'évolution créatrice* (Paris, PUF, 1907) 7–93.

[9] For an excellent account of these developments, see Vilmos Peschka's introduction to a Hungarian textbook on the scholarly discussion of the modern developments in Western legal theory (from the socialist period): V Peschka, 'A polgári jogelméleti gondolkodás a XX. század első felében' in Cs Varga (ed), *Jog és filozófia* (Budapest, Akadémia Kiadó, 1981) 23–26.

[10] See Z Péteri, 'Gustav Radbruch und einige Fragen der relativistischen Rechtsphilosophie' (1960) 2 *Acta Iuridica Academiae Scientiarum Hungariae* 113–60.

II. A NEW WAVE OF INSTITUTIONALISATION

As a preliminary point, it should be pointed out that the formation of this new paradigm was decisively supported by the fact that, around the turn of century, many new scholarly institutions focusing on issues of comparative law started to function. This was the era when the basic institutional structure of comparative law was established. This – second – wave of institutionalisation expanded the professional opportunities of scholars engaged in comparative law, because it provided a stable framework for international cooperation. Specialised research institutions were established in this period alongside the already existing societies and faculties, facilitating regular information gathering and supporting research activities. Hence, the period between the 1900 Paris Congress and the outbreak of World War II was characterised by a considerable advancement in institutionalisation. This process manifested itself mainly in the foundation of various national comparative law research institutes, and in the creation of the first really international institution, the International Academy of Comparative Law.

On the one hand, the university positions of comparative law were strengthened in this period: in 1892, at the law faculty of the University of Paris (*Faculté de droit à Paris*) two new departments of comparative law were established;[11] then, in 1905, another position of professor of comparative civil law was created. The position was first filled by Raymond Saleilles, until his death in 1912.[12] Besides the establishment of comparative law departments, two institutions specifically dedicated to the study of comparative law were also created. Édouard Lambert founded his Institute of Comparative Law at the University of Lyon in 1920,[13] and Henry Lévy-Ullmann did the same at the University of Paris in 1931.[14] Both Institutes operate to this day. These institutions, besides teaching courses related to comparative law, dealt with scholarly administrative tasks as well, such as organising conferences and meetings, and publishing series of books dedicated to the comparative study of law.

In Germany, the 1916 foundation of the first Institute of comparative law is connected to Ernst Rabel. The Institute, the tasks of which included informing the Bavarian courts of foreign legal issues, could not then perform its duties effectively, due to the lack of relevant resources and infrastructure.[15] It became

---

[11] They were called *Droit Civil Français Approfondi et Comparé* and *Droit Commercial Maritime et Législation Commercial Comparé*. See H Lévy-Ullmann, 'The Teaching of Comparative Law: Its Various Objects and Present Tendencies at the University of Paris' (1925) 2 *Journal of the Society of Public Teachers of Law* 16–21, 18.

[12] ibid 19.

[13] For details of the institute, see S Basdevant-Bastid, 'L'Institut de droit comparé de Lyon' in *Introduction à l'étude du droit comparé – Recueil d'Études en l'honneur d'Édouard Lambert* (Paris, Sirey-LGDJ, 1938) 11–15. The website of the institute may be found at www.gdc.cnrs.fr/idcel/.

[14] For further details about the institute, see R David, 'Lévy-Ullmann et le droit comparé' in LFJ de la Morandière and M Ancel (eds), *L'oeuvre juridique de Lévy-Ullmann. Contribution á la doctrine moderne sur la science du Droit et le Droit comparé* (Paris, Centre français de droit comparé, 1952) 75–84, 83–84. The website of the institute may be found at www-u-paris2.fr/idc/.

[15] Rheinstein, 'Comparative Law and Conflicts of Law in Germany' (n 3) 241.

apparent that a more substantial financial infrastructure was needed. However, it only became available one decade after the crisis and collapse following World War I. The *Karl-Wilhelm-Gesellschaft* (now the *Max Planck Gesellschaft*), coordinating both state and private resources as a funder of sciences, founded two institutes in 1926, and the Institute dealing with comparative private law (*Institut für auländisches und internationales Privatrecht*) came to be led by Rabel.[16] The Institute, besides dealing with the organisation of traditional scholarly activities – publishing journals and books, as well as organising scholarly events – also performed more practical tasks; for instance, it collected foreign legal information and assisted the authorities when a question of foreign law was raised. In this way, among other achievements, it helped the public administration in cases relating to foreign laws, prepared certain legal reforms and constantly monitored the development of foreign law.[17]

The International Academy of Comparative Law was founded in Geneva on 13 September 1924 (*Académie internationale de droit comparé*).[18] The primary goal of this body, which initially consisted of 30 members, was the international coordination of comparative legal studies. For this purpose, they decided to organise regular congresses on comparative law every four years, and they also started to publish a journal with the title *Acta Academiae Universalis Jurisprudentiae Comparativae*. Several memoirs and the *communis opinio doctorum* revealed that the Hungarian emigrant professor Elemér Balogh contributed immensely to the foundation of the Academy,[19] and, in honour of his organising work, he held the title of perpetual secretary general (*secrétaire général perpétuel*) until his death in Paris in 1955.

The Academy's role is certainly to be regarded as outstanding in the history of comparative law. The congresses that were organised and the scholarly and personal relations developed at these events made it possible for the comparatists of the world to keep regularly in touch. The widening and further intensification of these relations contributed greatly to the gradual development of a scientific community that was much bigger than that of the previous paradigm of no

---

[16] E Wahl, 'Le Kaiser-Wilhelm-Institut für Auslaendisches und Internationales Privatrecht à Berlin' in *Introduction à l'étude du droit comparé – Recueil d'Études en l'honneur d'Édouard Lambert* (n 13) 673–680, 676. The website of the institute may be found at www.mpipriv-hh.mpg.de/index.shtml.

[17] The work of the institute is presented in detail by Rabel in E Rabel, 'On Institutes for Comparative Law' (1947) 47 *Columbia Law Review* 227–37. See also Rheinstein, 'Comparative Law and Conflicts of Law in Germany' (n 3) 244–45; and Wahl, 'Le Kaiser-Wilhelm-Institut für Auslaendisches und Internationales Privatrecht à Berlin' (n 16) 677–79.

[18] Website of the Academy at www.iuscomparatum.org.

[19] HC Gutteridge, *Comparative Law* (Cambridge, Cambridge University Press, 1949) 19. On the life and oeuvre of Balogh, see G Hamza, 'Elemér Balogh (1881–1955): The Forgotten Great Scholar of Roman Law and Comparative Law' (2008) 3 *Nordicum-Mediterraneum* 12–17. On Balogh's role in the activities of the International Academy of Comparative Law, see I Szabó, 'Elemér Balogh et l'Académie internationale de droit comparé' in I Szabó and Z Péteri (eds), *Comparative Law – Droit comparé. Selected Essays for the 10th International Congress of Comparative Law* (Budapest, Akadémiai Kiadó, 1978) 11–22.

more than 10 scholars at the same time Europe-wide. Due to the intensive organisation of scholarly activities under the auspices of the Academy, the previously rather isolated scientific community, which consisted of only a few scholars gathering around university faculties and journals, was replaced by a much wider one, whose members regularly kept in touch with each other, even personally. Moreover, these scholars were able to exchange their ideas in the publications of the Academy and on the pages of other journals, and so the institutional conditions for puzzle-solving research were set up. Furthermore, this recently established structure and the openness of the comparatists' scientific community must not be disregarded from the aspect of general legal thinking either, as it contributed to the formation of a growing general interest in questions of comparative law.

The Academy, as Balogh pointed out, never intended to favour one particular concept of comparative law. In reality, it was open to all forms of research that dealt with at least one foreign legal system. According to the Academy's rules, studies focusing on foreign law had to be restricted in two ways: simple presentations of foreign law obviously did not belong within the scope of the Institute, neither did those projects on sociology that only looked at legal systems as societal phenomena.[20] As a result of this declared openness, the Academy did not attach any single goal for comparative law to pursue in all cases; in fact it declared that comparative law has many different goals.[21] Therefore, in Balogh's eyes, comparative law was to be divided into three main schools[22] – the historic-evolutionist school, the tradition focusing on the improvement of national law, and the approach aiming at the unification of laws on the premise that some kind of *droit commun* has to exist. All these interests were reflected in the work of the Academy, although to different extents. This methodological openness, coupled with Balogh's legendary organisational skills, most probably played a key role in enabling the Academy to integrate the comparatists of the Western World without being influenced by one single interest group.

III. THE 1900 PARIS CONGRESS OF COMPARATIVE LAW

Undeniably, the formation of the second paradigm of comparative law was strongly connected to the first international congress of comparative law, organised as part of the Paris World Fair of 1900.[23] While scholarly initiatives from

---

[20] E Balogh, 'Lévy-Ullmann, Vice-Président de l'Académie Internationale de Droit comparé' in LJ de la Morandière and M Ancel (eds), *L'oeuvre juridique de Lévy-Ullmann* (n 14) 119–35, 123.

[21] Balogh considered this pluralism to be the most important feature of comparative law. See ibid 122, fn 10.

[22] See in detail ibid 123–36.

[23] For an excellent analysis and deconstruction of the intellectual (and political) context of this congress, see M Fournier, *Comparative Law Gets Entitled: The 1900 Paris Congress in Contexts* (Victoria, University of Victoria, 2018).

decades earlier[24] had already anticipated certain tenets of this new emerging paradigm, its fundamental axioms appeared for the first time in both an overt and a structured form at this Congress. Further, these new tenets – forming the basis of many exemplars applied in future research – were mostly developed as counterpoints to the older view, the historic-evolutionist paradigm. For this reason, the Congress has to be considered a unique point, a paradigm-shifting event in the history of modern comparative law that symbolises the 'victory' of the new way of thinking about comparative law studies – although, naturally, the reconfiguration of basic tenets occurred over a longer period.

Even the fact that this Congress was organised in Paris points to an essential feature of the second paradigm of comparative law, which would become dominant in the following decades. It is clear that, contrary to the German- and British-minded nature of the previous paradigm, it was French legal scholarship that played a leading role in creating and animating this paradigm.[25] During the development of the second paradigm, the institutional centre of comparative law was gradually transported to France, more precisely to Paris and Lyon: the headquarters of the *Société de législation comparée* and Lévy-Ullmann's Institute was located in Paris, while Lyon provided a home for Lambert's Institute. Due to this shift in the geographical orientation of comparative legal studies, the three and a half decade-long period of the second paradigm – the pre-World War I period and the inter-war period – might even be called 'the golden age of French comparative law'.[26]

Organising such an inviting and important event as the Paris Congress required serious preparatory work. The *Société de législation comparée* decided on the plan for the Congress at the beginning of 1899, and it succeeded in inserting the conference into the programme of the 1900 World Fair by November 1899. After this, the organising committee, led by George Picot, then President of the *Société*, was formed. The committee handed over the daily tasks relating to the organisation to an individual body[27] (*Bureau*), which had its own presidents, vice-presidents and secretaries. The two major steps in its preparation were drafting the statutes of the Congress[28] and sending out invitations.[29]

The aims of the organisers were clear from the content of the invitations and the preparatory report by Raymond Saleilles on the reasons for the event and its

---

[24] See, eg, Glasson's writing from 1880 in E Glasson, *Le mariage civil et le divorce dans les principaux pays de l'Europe* (Paris, G Pedone-Lavrier, 1879); or Zachariae and Mittermaier's work from almost a century earlier, in W Hug, 'The History of Comparative Law' (1932) 45 *Harvard Law Review* 1027–70, mainly fnn 133 and 136.

[25] LJ Constantinesco, *Traité de droit comparé I. Introduction au droit comparé* (Paris, LGJD, 1972) 127.

[26] Ancel, 'Cent ans de droit comparé en France' (n 2) 10.

[27] For the list of names, see *Congrès international de droit comparé. Procès-verbaux des scéances et document. Tome premier* (Paris, LGDJ, 1905) 2–4.

[28] ibid 4–7.

[29] G Picot and F Daguin, 'Circulaire' in *Congrès international de droit comparé. Procès-verbaux des scéances et document. Tome premier* (n 27) 7–9.

goals. The organising committee requested Saleilles to prepare a longer piece on the nature of comparative law.[30] Saleilles emphasised that the basic problem of private law scholarship in his era was that the connection between teaching private law and the development of social sciences was almost entirely absent at the turn of century. While social sciences and some areas of law – such as public law and criminology – had kept up with the new developments and were able to insert the discussion of foreign legal solutions and the results of social sciences and theoretical development into teaching, private law stuck to simple textual analyses, so it was still dominated by the explanatory method (*méthode exégé-tique*).[31] Saleilles argued that this disadvantage could only be reduced through studying foreign law, and the widespread use of comparative law seemed to be an essential prerequisite to achieving this.

In order to apply the insights of comparative law, a conceptual definition was also necessary. However, as Saleilles argued, the task of conceptual clarification was made even more difficult because one could not rely on the previous forms of comparative law – in the terms of this book, the first, historical-evolutionist paradigm – as these earlier initiatives appeared unable to explain the main problem of Saleilles' period, namely, the effect of foreign law on national law, to an adequate extent. The historical-evolutionist paradigm of comparative law, aiming at revealing the developmental history of legal evolution, had no proper scholarly vocabulary with which to approach the new phenomenon of foreign (so to say, external) legal impacts, due to its philosophical and histori-cal foundations.[32] Thus, in order to enable comparative law to handle the novel questions of the age, it had to be thoroughly conceptualised and elaborated, and its subject-matter and methodology needed to be defined. According to Saleilles, this conceptual clarification could only be done by the participants at the Congress.[33]

This conceptual ambition to draft a new structure for comparative legal stud-ies determined the whole event. The five-day Congress – between 31 July and 4 August 1900 – met in six different sections.[34] To emphasise the main ambition, the statute afforded a privileged place to the first, conceptual section, which was intended to focus on theoretical questions. Article 8 of the statute of the Congress declared that, with respect to the relevance of the general questions covered by the first section, no other section could be held parallel to that one.

Beside some foreign invitees, almost all French lawyers engaged in compar-ative law participated in the Congress.[35] The significance of this Congress

---

[30] R Saleilles, 'Rapport sur l'utilité, le but et le programme du congrès' in *Congrès international de droit comparé. Procès-verbaux des scéances et document. Tome premier* (n 27) 9–17.

[31] ibid 10.

[32] ibid 13–14.

[33] ibid 14; Picot and Daguin, 'Circulaire' (n 29) 7–8.

[34] 1st section: general theory and methodology; 2nd section: international private law; 3rd section: commercial law; 4th section: private law; 5th section: common law; 6th section: criminology (Art 8 of the statute of the Congress).

[35] See Lévy-Ullmann, 'The Teaching of Comparative Law' (n 11) 18.

from the viewpoint of the scholarly development of comparative law can be understood primarily from the work on the above-mentioned first section. It is certainly not an exaggeration to state that this section had a decisive impact on the further development of comparative law. In sum, the panellists of this section successfully formulated both the problems of the period – the anomalies, again in Kuhn's terminology – and the scientific crisis underlying them, and they were also able to find relevant answers to these. The work on the first section was guided by two professors, Professor Raymond Saleilles from Paris and Professor Édouard Lambert from Lyon. Later, they both became leading figures in the newly emergent paradigm of comparative law.

Three decades later, at a session at the International Academy of Comparative Law, Lambert voiced a criticism of the first Congress in his exposé, and he also suggested organising another congress. In his opinion, a major deficiency of the Congress was that in reality it was not international, as only members of the *Société* and a few other European legal scholars participated. He argued that this deficiency should be avoided in future comparative law activities. Another problem was, in Lambert's eyes, the lack of continuous scholarly cooperation, which was due to there being no regular events following the 1900 Congress. However, what is even more interesting than the preceding two critical remarks is that Lambert also pointed out that the Congress could not devise a 'closed and coherent' concept of comparative law, so in reality it did not achieve its goals. This critique from the person who prepared the main report of the Congress, which was an essential document as regards the intellectual history of comparative law, comes as a surprise; however, it also indicates the importance of puzzle-solving scholarly activities.[36]

These critical remarks help us to perform a neutral evaluation of the role of the Congress. One might conclude that the 1900 Paris Congress is to be regarded as a symbolic moment in the birth of the second paradigm, when the deficiencies of the first paradigm's assumptions became visible and clear against the new set of legal problems – with special regard to the issue of foreign legal impact – at the turn of century. While the new initiatives of the Congress did not result in a finished conceptual framework, they did nevertheless open up the perspective of a new way of research. As such, the Congress created a qualitatively new conceptual framework – a new paradigm – one that was capable of initiating a new way of puzzle-solving research, as was endorsed by Lambert's later critical remarks.

IV. THE ESTABLISHMENT OF THE NEW PARADIGM

As can be seen from the Congress programme, the crisis inspiring the organisation of the Congress was due to the inability of the historic-evolutionist paradigm to handle contemporary legal issues. In addition, the teaching of

---

[36] See E Lambert, *Le rôle d'un congrès international de droit comparé en l'an 1931* (Paris, Giard, 1929) 7.

private law had become anachronistic at the French law faculties of that time, as it could not go beyond the earlier, national legal text-orientated approach. This inability was worsened further by the fact that the authors working within the framework of the first paradigm did not aim to lay down the conceptual foundations of comparative law explicitly, as an individual field of scholarship. It was therefore not easy to differentiate the historic-evolutionist paradigm of comparative law from the dynamically developing legal history or sociology of the era, in terms of either its goals or its methods.[37]

As a result of many anomalies mentioned earlier, a scientific crisis took hold of comparative legal studies in the last decade of the nineteenth century. The way out of this situation was found by two influential personalities of the Congress: Saleilles and Lambert. Basically, they paved the way for a new paradigm, which would be able to meet these new claims and requests. In his preparatory report, Saleilles tried to prove the autonomy of comparative law as a distinct field of legal scholarship, and also drafted a new perspective that was qualitatively different from the horizon of the theory-minded and frequently speculative historical-evolutionist paradigm. On the other hand, Lambert, after going through all the reports sent in to the Congress, prepared a general report in which he elaborated in detail the hypotheses and methodology of the new paradigm of comparative law, thus creating a new set of exemplars for the paradigm.

The efforts of these two French scholars literally saved comparative law – which fell into crisis due to the changed circumstances of the period – from being dissolved in legal history or sociology, and thus from losing its own scholarly character. At the same time, they also set forth a qualitatively new research programme for a renewed comparative law, thus providing considerable room for puzzle-solving research within the paradigm.

A. Comparative Law as an Autonomous Field of Legal Scholarship

Saleilles' preparatory report focused on conceptual questions; consequently, his understanding approached the fundamental questions of comparative law from a conceptual perspective. His starting point was the declaration that comparative law, until the turn of century, had not been considered as more than a possible complementary tool for a general critique of law, and this kind of scholarly activity often did not mean more than juxtaposing various legal texts without any detailed and analytical explanation. Authors engaged in this kind of 'comparative law research' simply presented certain rules of foreign legal systems but did not try to understand or explain either the similarities or the differences.[38]

---

[37] cf M Weber, *Staatssoziologie* (Berlin, Duncker und Humblot, 1956).

[38] R Saleilles, 'Conception et objet de la science du droit comparé' in *Congrés international de droit comparé. Tenu á Paris du 31 Juillet au 4 août 1900. Procés-verbaux et documents* (Paris, LGDJ, 1905) 167–89, 167.

However, as Saleilles argued, this activity could not be considered an autonomous scholarly field, because, in his opinion, 'science' has to fulfil four criteria: it must possess its own subject, its own laws and individual methods, and it cannot lack scientific discipline either.[39] As such, one can only establish the 'science of comparative law' if it can be linked with a *sui generis* subject-matter and a particular method of study.

Saleilles argued that if one wants to accept comparative law as an autonomous field of legal scholarship, fulfilling the above-mentioned criteria, as a first step, it has to be separated from the other fields of study that already exist and have similar goals and presumptions to a certain extent. According to Saleilles, the discussion of other fields of scholarship – comparative history of institutions, sociology and legal politics[40] – is unavoidable in order to define the specific goals and methods of comparative law. This study is also useful because, while comparing comparative law to the other similar fields mentioned above, the specific features of comparative law would become more visible. This contrast would help gain a better understanding of the specific nature of comparative legal studies as an individual discipline.

Saleilles submits that the comparative history of institutions is the equivalent of comparative legal history, the starting point of which is that different peoples at the same level of civilisation organise themselves in practice with the help of the same legal institutions.[41] Unsurprisingly, a main methodological principle of the historical-evolutionist paradigm can easily be recognised at this point. When pointing this out, Saleilles criticises the previous paradigm; moreover, he also exposes those problems – anomalies – that this paradigm could not address and answer appropriately. In Saleilles' view, the historic-evolutionist approach – that is to say the first paradigm – disregarded the option of reception and borrowing law – the circulation of legal models – because it presupposed the existence of similarity when conceptualising the laws of evolution. Moreover, Saleilles concludes, the approach was too black-letter-law-orientated, so it was not interested in the real operation of law.[42]

Sociology aims at identifying and examining natural laws of development, and this general and comprehensive interest is what differentiates it from comparative institutional history.[43] The sociological examination of law had not led to satisfactory results thus far and, according to Saleilles – following Jhering's position – it can be said that the conclusions of Savigny and Puchta were too narrow and artificial.[44] Legal development cannot be explained only on the basis of national legal history tracked back to customary law: external effects – such

[39] ibid.
[40] ibid 169 and 172. It has to be mentioned here that Saleilles, in accordance with the choice of words of the era, talked about legislative politics.
[41] ibid 169.
[42] ibid 169–70.
[43] ibid 170.
[44] ibid 171.

as reception of law or international influence – that are capable of influencing the course of legal development should be examined as well. Moreover, the study of various peoples, separated from the whole of humanity, is also unthinkable, argues Saleilles, because in this case the same mistake would be made as when we try to understand the individual alone, without taking the community into consideration.[45] However, the most important difference between sociology and comparative law is that sociology always examines things that already exist, whereas comparative law has to study how 'things' should be, stemming from a society's needs (*le devoir social*).[46] Due to this, in Saleilles' view, comparative law cannot have only a simple descriptive function; it has more to do besides.

The differentiation of comparative law from the politics of law is an easier task. Saleilles stresses that comparative law may submit that certain rules match the needs of the economic-social context, but the introduction of these rules into the national legal order is not its task. It is the politics of law that should gear the abstract model developed by comparative law to the reality of the national legal order, taking different aspects that are pragmatic and fall out of the scope of scholarly activity into account.[47]

Comparative law can therefore be found somewhere in the surroundings of these fields of study, and it is partly interconnected with all of them; for example, it relies on the laws discovered by sociology, or it may be able to support the politics of law, but – and this is Saleilles' main point – it is not identical to either of them. To summarise his conceptual conclusions, comparative law draws from the results of these areas, but its aim and method make it an autonomous field of study.

The role of comparative law is to define the relative ideal types of legal institutions (*type d'idéal tout rélatif*).[48] In order to understand the meaning of this concept properly, the author's concept of legal development has to be discussed first. Saleilles, influenced by Jhering's ideas,[49] considered legal development as a process that should be in harmony with the social context, and this insight deeply influenced his approach. In his view, no one can talk about a law that is generally suitable for all historic situations because, in harmony with the changes in social-economic needs, the demands and expectations regarding legal regulation also change. Hence, a comparatist should always aim at 'discovering' and defining the appropriate rules for the given social-economic setting (*l'état social*). The totality of laws in harmony with the social-economic condition is called 'relative ideal law' in Saleilles' approach.

---

[45] ibid.

[46] ibid 171–72.

[47] ibid 173.

[48] ibid. Constantinesco points out that Saleilles observed overarching similarities when studying Italian, Swiss and German contract law, and these similarities led him to the realisation that legal systems at the same level of civilisation possess similar, often almost the same, legal solutions and legal institutions: Constantinesco, *Traité de droit comparé I* (n 25) 135.

[49] Constantinesco, *Traité de droit comparé I* (n 25) 132.

This relative ideal law as a research goal entails many methodological consid- erations and consequences. According to Saleilles, an important methodological principle can be formulated easily: a comparative study always has to start with the facts and not with the ideals of legal development.[50] The world of facts, where laws also function, should be regarded as a key point from the perspective of the research – and this is why sociology may have a role in comparative law as well. Moreover, in Saleilles' view, research has to be narrowed down to those countries whose social orders are similar, because intelligible questions about the effectiveness of law can only be raised with respect to such countries.[51]

Therefore, the comparatist has three important tasks. The first two concern the study of foreign law. First, the researcher has to examine foreign law making with a critical eye, with special regard to the relevant social-economic aspects and, second, he or she has to find the interrelated points and common tendencies among the legal orders studied. As the third step, comparatists have to choose one specific national institution among the various legal models examined that they can consider to be the relative ideal type.

Having determined the 'ideal' legal institutions from the variety of national legal orders, one is able to recognise many different principles that are identical in these legal orders; and thus they may reveal the '*droit commun international*' or, in other words, the '*droit idéal relatif*',[52] which can become the objective basis for further developing the national legal orders.[53] This ideal legal order uniting the legal heritage of civilised nations (Saleilles sometimes, very often revealingly, calls it '*droit commun de l'humanité civilisée*' – the common law of civilised humanity – as a subsidiary source) may be capable of facilitating legal reforms, the development of jurisprudence and judicial interpretation.[54] Saleilles also emphasises that building up a national legal order exclusively based on this 'ideal law' is simply impossible, because every legal order is rooted in many historical and local elements that are unalterable. Despite this general reservation as to the scope of his inquiries, Saleilles argues that many areas of law can benefit from research into this ideal legal order.[55]

In this way, Saleilles successfully establishes the autonomous scholarly iden- tity for comparative law, as he defines as its main goal the orientation of future legal development or, in other words, the scholarly support of the improve- ment of national legal institutions. In addition, he also attaches an independent subject and method to this far-reaching goal – the discovery and study of the *droit commun de l'humanité civilisée*.

---

[50] Saleilles, 'Conception et objet de la science du droit comparé' (n 38) 147.
[51] ibid.
[52] Stammler's impact can be recognised here. See Constantinesco, *Traité de droit comparé I* (n 25) 135, fn 49.
[53] Saleilles, 'Conception et objet de la science du droit comparé' (n 38) 177 and 179.
[54] ibid 181–82.
[55] ibid 176.

From the perspective of contemporary legal theoretical debates, another statement by Saleilles may also be interesting. Saleilles submits that this 'ideal common law', revealed and created by comparative law, can be a perfect substitute for natural law, which – as an ideal construction – he considered too abstract and sterile. In Saleilles' eyes, this *droit commun de l'humanité* would be able to provide – at the same time – ideal and manageable models rooted in the world of facts and responsive to the real social-economic needs of nations.[56]

B. Comparative Law and Common Legislative Law

The main scholarly achievement of Saleilles' preparatory report is the separation of comparative law from comparative institutional history and sociology. Compared to Saleilles, Lambert examined comparative law from a different, somewhat less idealistic perspective; he did not attach such 'large-scale' goals, which touch upon humanity and the ethos of natural law, to comparative law (which he also thought of as an autonomous field in legal scholarship) as Saleilles did.[57] He did not intend to establish a similarly 'sublime' concept of law, and he defined the roles of comparative law on a much more practical level. Perhaps due to this, Lambert's understanding was more easily acceptable to the scholarly audience. As a result of this more practical outlook, and because of his outstanding role in the community of French comparatists, he is also considered to be the founding father of modern French comparative law, alongside Saleilles.[58]

i. The New Methodological Principles of Comparative Law – Lambert's Interpretation

From the viewpoint of this study, the most relevant contribution of Édouard Lambert – who dealt with Roman law and general history of law in the early

---

[56] ibid 181.

[57] Alexandre Otetelisanu, professor at the law faculty of Bucharest dealing with comparative private law, critically analyses the difference between the concepts of Saleilles and Lambert. His opinion most probably expresses the concerns of the wider professional public, and his main argument is that Saleilles' universalism, which argues that the legal thinking of civilised humanity has a common core, practically means the revival of natural law thinking. See in detail A Otetelisanu, 'Les conceptions de ME Lambert sur le droit comparé' in *Introduction à l'étude du droit comparé. Recueil d'Études en l'honneur d'Édouard Lambert* (n 13) 39–46, 42–43. When presenting the different types of comparative law, a contemporary author from Japan connected the new ideas on doing comparative legal studies with the 'new natural law' (*le nouveau droit naturel*) due to the impact of Saleilles' universalism. See N Sugiyama, 'Essai d'une conception synthètique du droit comparé' in *Introduction à l'étude du droit comparé. Recueil d'Études en l'honneur d'Édouard Lambert* (n 13) 50–60, 60.

[58] See also P Garraud, 'Preface' in *Introduction à l'étude du droit comparé – Recueil d'Études en l'honneur d'Édouard Lambert* (n 13) xxi–xxv, xxv; and P Garraud, 'Hommage à Édouard Lambert'

stage of his career,[59] and then became one of the leading figures of the second paradigm of comparative law[60] – is that he 'diagnosed' the crisis that engulfed the former initiatives of comparative law, and he also pointed out the directions for further development. The starting point of his understanding is therefore to differentiate between the 'earlier' and 'novel' understandings of comparative law. Basically, in his general report on comparative law prepared for the 1900 Congress, he devised the structure and hypotheses of the new paradigm, including the research goals and methods that would have a pre-eminent role in future puzzle-solving research.

Starting from Bernhöft's work – an influential proponent of the first paradigm – Lambert differentiates between the ethnological-historical and the dogmatic understanding of comparative law.[61] The representatives of the first view – here Lambert specifically mentions Maine, Pollock, Bachofen, Bastian, Bernhöft, Post and Kohler – subordinate comparative law to scientific and speculative purposes entirely, and this way of carrying out comparative law research is to be regarded as one branch of social sciences, such as linguistics or religious studies.[62] The main goal of these scholars was to reveal the natural laws behind legal phenomena, and also to understand the institutional forms connected to the different economic and social phases on the path of human evolution.[63] In order to achieve that, this approach wished to examine as a subject of its research all the legal systems of human history, be they ancient or still existing.[64] Moreover – to use Lambert's expression – 'comparatists with a strong historical interest', through paying attention to generalities, mainly examined judicial legal orders that contrasted with one another, and they wanted to become familiar with the main features of these legal orders, not in their entirety or in detail.[65]

At this point, Lambert draws up his critique of the historical-evolutionist paradigm, which is similar to Saleilles' preparatory work, and this refers, again, to the crisis already mentioned. While looking for the general laws of

---

in *Introduction à l'étude du droit comparé. Recueil d'Études en l'honneur d'Édouard Lambert* (n 13) 3–5, 3. According to Dean Garraud, Lambert was one of the 'greatest masters' who taught in Lyon, 'l'un des plus grands parmi les maîtres qui y ont enseigné'.

[59] His studies of the originality of the Law of the Twelve Tables were important pieces of his legal history work. See, eg, E Lambert, *L'histoire traditionalle des XII Tables et les critéres d'inauthenticité des traditions en usage dans l'école de Mommsen* (Lyon, Rey, 1903). For details of Lambert's work, see the work of Pierre Garraud pieces cited in n 58 and the list of publication in the *Récueil*.

[60] As for the general assessment of his oeuvre as a French scholar, see the thought-provoking discussion by Kennedy of the second wave of legal globalisation inspired by the idea of the 'social'. See Kennedy, 'Three Globalizations of Law and Legal Thought: 1850-2000' in DM Trubek and A Santos (eds), *The New Law and Economic Development. A Critical Appraisal* (Cambridge, Cambridge University Press, 2010) 19–73, 37–50.

[61] E Lambert, 'Conception générale et définition de la science du droit comparé, sa méthode, son histoire; le droit comparé et l'enseignement du droit' in *Congrés international de droit comparé. Tenu á Paris du 31 Juillet au 4 août 1900. Procés-verbaux et documents* (n 38) 26–60, 31.

[62] ibid 32.

[63] ibid 50.

[64] ibid.

[65] ibid.

legal development, the historical-evolutionist paradigm can only be capable of discovering the most basic standards of the legal orders studied. This was why the study of a 'certain kind of skeleton of legal systems'[66] might have seemed to be sufficient for these scholars. However, Lambert argues, the philosophical and conceptual examination of such comprehensive and theoretical issues as legal development through human evolution is simply insufficient to understand the legal problems of the turn of century as thoroughly as their contemporaries expect. The list of these main problems includes the revision of codifications, the refinement of legal politics, the struggle to find answers to the new challenges of the era (internationalisation and socialism) and the apparent development of judicial law on the Continent. A new approach to comparative law therefore has to be found, which could make answering the previous questions possible. It is also evident that this new approach has to be substantially different from the historical-evolutionist paradigm. Lambert – similarly to Saleilles' intentions – therefore also wanted to give comparative legal studies a new scholarly identity.

This new and different approach is manifested in the 'novel' understanding of comparative law passionately propagated by Lambert, which should have been qualitatively different from the historical-evolutionist paradigm. As a prelimi-nary note, Lambert warns that this new understanding of comparative law has only appeared in fragments in the reports submitted to the Congress, but its main points can be identified with the help of these.[67] An essential characteristic of the 'novel' understanding of comparative law is that it does not consider comparative law as a field of the social sciences; rather, it is approached as a distinct branch of legal scholarship. Thus, the main goal of this 'novel' way of carrying out compara-tive law research is not an abstract understanding of broad historical or social phenomena related to the general laws of legal development but the 'action' in the field of legal studies.[68] This 'action' is meant to bring the examined legisla-tions ever closer together, which can be achieved by revealing the common bases and rules hiding behind the 'illusory diversity of legislations'.[69] These common rules form the body of the so-called 'common legislative law' (*droit commun légis-latif*), and Lambert argues that their discovery and application might drastically decrease both the superficial and temporary differences between legal orders.[70]

The methodology of comparative law, in Lambert's vision, therefore has to be largely transformed, and the methodological basis of this new way of conduct-ing comparative legal studies already contradicts the very foundations of the historical-evolutionist paradigm. In the first place, Lambert emphasises that in order to carry out fruitful and successful research, comparatists have to restrict their work to legal systems that are 'related to each other'.[71] Lambert considers

---

[66] ibid.
[67] ibid 36.
[68] ibid 32.
[69] ibid 38.
[70] ibid.
[71] ibid 44 and 48.

the Latin and German legal systems to be of this sort, as they are linked by several common historical and other features.

Lambert explained in detail what these features are. Among others, one can find historic specificities: historical factors substantially influencing legal development, such as the existence of feudal law, which was universal in the mediaeval period, including some Roman or canon law components. Moreover, there are scholarly features, such as modern Roman jurisprudence (*usus modernus pandectarum*), which was widespread throughout Europe, and economic elements, such as the market-based economic system. All of these contributed to the formation of both the Latin and the German legal orders, so these systems are to be researched with the purpose of discovering common legislative features, not those that are rather distant from each other in either geographic or historical terms.[72] Lambert also mentions specific restrictions on comparative research, as he argues that the common law of England has to be examined only additionally; Islamic and Slavic laws and customary legal systems are also excluded from the scope of comparative legal studies, because they were formed under civilisations fundamentally different from the common heritage forming the basis of the Latin and German legal systems.[73] Here, Lambert makes a very important distinction when he determines that, in contrast with historical comparativism – the research scope of which included both the areas of common law and civil law – there is no place for common law in his concept of comparative law.

Specifically, in Lambert's view, comparative legal studies, understood as an element of positive law aimed at discovering common legislative law (*droit commun législatif*), can only be concerned with private law.[74] With this step, he narrows down the scope of comparative law still further, but he also defines its limits, in contrast with the really ephemeral historical paradigm aimed at comparing practically everything that has been part of the course of legal history at some point.

Moreover, Lambert argues that the 'legal comparatist' cannot be satisfied with studying only the 'skeleton' of a given legal order, as could the 'historical comparatist', but should aim for a broad and all-encompassing knowledge of the legal order studied. The narrow study of the legal provisions set forth in the various Western European codes is obviously insufficient, but the researcher also has to be familiar with the everyday practice of law, which shapes laws to the needs and changes of the social and economic environment. The ordinary work of the courts and authorities is where the 'face' of a legal order slowly emerges over time.[75] Lambert adds to the previous criteria that research cannot be finished at this point, because one also has to aim at getting to know the legislative environment of the legal order studied, which manifests itself in the

[72] ibid 44.
[73] ibid 48.
[74] ibid 47.
[75] ibid 50.

spirit of and reason for unique legal solutions. This is clearly a very ambitious research programme, which focuses on the needs of practice in contrast to the abstract and speculative historical-evolutionist goals and their methodological requirements.

Lambert's vision, when explaining the bases of his new understanding of comparative law – and thereby the creation of some new exemplars for puzzle-solving research – is highly relevant from the perspective of the theory of paradigms. Nevertheless, it should also be stressed that he never denied the scholarly relevance of the previous paradigm, not for one moment; he merely stated that these two different views cannot fit into one frame.[76] The historical-evolutionist ambitions in comparative legal studies have to be placed among the social sciences, while the novel research framework – the new paradigm – representing the hypotheses developed by him, is to be regarded as a field of legal scholarship, with an ambition to give useful and practical answers to the previously discussed anomalies. That is, he envisaged a radically different approach to comparative legal studies, and this intent to set up a new framework for comparative law resulted in the paradigm shift.

Lambert's ideas on the new understanding of legal comparison were welcomed and praised within the European legal academia, and in this way the paradigm shift occurred within the community of those legal scholars who intended to apply the comparative method for the study of specific legal phenomena instead of speculating on 'big issues' of legal development.[77]

ii. New Emphases in Lambert's Oeuvre – The Start of Puzzle-solving Research

Lambert's monumental work *La fonction du droit civil comparé* was published in 1903. This volume was created as an introduction to a multi-part series of monographs, which would incorporate all areas of private law. From the viewpoint of the intellectual history of comparative law, the most intriguing part is the one in which Lambert writes about comparative law. Here, he mainly follows the line of thought presented in his general report for the 1900 Paris Congress; however, he also deviates from it at two points, and these differences suggest a further shift in his understanding of comparative law. These refinements may even be regarded as the first steps in puzzle-solving research in the new paradigm.

Lambert had already indicated in his main report that a main problem of comparative law is of a terminological nature, as there are no relevant 'technical terms' to differentiate between the two branches of comparative law, between the old and the new paradigms. The confusion caused by this is responsible for all

---

[76] ibid 46.
[77] The pieces by Garraud, Otetelisanu and Sugiyama – inter alia – may prove it convincingly. Interestingly, Sugiyama stresses that Lambert's approach should be regarded as the main way of performing comparative legal studies in the era. See Sugiyama, 'Essai d'une conception synthétique du droit comparé' (n 57) 53 ('[La] tendance predominant dans le droit comparé' writes Sugiyama).

the mistakes and misunderstandings regarding the nature of comparative law.[78] However, even though this terminological issue was obvious to him, Lambert made suggestions regarding a proper terminology after the Congress, as in this new book he introduced two terms to mark the two different approaches: he argued that the older approach might be called comparative (legal) history (*l'histoire comparative*), while the new one might be named comparative legislation (*législation comparée*).

Nevertheless, he completely rephrased the definition of *législation comparée*, because he argued that it was not a simple scholarly activity but rather an art (*le droit civil comparé, conçu comme art*), the aim of which was to reveal the common elements hiding in the background of the various legal orders.[79] By declaring comparative law to be an art, Lambert most probably wanted to emphasise the added value implied in his definition of common legislative law, which puts a strong emphasis on the relevance of creativity when looking for the common elements in the legal orders being compared, and he thereby intended to liberate comparative law from the cords of the schematic and strict understanding of science.

The other relevant point of the 1903 publication from the aspect of the intellectual history of comparative law is the part in which Lambert turns directly against Sailelles' views. This is definitely new in comparison with the Congress, where he only discussed Saleilles' ideas positively. In *La fonction du droit civil comparé*, Lambert considers Saleilles' concept of the common law of humanity simply unacceptable. One problem with this concept, it is argued by Lambert, is that it does not entirely break with the natural law approach, as it keeps the idea of universalism that pervasively characterises natural law theories.[80] Lambert's other plea is also connected to the question of universalism. In his view, his common legislative law embraces a much narrower segment of law than the universalist concept of Saleilles,[81] because it only focuses on Latin and German legal systems. He considers this restriction necessary, because talking about real common elements is only reasonable in legal systems that are similar to each other in their civilisation. If, in contrast, we were to examine the whole of civilised humanity, as Saleilles did, we would barely find any points in common.[82] Lambert, based on realism, therefore rejects Saleilles' concept built upon idealist hypotheses, and his critique draws attention to the exaggerations of idealism found in universalism.[83]

Following the publication of *La fonction du droit civil comparé*, the emphases of Lambert's work gradually shifted even more. In his oeuvre, the clarification

---

[78] Lambert, 'Conception générale et définition de la science du droit comparé, sa méthode, son histoire; le droit comparé et l'enseignement du droit' (n 61) 60.
[79] E Lambert, *La fonction du droit civil comparé* (Paris, V Giard et Brière, 1903) 916–17.
[80] ibid 918.
[81] ibid 920.
[82] ibid 919.
[83] See ibid 926–27.

of the theoretical questions of comparative law and the elaboration of some components of common legislative law were put in the shade, and after 1920, the founding of the Institute in Lyon, he focused on his teaching and the organisation of scholarly activities.[84]

V. THE DEVELOPMENT OF THE PARADIGM – FUNCTIONALISM, GLOBAL LAW AND SCEPTICISM

A. The 'Re-founding' of German Comparative Law

The dramatic effects of World War I and the subsequent political and social insecurities had a serious effect on German jurisprudence at the start of the inter-war period. The insecurity of German jurisprudence stemmed from existential problems,[85] and the application of the Treaty of Versailles put further pressure on German legal scholarship, which traditionally had a national law-orientated scope and was mostly disinclined to study foreign laws. The peace treaty bringing World War I to a close established the so-called Mixed Courts, the role of which was to settle the validity and effects of the German private law treaties signed by the Allies prior to the War. The German judges and the parties in the proceedings were completely unprepared for this, since the Versailles Treaty, which was drawn up by French and British lawyers, provided a qualitatively different legal frame for these disputes. Moreover, this insufficient knowledge of English and French legal concepts in some cases led to considerable losses,[86] harshly pointed out the deficiencies of the inward-looking German legal scholarship. This unfavourable situation increased the need for an efficient comparative understanding of law, and also made it evident that these – sometimes really technical – problems could not be resolved within the earlier framework of the historical-evolutionist paradigm.

Following the social and 'legal' shocks of World War I, Ernst Rabel, an already renowned legal historian who was initially engaged in the study of Roman law, was the one who started to re-establish German comparative law in order to enable it to handle these new and qualitatively different sorts of legal issues.[87] In 1916, Rabel had founded the first Institute of Comparative Law on

---

[84] Regarding the goals of the Lyon Institute, see Basdevant-Bastid, 'L'institut de droit comparé de Lyon' (n 13) 12.

[85] DJ Gerber, 'Sculpting the Agenda of Comparative Law: Ernst Rabel and the Facade of Language' in A Riles (ed), *Rethinking the Masters of Comparative Law* (Oxford, Hart Publishing, 2001) 190–208, 193–94.

[86] Rheinstein, 'Comparative Law and Conflicts of Law in Germany' (n 3) 241–42.

[87] Rabel's life, work and Institute are presented in detail by M Rheinstein, 'In Memory of Ernst Rabel' (1956) 5 *The American Journal of Comparative Law* 185–96. See also Gerber, 'Sculpting the Agenda of Comparative Law: Ernst Rabel and the Facade of Language' (n 85); and E von Caemmerer and K Zweigert, 'Évolution et état actuel de la méthode du droit comparé en Allemagne' in *Livre centenaire de Société de législation comparée II* (Paris, LGDJ, 1969) 267–81, 272–77.

the Continent at the University of Munich, and then in 1926 he became the director of the Institute established using state and private funds under the aegis of the *Kaiser-Wilhelm-Gesellschaft*, engaged in foreign and international private law.[88] Besides his work at the Institute, he also taught at the Faculty of Law in Berlin, and between 1932 and 1933 he was dean of this faculty. Rabel emigrated to the United States in the Spring of 1939, at the age of 65, and, except for some occasional visits, he did not return to Germany until his death.[89]

Rabel distinguished three understandings of comparative law in his writings. He differentiated between the (i) historical and (ii) philosophical approaches to comparative legal studies and (iii) comparative law focused on contemporary legal systems.[90] In his seminal paper, Rabel called the third type 'systematic-dogmatic comparative law', and during his scholarly activities he focused on this area alone.[91] This approach, since it focused only on existing and 'civilised' legal systems, was in complete harmony with the French initiatives discussed earlier that were dominant during that era.

In Rabel's opinion, when studying contemporary legal orders by applying the comparative method, one necessarily has to overcome the traditional approach, which regards law as only a set of legal rules. This insight led Rabel to his most important methodological innovation: the introduction of the so-called functionalist/contextual[92] method to comparative legal methodology. This development, which signified a fundamental change in perspective for comparative legal studies (as it was intended to shift the researchers' attention from legal texts to the tasks and context of legal institutions), made a deep impact on comparative law in the decades following World War II.

It is important to note here that Rabel explained that, with the introduction of the functionalist/contextual method, he did no more than apply the research method of his master, Ludwig Mitteis. Mitteis was a legal historian engaged in studying Roman law with the help of primary sources at the turn of the nineteenth–twentieth century; and while researching Roman law he developed a method for understanding the functions of classical legal institutions.[93] Hence, in this sense, this methodological starting point was not new at all. What should be considered new was that Rabel wanted to apply this method, originally

---

[88] Rheinstein, 'Comparative Law and Conflicts of Law in Germany' (n 3) 244.

[89] See in detail I Schwenzer, 'Development of Comparative Law in Germany, Switzerland and Austria' in M Reimann and R Zimmermann (eds), *The Oxford Handbook of Comparative Law* (Oxford, Oxford University Press, 2006) 69–106, 82–84.

[90] Gerber, 'Sculpting the Agenda of Comparative Law: Ernst Rabel and the Facade of Language' (n 85) 196–97. Rabel's fundamental writing on methodology was published in 1924. E Rabel, 'Aufgabe und Notwendigkeit der Rechtsvergleichung' (1924) *Rheinische Zeitschrift für Zivil- und Prozessrecht* 279–301.

[91] Rheinstein, 'Comparative Law and Conflicts of Law in Germany' (n 3) 244.

[92] Gerber, 'Sculpting the Agenda of Comparative Law: Ernst Rabel and the Facade of Language' (n 85) 199.

[93] ibid 192.

developed for a better understanding of classic Roman law, to the comparative study of contemporary legal systems. Putting his method into contemporary perspective, Rabel even notes that Édouard Lambert also started from similar hypotheses.[94]

As Rabel's student Max Rheinstein (who had a considerable impact on the development of North American comparative law[95]) pointed out, the functional/contextual method lies on two methodological postulates – again, these can be interpreted as new exemplars for comparative law research. The first postulate is that it is insufficient for a researcher to focus only on legal texts because they can simply lead to inaccurate results. The comparatists have to do more; they have to breathe life into the examined legal systems, so they have to get to know the spirit of legal systems.[96] Comparative legal research should therefore necessarily comprise various segments of legal life: starting from legal texts and the judicial and business practice related to them, through the methods of legal argumentation and thinking, to the role that law plays in the life of a nation. These components can be those dimensions for which a proper knowledge is indispensable for understanding the reality of law.[97] Naturally, such deep familiarisation with a legal system is a huge task and assumes a broad collection of sources, hence it is very demanding.

Rabel's second postulate can be derived from the nature of the above-mentioned task. Rabel argues that comparatists have to start their research with a given problem segment or sub-question, and they always have to take into account that the issue studied is an integral part of the legal system examined, so it is not an isolated entity that can stand on its own.[98] When comparatists address such sub-questions, they have to examine what kind of problems the legal institution wishes to solve and what solutions it offers.[99] Researching such problem segments can point to the fact that legal systems often use different legal techniques to achieve a particular goal, so the main differences between legal systems are to be found at the level of the technique and not the problems to be solved by specific legal provisions. Rabel thinks that this functional approach is the proper basis of creative criticism, and it leads to fruitful results during the course of legal reforms.

In this way, the most significant innovation of Rabel's method is that it shifts the focal point of comparative legal research from general questions to very well-defined problem segments; and he also convincingly proves that when examining a legal institution, it is not the legal text and the hierarchical position of the legal institution in the legal order that has to be the prime object of examination but

---

[94] ibid 201.

[95] W Ewald, 'Rats in Retrospect' in S Besson, L Heckendorn Urscheler and S Jubé (eds), *Comparing Comparative Law* (Geneva, Schulthess, 2017) 19–34, 28.

[96] Rheinstein, 'Comparative Law and Conflicts of Law in Germany' (n 3) 247.

[97] ibid.

[98] ibid.

[99] Schwenzer, 'Development of Comparative Law in Germany, Switzerland and Austria' (n 89) 78.

rather its function and purpose. Examining the function and purpose can high-light how, underneath the superficial legal diversities, due to the similarity of their economic structure, modern legal systems may actually be quite similar.[100]

Rabel used this method during his work on his monumental book, during the period he spent in the *Unidroit*, to develop the plan for the unification of international sales of goods. This plan only became the focus of attention again in the 1960s, due to hardships of Word War II. However, it later became the basis of the international treaties dealing with international sales of goods until the Vienna Convention of 1980.[101]

B. Developing the Institutional Background and the Attraction of 'Global Law'

After the 1900 Congress on comparative law in Paris, French initiatives in the field of comparative law gradually took the leading role in the international comparative law movement. This was not independent from the fact that French scholars played an important part in elaborating a new framework for compara-tive law, by which they set up the bases for a new, more up-to-date and receptive paradigm. Because of this, in the French comparative legal studies of the inter-war period, institution building and scholarly organisation were given equal rank as scholarly work. The *Société de législation comparée*, which was one of the centres of comparative law activity, for example, deliberately aimed at ending its Paris-centred nature. In this spirit, so-called affiliations were estab-lished in Lyon and Strasbourg, and abroad as well, in Bucharest and Havana, with the purpose of further connecting those areas to the international circula-tion of the French-dominated movement of comparative law.[102]

After Saleilles' death in 1912, Lambert became the leading figure in French comparativism. As it has already been explained, he founded his Institute in Lyon in 1920, and at the same time teaching and organising scholarly activities became central to his ordinary duties. During his almost two decades as director of the Institute, he raised generations of French and foreign legal scholars.[103] Moreover he also helped and supported the publication of more than 50 mono-graphs of a comparative law nature,[104] which often deal with 'current' and

---

[100] Rheinstein, 'Comparative Law and Conflicts of Law in Germany' (n 3) 250.

[101] E Rabel, *Das Recht des Warenkaufs. Eine rechtsvergleichende Darstellung*, vol 1 (Berlin, De Gruyter, 2011) originally published in 1936.

[102] P Goulé, 'La Société de législation comparée (Paris)' in *Introduction à l'étude du droit comparé – Recueil d'Études en l'honneur d'Édouard Lambert* (n 13) 696–701, 701.

[103] As to Lambert's Egyptian students and activities, see A Shalakany, 'Sanhuri, and the historical origins of comparative law in the Arab World' in A Riles (ed), *Rethinking the Masters of Compara-tive Law* (Oxford, Hart Publishing, 2001) 152–88.

[104] The full list of the Institute's publications can be found in the *Introduction à l'étude du droit comparé – Recueil d'Études en l'honneur d'Édouard Lambert* (n 13) 17–21. Sixty volumes were published in the first two years of the Institute's operation.

less-researched topics, even including Soviet and national socialist law. Due to these scholarly results and Lambert's frequent visits abroad, the Lyon Institute became an internationally renowned centre of comparative law. Lambert's famously open, polite and informal personality made it possible for him, during his travels abroad, to build several friendly and professional relationships, and to benefit from them in the future, as the unofficial ambassador of French comparative law.[105]

A major French comparative law endeavour in the second half of the 1930s can be connected to Lambert's name too. In 1936 the 70-year-old Lambert retired, and this gave rise to the idea of publishing a *Liber Amicorum*. As a salute to the 'master', the editors did not want to put together a simple *mélange* volume; they wanted instead to publish a comparative law handbook based on a pre-determined syllabus.[106] This quite ambitious plan was realised with the help of enormous international assistance. Three books, containing studies written by more than 170 authors – French and foreign – were published, and the three volumes therefore covered practically all the possible aspects of comparative law, ranging from the history of comparative law to the latest developments connected to the emergence of new economic law. In the end, this '*Liber Amicorum* trilogy' not only forged an abiding memory for Lambert, it also became the veritable proof of how lively comparative legal studies were in this era.

Another influential French figure in the comparative legal studies of the inter-war era, besides Lambert, was Henri Lévy-Ullmann, director of the Legal Institute at the University of Paris. Lévy-Ullmann had at least as deep an impact on the development of French comparative law, and thereby on the general development of the second paradigm, as did Lambert. His scholarly organisational activities complementing his academic work helped the further acknowledgement of the 'independence and originality' of comparative law in the French legal academia.

As a young professor at the University of Montpellier, Lévy-Ullmann participated in the 1900 Paris Congress, where he edited the main report summarising the work of the private law section, and he was also a member of the first section discussing conceptual questions.[107] His teaching and research activities covered several fields: among other things, he participated in preparing the translation and commentary of the German Civil Code (BGB), supervised by Bufnoir and Saleilles;[108] his was the very first comprehensive piece of French

---

[105] Garraud, 'Hommage à Édouard Lambert' (n 58) 5. According to Garraud, Lambert's gentle spirit and heart, his independence, his respect for the opinion of others, his politeness and goodwill, and his dignity, in both his family life and his professional life, were the features that explain his personal charisma and success in 'scholarly diplomacy'.

[106] Garraud, 'Préface' (n 58).

[107] Lévy-Ullmann, 'The Teaching of Comparative Law: Its Various Objects and Present Tendencies at the University of Paris' (n 11) 18.

[108] Balogh, 'Lévy-Ullmann, Vice-Président de l'Académie Internationale de Droit comparé' (n 20) 119.

writing on English law,[109] which gained him significant respect in the world of *common law*, and from 1919 he taught comparative law, private law and international private law as a professor of the Paris faculty of law.[110] As professor, with the help of Henri Capitant, in several stages, he created the Comparative Law Institute of the University of Paris (*Institut de droit comparé*), and when doing so he followed the 'Lyon model' set up by Lambert. The Institute became independent from the faculty of law in 1932.[111]

Presentation of his ideas on the conceptual dimension of comparative law is made difficult by the fact that Lévy-Ullmann never wrote an all-encompassing work on comparative law.[112] His insights on the theory of comparative law can often be found in publications distant from each other in both space and time. Nevertheless, the collection of these ideas gives us the contours of his thoughts. In his university note called 'Comparative private law', written in the second half of the 1930s, he defines comparative law as follows: 'a branch of jurisprudence, the purpose of which is to bring the rules, institutions and legal orders of the most significant civilised countries closer to each other'.[113] This understanding suits the general hypotheses developed by Saleilles and Lambert, and basically means inserting the views of the Congress – according to which an unconscious community of law exists beneath the surface of superficial contradictions in the laws of the civilised nations – into the definition of comparative law, 30 years after the event.

In the definition mentioned above, Lévy-Ullmann puts the emphasis on the term 'legal orders', which already refers to the internal development – a sign of puzzle-solving studies – of the paradigm that started to take shape at the 1900 Congress. Laws and legal institutions cannot be understood without being familiar with the entire legal order, and the legal order itself is not identical to the sum of positive laws, argued Lévy-Ullmann. The concept of a legal system is inseparable from the 'human side' of law, and by this 'human side' he meant the totality of those sociological and psychological factors that determine the evolution of legal orders.[114]

Hence, comparative law cannot be narrowed down to studying positive legal provisions and rules, and it is not sufficient either to take only certain sociological and economic facts into account, as suggested by Saleilles or Lambert; rather, legal rules have to be examined with respect to their sociological and

---

[109] Sir William Holdsworth, one of the most respected English professors of the period, wrote the Preface to the book and, recommending it to the readers, he declared that this was 'the best introduction to English law that he knows of'. HC Gutteridge, 'Lévy-Ullmann' in de la Morandière and Ancel (eds), *L'oeuvre juridique de Lévy-Ullmann* (n 14) 17–18, 18.

[110] LFJ de la Morandière, 'Henri Lévy-Ullmann' in de la Morandière and Ancel (eds), *L'oeuvre juridique de Lévy-Ullmann* (n 14) 11–15, 13.

[111] David, 'Lévy-Ullmann et le droit comparé' (n 14) 83.

[112] ibid 75.

[113] See I Zajtay, 'Henri Lévy-Ullmann professeur de droit comparé' in de la Morandière and Ancel (eds), *L'oeuvre juridique de Lévy-Ullmann* (n 14) 105–10, 105.

[114] ibid 106.

psychological context, which can be derived with the help of historical studies. Many examples of this 'contextual approach' can be discovered in Lévy-Ullmann's works presenting and discussing English common law.[115]

Lévy-Ullmann's ideas on the goals of comparative law achieved their final form after World War I. At the Congress, in harmony with the general opinion, he considered that revealing a widely shared common law – in his words common international law (*droit commun international*) – would be the main task of comparative law.[116] However, after World War I, this focused view gave way to a more pluralistic approach.

Lévy-Ullmann sorted the tasks of comparative law into three groups; he concluded that comparative law possesses practical, scholarly and humanitarian goals.[117] From a practical point of view, comparative law is essential for those who are interested in international relations, whether they are businessmen or politicians, because familiarity with other nations' laws is indispensable in international life. From a scholarly dimension, comparative legal studies can help historical research, can be given a role in university education and can contribute to the evolution of international law, because the common solutions of civilised people can serve as models and are also able to inspire the course of legislative work.

Compared to the previous tasks, the humanitarian goals of comparative law exceed the legal issues, because Lévy-Ullmann urges that comparative law can contribute, in fact must contribute, to the mutual understanding among nations, as 'nothing can facilitate more the understanding of the soul of a nation than studying the legal language and positive institutions of a people'.[118] Based on this, we can conclude that the goals and tasks of comparative law are certainly more complex than those set during the 1900 Congress that inspired the paradigm shift, and the purposes connected to positive law are complemented with broader – meta-legal – aspirations too.

In accordance with these goals, Lévy-Ullmann formulated several methodological conclusions.[119] He deliberately drew attention to the fact that in comparative legal studies one always has to rely on sources, and only comparable phenomena should be compared. Moreover, in light of the 'contextual view' mentioned above, he also submitted that knowing the atmosphere and the context of law (*le milieu*) is also a prerequisite of comparative law. Under *milieu*, Lévy-Ullmann understood the totality of political, economic, philosophical and social elements. Such a broad understanding of the concept of

---

[115] ibid. Zajtay notes that, on this basis, Lévy-Ullmann unequivocally rejected the simple transposition of laws.

[116] See also in *Introduction à l'étude du droit comparé – Recueil d'Études en l'honneur d'Édouard Lambert* (n 13) 131.

[117] David, 'Lévy-Ullmann et le droit comparé' (n 14) 76–77.

[118] Lévy-Ullmann's statement, as cited by David, ibid 77.

[119] Ibid 78.

milieu exceeds Lambert's concept of the 'legislative environment', and implies an approach to legal scholarship that considers law as an integral part of its external environment.

Lévy-Ullmann also studied international business practice, and he saw the realisation of certain aspects of a hoped-for international common law in it. In his view, the world of international commerce, which does not strictly belong to any specific nation, had already created its own types of treaties, conciliation mechanisms and unique professional sanctions by the beginning of the twentieth century, and in this way it laid the foundations of an autonomous legal order largely independent of national law.[120] This law, which is rooted in international business law, was called 'global law' (*droit mondial*) by Lévy-Ullmann,[121] and he thought that it could be found in the juncture of international business law, international common law and international private law. This legal order develops with the supranational unification and approximation of those national legal areas that are relevant from the point of view of world trade.[122] Clearly this idea of 'global law' was ahead of its time;[123] however, it should also be recognised that it was obviously implied in Lévy-Ullmann's theoretical and methodological points, since 'global law' has to be considered the product of almost identical civilisations – the Anglo-Saxon and Continental – and a basically similar context – the world of international trade.

C. The English Initiatives of the Period – Deviating from Maine's Heritage

In England, scholars with a comparative legal studies interest were united through the Society of Comparative Legislation and its journal – both founded in the last decades of the nineteenth century. This Society was openly inspired by the model of the French *Société de la législation comparée*,[124] and this determined the emphases of its activities as well. Besides specialised committees – statute law, commercial legal and procedural legal committees coordinated the professional activity relating to certain areas of law – the Society had a committee dealing with general issues of comparative law and legal history as well, but

---

[120] P Lepaulle, 'Henri Lévy-Ullmann et le droit mondial' in de la Morandière and Ancel (eds), *L'oeuvre juridique de Lévy-Ullmann* (n 14) 111–18, 115.

[121] Lepaulle notes that in fact Lévy-Ullmann used this expression in more than one sense; among others, the expression *droit mondial* had a philosophical, 'neo-scholastic' connotation as well: ibid 111–12.

[122] See also Balogh, 'Lévy-Ullmann, Vice-Président de l'Académie Internationale de Droit comparé' (n 20) 127.

[123] Regarding today's global business law, see H Van Houtte, *The Law of International Trade* (London, Sweet & Maxwell, 2002) esp chs 2, 3, 4, 10 and 11. The theoretical perspectives are analysed in detail by G Teubner (ed), *Global Law without a State* (Aldershot, Dartmouth, 1997).

[124] JW Cairns, 'The Development of Comparative Law in Great Britain' in Reimann and Zimmermann (eds), *The Oxford Handbook of Comparative Law* (n 89) 131–73, 140.

the theoretical interest and the study orientation of the historical-evolutionist paradigm were gradually put into the shade in the decades after World War I.[125]

Despite the emergence of new inspiration arriving from France, in England the first paradigm did not entirely disappear, but by the second half of the 1930s – following the death of the authors who dominated the evolutionist paradigm, such as Sir Paul Vinogradoff – its findings were integrated into the curricula of those institutions that educated imperial officers as a special 'applied' form of historical comparative law. Obviously, this was due to the fact that in the education of colonial officers, there was a need to study non-European civilisations and the earlier stages of civilisations. On the other hand, the late representatives of this approach gradually 'melted' into the group of ethnologists carrying out various research projects into the customs of African and Asian peoples.[126]

The question that interested English comparatists at the turn of century was the legal development of the British Empire. As there were more than 60 different functioning local legal orders throughout the territory of the Empire,[127] and many among them were rooted in a completely different tradition from *common law* – for example Roman-Dutch law in South Africa and Hindi law in India – a sufficient knowledge of the legal orders of this diverse Empire was a vital interest of British public administration. As such, it was natural that the Society and its journal primarily attempted to collect, spread and process this enormous amount of information.

The authors of the journal mainly focused on two areas: due to the constantly widening internal economic relations of the Empire, they paid special attention to the different questions of private and commercial law.[128] Moreover, they examined the problems in detail, since the effective political and legal functioning of the British Empire would have been unimaginable without a thorough knowledge of the various constitutional settings of the colonial territories.[129]

As is apparent from these, in the decades preceding World War I, mainly practical questions relating to the functioning of the Empire became the centre of attention for English comparative legal studies. This shift in scholarly interest led to the ignoring of the historical-philosophical and evolutionist perspective, and thus an approach completely different from Maine's paradigm appeared and became institutionalised; it was mainly practical and private law-orientated, and – unsurprisingly – stood not too far from French comparativism.[130]

Harold Coke Gutteridge[131] was a representative of this understanding, and he was the author of the first monograph discussing the perspectives of

---

[125] ibid.
[126] ibid 137–38.
[127] ibid 134.
[128] ibid 140.
[129] ibid.
[130] This is also indicated by FP Walton's statement from 1934, 'comparative law now meant something different from evolutionary jurisprudence': ibid 132.
[131] About Gutteridge, see ibid 142–44.

comparative law in the common law world. Gutteridge's work is an excellent example of the second paradigm of comparative law, not only because of the encyclopaedic summary of the results of English comparative legal studies, but because its importance exceeds British relevance. This monograph often cites contemporary French and German publications of comparative law, and in most cases Gutteridge not only refers to them as illustrations, but also reflects on them in an often critical scholarly way.[132] These reflections make the English understanding of comparative law, which at some points differs from the Continental, predominantly French-minded one, easier. Moreover, the scientific debates of the second paradigm can also become known from the often polemic reflections, and thus, in the shadow of these reflective parts, the author leads the reader into the world of those questions that really bothered the comparatists of the era, so basically into their scholarly life. This makes it easier to identify the main members of this scholarly community and map the areas and issues studied.

Due to all this, one might even risk arguing that the evaluation of Gutteridge's work cannot be restricted only to its undeniable role in encyclopaedically presenting the results of English comparative law, but it had to be studied as a 'summarising' work, more or less broadly describing the scholarly community and academic life of the second paradigm.

Gutteridge attempts to define comparative law as a scholarly field on its own, by discussing a linguistic problem. In his view, the expression 'comparative law', widely used by English law scholars, is not the most suitable choice for this concept, as this term may lead to several misunderstandings. The most important problem with it is that, similarly to the expressions 'family law' or 'maritime law', the concept 'comparative law' suggests that it is in fact a separate, individual field of law.[133] Obviously this is untrue, and at this point Gutteridge adds that the German term *Rechtsvergleichung* describes the essence of comparative law much better, because it characterises this field of scholarly study from the perspective of action – so, by emphasising the activity behind it, the act of comparing laws. In no way can the use of the term 'comparative law', even if it may be misleading, be avoided, though, because it is very widespread in the English world and no other expression could take root alongside it.[134]

Gutteridge argues that comparative law should not be approached from different conceptual perspectives but from the viewpoint of its tasks and goals and, consequently, from the perspective of its scholarly definition. The real question is what the purpose of comparative law is. In contrast with the French authors of the era, Gutteridge thinks of comparative law as a method, and here

---

[132] In the first chapter, which presents the history of comparative law, Gutteridge makes a list of the already formulated concepts and creates his understanding based on them, which divides comparative law into a descriptive branch and an adopted branch. Among others, he examines the theses of Kohler, Pollock, Maine, Wigmore, Lambert, Hug, Sarfatti, Saleilles, Kantorowicz, Kaden and Rabel. Gutteridge, *Comparative Law* (n 19) 1–10.

[133] ibid 1.

[134] See also ibid 1–2.

he significantly differs from the position of his French colleagues. However, he also argues that we should not go too deep into the problem of method versus scholarship, because the substance of both expressions ('method' and 'scholarship') depends on the definition, and the definition is a purely philological issue and as such should be far from a practitioner of law.[135] The final conclusion at this point is that the comparative method is flexible enough to be used in all areas of law, so there is no branch of law or legal problem that could not benefit from the outcomes of comparative law.

Two areas of comparative law understood as methods can be differentiated from each other: descriptive comparative law and applied comparative law.[136] Descriptive comparative law is essentially the method of collecting of legal information: the scholar here basically collects and juxtaposes the rules of different legal orders relevant to a certain regulative area. Applied comparative law generally encompasses the activity called *législation comparée* by Lambert,[137] and the expression 'applied' refers to the fact that this comparative work has a specific purpose: it can be conceptual but practical at the same time, such as the reform of national law or the unification of law. Having differentiated between these two main functions, Gutteridge notes that applied comparative law is still under development, so its goals cannot be exhaustively listed nor its goals definitively enumerated.[138]

The next question to be clarified is what service comparative law can offer lawyers, that is, what its value is. According to Gutteridge, this question can only be answered in relation to a given area of law; giving a general answer to it is simply impossible. In his book, Gutteridge examines the following areas in detail: legal theory, legal history, constitutional and administrative law, criminal law, labour law, family law, property law, law of inheritance, contract law, commercial law, procedural law, law-making and legal reform, comparative law as a legal source in the jurisprudence of courts and international law. This list is a sign of the practical side of law coming to the fore, which is nuanced by his sceptical comments added to the theoretical and historical areas.[139] In contrast to this scepticism, Gutteridge is quite enthusiastic in presenting the new, practical perspectives opened up by comparative legal studies, and in detailing the benefits comparative law may add to a given area of law, although he admits that in certain areas comparative law can play only a limited role.[140]

---

[135] ibid 5.

[136] ibid 8–9.

[137] ibid 2.

[138] ibid 10.

[139] Such as 'that it is extremely dangerous, if not fallacious, to deduce the universality of a rule of law from its existence in all systems'; or '[it] is possible that enthusiasts may have exaggerated the value of comparative method in providing a means for the determination of abstract principles': ibid 27.

[140] Such an area might be, for instance, family law, property law and the law of inheritance: ibid 31–32.

An example might help in highlighting Gutteridge's line of thought on the value of comparative law. In his view, the application of comparative method had already been used fruitfully in the area of labour law. Similar problems appeared in the last decades of the nineteenth century in the developed industrial societies, and they basically needed the same solutions. This atmosphere gave birth to an international movement, the goal of which was to eliminate the different forms of injustice against workers. The international conferences of the International Association of Labour Legislation, founded in 1900, won the prohibition of night working for women and a ban on the industrial application of white phosphorus at the beginning of the twentieth century. With the founding of the International Labour Organization (ILO) this movement gained a new momentum, and the headquarters of the former movement in Ghent became the most important centre of comparative law regarding labour law.[141] According to Gutteridge, similar perspectives were in sight for international commercial law and the regulation of intellectual property.

One of the main ambitions of comparatists of the era was to discover common elements lying behind national legal orders, and to begin to build up a legal order applicable to all civilised nations. This aim was penetrated by the idea of universalism, according to which the common core of civilised legal systems could be universalised for these legal systems, so it offers generally applicable patterns.[142] English legal scholarship was generally sceptical about this idea, and occasionally even rejected it;[143] so it comes as no surprise that Gutteridge dedicates the last three chapters of his book to this issue. These chapters seek to present the reasons behind the moderate English standpoint, and so they contribute to the understanding of the British view, which is often accused of being obstructive or sceptical.[144]

The often disillusioning failures of the unification of law in the inter-war era can be traced back to more than one reason, according to Gutteridge. From a theoretical aspect, it is questionable whether the universalist starting point of lawyers supporting the unification of law is correct or not, because it is possible that it is no more than 'a devout aspiration, which is based partly on the legal and other cooperation between nations, but mainly on a presumption about the substantive unity of mankind'.[145] The universalist approach was questioned by many problems that are well known in everyday life. Divergent national mentalities, habits based on traditions, the different structures of legal institutions and differing legal techniques can all undermine this starting point.[146]

However, not only the conceptual problems should be blamed for the failures; they can be traced back to several other factors as well. Gutteridge argued that one

---

[141] ibid 31.

[142] On universalism, see M Ancel, 'La doctrine universaliste dans l'oeuvre de Lévy-Ullmann' in de la Morandière and Ancel (eds), *L'oeuvre juridique de Lévy-Ullman* (n 14) 181–202, 182–87.

[143] Cairns, 'The Development of Comparative Law in Great Britain' (n 124) 162.

[144] Gutteridge, *Comparative Law* (n 19) 162–64.

[145] ibid 6.

[146] ibid.

of the main reasons for the lack of success was the exaggeration of the importance of legal unification, and the under-estimation of the problems. The most enthusiastic representatives of legal unification often miscalculated the significance and potential of their cause, and this made it impossible to recognise how unpopular their goals were among lawyers and how uninteresting they were for the public.[147] This self-confidence stigmatised the whole process and has naturally led to an unfavourable result – the failure of a proposal worked out at a desk.

Besides this unfounded enthusiasm, the other psychological reason behind the failure of legal unification was national pride, which is manifested in unconditional respect for national law. Gutteridge argued that this is characteristic of all nations, not only of common law countries. Besides these psychological reasons, the process of law unification was also made difficult by many problems of a technical nature. The often hasty and professionally inadequate preparation, the 'one nation, one vote' rule dominating the international congress dealing with such issues, and the existence of competing national and international agencies dealing with the unification of law often simultaneously were all factors making the realisation of legal unification overly complicated.[148]

Thus, the English understanding, which was sceptical and critical of the unification of law, correctly pointed out its difficulties through analysing the various problems, and so it made the overarching ambitions born in the 'ecstasy of legal unification' summoned by the *droit commun* concepts more moderate and refined.[149] These comments all facilitate a better understanding of the reality of the unification of law – including of the *droit commun* concepts – and they also represent how puzzle-solving research improved the paradigm. As such, this scepticism is to be considered as an integral part of the paradigm, not a sign of problems and anomalies.

VI. CHARACTERISTICS OF THE SECOND PARADIGM

With the birth of the second paradigm of comparative law, the scholarly identity of comparative law changed substantially.[150] This new identity inspired a radical change in the exemplars determining how to conduct comparative legal studies, and in most cases it appeared in confrontation with the previous paradigm.[151]

---

[147] ibid 157.

[148] ibid 183–84.

[149] About the results of the unification of law before World War II, see AF Schnitzer, *De la diversité et de l'unification du droit* (Bâle, Verlag für Recht und Gesellschaft AG, 1946) 65–82.

[150] Rodolfo Sacco also emphasises that 'something new was born with Lambert and Saleilles'. He describes this transformation with the term 'rupture' to emphasise its qualitative nature and its novelty as compared to the previous works. See R Sacco, 'One Hundred Years of Comparative Law' (2001) 75 *Tulane Law Review* 1159–76, 1165.

[151] A good example of this approach is Lambert's main report at the Congress, which clearly differentiates between the 'old' and 'newer' understandings of comparative law. See Lambert, 'Conception générale et définition de la science du droit comparé, sa méthode, son histoire; le droit comparé et l'enseignement du droit' (n 61) 10.

Although some authors deliberately contrasted their new views with the principles of the previous paradigm, we still cannot say that, after the Paris Congress, comparatists consciously ended all relations with the earlier paradigm and with its representative authors, who were still alive. The emergence of the new paradigm happened in a much more sophisticated manner than if the advocates of the new understanding had just radically rejected the previous one. The main representatives of the new attitude often referred to the historical-evolutionist paradigm and its most prestigious authors – Bernhöft, Maine or Kohler – in their paradigm-creating writings, but they immediately declared that they did not want to follow their approach. Some of them referred to the essentially social scientific – thus not legal in strict terms – nature of the earlier paradigm,[152] while others merely mentioned its doubtful methodological principles.[153] The followers of the new paradigm united under the name of *droit comparé* never denied the merits of the historical-evolutionist paradigm, but they proclaimed that they did not want to work within its frames, as in most of the cases they did not consider the previous paradigm to be a real field of legal scholarship.

An essential characteristic of the second paradigm is its clear claim for methodological clarification and precision. Scholars thinking along this paradigm put a much stronger emphasis on developing a proper methodology than the authors influenced by the previous paradigm. This was especially important, because they argued that the greatest imperfection of the previous paradigm lay in its underdeveloped methodology. The emerging new methodology was the result of merging many basic thoughts, and these junctions are relatively easy to identify.

The most relevant methodological starting point for the representatives of the new thinking was that comparative law is not a philosophical but a practice-orientated scholarly field, and one of its main goals was to help the improvement of national law. This presumption, which was practical and meliorist at the same time, defined the subsequent methodological theses. A major one among these is the fact that comparatists cannot aim at getting to know all the legal orders of the world: they have to be satisfied with only studying the developed countries belonging to the same sphere of civilisation. With this shift in perspective, the previous research scope – practically unlimited in both space and time – became narrowed to the countries belonging to Western civilisation. Another basic claim was that they only wished to focus on private law, that is, on a very restricted area, so they did not want to research all areas of law.[154] It is also important to

---

[152] This argument occurs the most in Lambert's and Balogh's publications. See ibid 11; and Balogh, 'Lévy-Ullmann, Vice-Président de l'Académie Internationale de Droit comparé' (n 20) 123.

[153] Saleilles and Gutteridge do this as well on several occasions. See Saleilles, 'Conception et objet de la science du droit comparé' (n 38); or Gutteridge, *Comparative Law* (n 19) 27.

[154] This is proved by the fact that the legal work of all cited authors is connected to private law or commercial law. Lambert planned to write a broad piece on the questions of comparative private law (*Études du droit commun législatif. La fonction du droit civil comparé* (Paris, LGDJ, 1903); the main

add that the representatives of the paradigm mainly searched for the similarities lying behind the different legal systems and did not focus on examining the differences, as proved by the different *droit commun* concepts.[155]

Hence the research scope of the second paradigm was restricted to the private laws of developed countries belonging to Western civilisation, as opposed to the temporal and spatially unlimited scope of the previous paradigm. An important development in the internal evolution of the paradigm – another good sign of puzzle-solving research – is that the view initially only focusing on the Continent was widened to include the common law systems after World War I, so the research 'area' of the paradigm that reached the peak of its development in the last decade before World War II consisted of Continental and Anglo-Saxon legal orders.[156]

The limitations of the research subject to such an extent helped progress in the direction of more precise, detail-orientated research. This understanding, focusing on details, led the engaged scholars to the seemingly most surprising statement of the new paradigm in this period. The representatives of the paradigm all argued – some of them enthusiastically, others moderately – that studying only the law in a strict – black-letter-law-focused – sense is not enough in itself for comparative law aspirations; both its broader legal and its social-political contexts have to be taken into account, if one really wants to understand the examined legal problem. This insight led to Lévy-Ullmann's contextual approach, based on a concept of legal order that includes the 'human side', and to Rabel's functionalist method. This understanding meant a real shift in perspective compared to both the mind-set of the previous paradigm and general positivism determining the period's legal thinking, and foretold the strengthening of the new – cultural – direction of legal scholarship.

Obviously this paradigm also had its own internal debates, which inspired the puzzle-solving research within the context of the paradigm. One may identify two main issues from this viewpoint. Although French authors unequivocally committed themselves to the autonomy of comparative law as a distinct scholarly field, their position did not become generally accepted because English comparative law scholars considered comparative law to be a method. The goals

---

research area of Saleilles was contract law and the question of legal persons (*Essai d'une théorie générale de l'obligation d'après le projet de Code Civil allemande* (Paris, Libraire Cotillon, 1890) and *De la personalité juridique: histoire et théories* (Paris, Rousseau, 1922); Rabel's main work attempted the comparative analysis of the sales of goods (*Das Recht des Warenkaufs I–II* (Berlin, Walter de Gruyter, 1936, 1957); Lévy-Ullmann taught comparative private law and dealt with international commercial law (*Éléments d'introduction générale à l'étude des sciences juridiques I–II* (Paris, Sirey, 1928); and Gutteridge also taught commercial law and published in this area (for his most important papers, see Cairns, 'The Development of Comparative Law in Great Britain' (n 124) 143, fn 41).

[155] M Ancel, 'Le comparatiste devant les systèmes (ou "familles") de droit' in H Bernstein, U Drobnig and H Kötz (eds), *Festschrift für Konrad Zweigert* (Tübingen, JCB Mohr, 1981) 355–62, 360.

[156] M Ancel, 'Les grand étapes de la recherche comparative au XXe siècle' in K Zweigert and HJ Puttfarken (eds), *Rechtsvergleichung* (Darmstadt, Wissenschaftliche Buchgesellschaft, 1978) 350–60, 354; and Z Péteri, 'Paradigmaváltás a jogösszehasonlításban?' in K Raffai (ed), *Placet experiri. Ünnepi tanulmányok Bánrévy Gábor tiszteletére* (Budapest, Print Trade, 2004) 228–38, 234.

of legal unification inspired by the various *droit commun* concepts that had taken shape in French comparative law thinking also received serious criticism from the other side of the Channel, which led to the realisation that many unforeseen problems could accompany such a broadly formulated attempt. These debates mutually stimulated the authors representing opposing views, thus keeping the paradigm under development and refinement. Moreover, they made the picture emerging from these debated questions more nuanced. The paradigm of *droit comparé* could only become complete through the enthusiasm of the French founding fathers and the scepticism of the later English scholars because both camps recognised each other's existence.

4

The Third Paradigm –
Post-World War II Comparative Law

I. INTRODUCTORY REMARKS: THE NEW WORLD ORDER AND COMPARATIVE LAW SCHOLARSHIP

THE DEVELOPMENT OF comparative law thinking after 1945 was fundamentally influenced by the birth of the bipolar world order and the emergence of the Soviet Bloc as a distinct political and legal entity.[1] This statement may sound bizarre at first, since it seems to have no connection to the inner – academic – sphere of any scholarship or science. However, it can easily be justified due to the very nature of comparative law activities.

Essentially, because of its scope and research interests, comparative law has always been a scholarly field that is open and sensitive to the development of foreign laws. Therefore, naturally, comparative law scholars reacted to the transformation of the world order following World War II almost immediately. The rise of the Eastern Bloc not only meant the imposition of Soviet-styled socio-political systems beyond the borders of the Soviet Union in Europe, but also implied the expansion of such a vision of law in ways that overtly opposed the Western conception of law. Furthermore, since this vision was not limited to one country only, the Soviet Union, as had been the case during the inter-war period, it swiftly became the dominant legal ideology within the Soviet sphere of influence, and the international comparative law movement could not simply ignore the laws of those countries that endorsed Soviet-styled socio-political principles.[2]

---

[1] For a comprehensive and critical discussion of the impact of the bipolar world on the development of comparative law as a discipline, see U Mattei, 'The Cold War and Comparative Law: A Reflection on the Politics of Intellectual Discipline' (2017) 65 *The American Journal of Comparative Law* 567–608.

[2] See Ancel, 'Les grands étapes de la recherche comparative au XXe siècle' in K Zweigert and HJ Puttfarken (eds), *Rechtsvergleichung* (Darmstadt, Wissenschaftliche Buchgesellschaft, 1978) 350–60, 356; M Ancel, 'La confrontation des droits socialistes et des droits occidentaux' in Z Péteri (ed), *Legal Theory – Comparative Law. Studies in Honour of Professor Imre Szabó* (Budapest, Akadémiai Kiadó, 1984) 13–23, 16; R David, 'Rapport écrit' in M Ancel (ed), *Livre du centenaire de la Société de législation comparé* (Paris, LGDJ, 1975) 145–51, 146; C Osakwe, 'Introduction: The Greening of Socialist Law as an Academic Discipline' (1987) 61 *Tulane Law Review* 1257–78, 1262–63; Z Péteri, 'Goals and Methods of Legal Comparison' in Z Péteri (ed), *The Comparison of*

The inevitable study of Socialist legal orders motivated most comparative law scholars to rearrange and improve their settled premises and methodology, originally coming from the frame of the *droit comparé*. This step-by-step process of readjustment to a new research issue, namely the study of Socialist law in general, gradually led to a qualitative transformation of the earlier research methodology amounting to a paradigm shift. However, it should be stressed that this paradigm shift was unlike the one that occurred between the historical-evolutionist and the *droit comparé* paradigms, when the French founding fathers of the novel approach promoted a new definition of comparative law and revised its methodological background relatively quickly during the days of the Paris Congress.[3] In the case of this third paradigm, the subject of comparative law studies, the reconfiguration of the external context stimulated the establishment of a new paradigm. In parallel with the qualitative transformation of the scholarly subject, the premises of the methodology also had to change, to such an extent that these refinements caused the earlier paradigm to begin to disintegrate.

All the research problems and methodological insights that arose during the comparison of Socialist legal orders with the Western ones revealed issues that could not properly be handled within the frame of the *droit comparé* paradigm, and these gradually led to the formation of a new paradigm of comparative law. This process had been supported by the so-called *détente* period beginning in the 1960s, since it explicitly encouraged the exchange of ideas between the two opposing blocs of world politics, and thereby also hastened a mutual and objective discussion of world legal orders.[4]

All in all, the scientific community of comparatists attempted to resolve the various anomalies related to the study of Socialist law – specifically that the second paradigm was unable to give adequate answers to questions such as the tools and methods of comparing Socialist laws to Western laws, and the role of Marxist ideology in Socialist laws and their relation to the intellectual background of Western European laws – with the help of a 'silent' scientific revolution. This 'silent revolution' happened with little drama; there were no major international comparative law congresses, for instance, but the continuous questioning of the previous settled ways of thinking, and thereby the discovery and study of a growing number of anomalies, amounted to the development of new structural premises and the continuous refinement of scholarly works rooted in them.

Law – La comparaison de droit (Budapest, Akadémiai Kiadó, 1974) 45–58, 47; G Eörsi, *Összehasonlító polgári jog* (Budapest, Akadémiai Kiadó, 1975) 16.

[3] Ancel, 'Les grands étapes de la recherche comparative au XXe siècle' (n 2) 356–58.

[4] On various phases of the discussion on the comparability of Western and Socialist law, see U Drobnig, 'The Comparability of Socialist and Non-Socialist Systems of Law' (1977) 3 *Tel Aviv University Studies in Law* 46–51; and Ancel, 'La confrontation des droits socialistes et des droits occidentaux' (n 2) 17–19. On the American view of this issue, see Osakwe, 'Introduction: The Greening of Socialist Law as an Academic Discipline' (n 2) 1258–62.

This novel paradigm is to be presented through two different but intertwined research issues. The structural premises and new exemplars of the emerging paradigm were crystallised during the study of these issues, and the puzzle-solving research setting up the corpus of the paradigm was built on these. These new research issues either opened up new horizons for comparative law studies, or they resulted in a qualitative improvement of the earlier theses, exemplars and ideas. This chapter will discuss the issue of the taxonomy of legal orders of the world first, and then it will also present the development of the function-alist methodology of comparative law. By doing so, it reveals both the main trends of post-World War II comparative legal studies and the framework of the new paradigm including the sets of 'exemplars' widely used by the scholarly community.

II. THE TAXONOMY OF THE WORLD'S LEGAL ORDERS

A decisive issue of the third paradigm of comparative law was certainly the taxonomy of the world's legal orders. This problem became a central theme of comparative law scholars in the decades following World War II, since only by refining the taxonomy of legal systems could Socialist law be integrated into the international discourse of comparative law as such. Basically, finding a place for Socialist laws on the world map of legal orders enabled both Western and Eastern comparative law scholars to participate in the general scholarly discourse of comparative legal studies.

Of course, the issue of the taxonomy of the world's legal orders had already been raised by some authors before World War II. However, these attempts were rather sporadic and irregular, and they were not related to any specific para-digms of comparative law in essence.[5] Thus, contrary to these earlier attempts, a more theoretically refined approach to the taxonomy of legal orders took shape from the 1950s, began to develop dynamically thereafter and swiftly became a research issue with a key role in the third paradigm.[6]

The earliest attempts at taxonomy as part of post-World War II comparative law provided a general critique of the previous concepts – rooted predominantly in the inter-war period – on the classification of the world's legal systems. These critiques showed that the authors of these new approaches sought to develop a qualitatively different account of the classification of various national legal orders

---

[5] For a detailed discussion of the earlier attempts of taxonomy, see LJ Constantinesco, *Traité de droit comparé III. La science de droits comparés* (Paris, Economica, 1983) 93–105; P Arminjon, B Nolde and M Wolff, *Traité de droit comparé I* (Paris, LGDJ, 1950) 42–47; Cs Varga, '*Theatrum legale mundi*: On Legal Systems Classified' in Cs Varga, *Comparative Legal Cultures* (Budapest, Szent István Társulat, 2012) 49–76.

[6] Certain authors even argue that comparative law as an independent field of scholarship should be dedicated to the classification and taxonomy of legal orders. See Arminjon, Nolde and Wolff, *Traité de droit comparé I* (n 5) 42.

in order to correct the deficiencies embedded in the previous fragmentary concepts. These critical remarks may be summarised in two main points as follows.

First, the new approaches recognised that comparative law cannot strive for the taxonomy of all the legal orders that ever existed. Comparative law is simply unable to prepare schemes of classification that would be capable of bringing together the complexity of every field of law and each legal order that ever existed. On the contrary, to produce results of real scholarly value, the classification of legal orders should be limited in terms of both time and subject. Most of these comparatists agreed that classificatory attempts must be limited to a specific field of law, most typically to private law,[7] and solely historically modern legal orders must be studied.[8] This position also implied that this paradigm had generally lost interest in dealing with the earlier ages of legal history.

The second point in this criticism was focused on the obscure or superficial nature of those criteria – for instance race,[9] historical origin,[10] or the contrast between codified and customary law[11] – that were used by the previous scholars to ground their classifications. These criteria were all considered useless; therefore, the post-World War II authors urged the development of a scheme of classification that would be able to provide a solid basis, grounded in a coherent theory, for prospective research. That is, a conceptually appropriate basis had to be constructed for future classifications, and this task swiftly became one of the most relevant challenges for the newly emerging paradigm of comparative law.

A. The First New Try: The Arminjon–Nolde–Wolff Manual

The first attempt at classification that was undeniably related to the new post-World War paradigm of comparative law appeared in the comparative law manual authored by Pierre Arminjon, Boris Nolde and Martin Wolff, published in 1950. From our point of view, this may be regarded as the 'missing link' between the previous incoherent taxonomical attempts and the emergence of the new attitude. Definitely, because of this, it had a certain transitory quality in this respect.

As a first step, the authors provide a detailed critical assessment of the available literature on the issue of classification. Thereafter, they set forth their approach stemming from this criticism.[12]

In the course of elaborating their own proposal for the classification of the world's legal orders, the authors also make some methodological remarks. These

---

[7] ibid 47.

[8] ibid. R David, *Traité élémentaire de droit civil comparé* (Paris, LGDJ, 1950) 216.

[9] For example, see the work of Sauser-Hall in 1993. For details, see Arminjon, Nolde and Wolff, *Traité de droit comparé* I (n 5) 44.

[10] For example, see the works of Glasson (1880) or Martinez-Paz (1934). For details, see Arminjon, Nolde and Wolff, *Traité de droit comparé* I (n 5) 45–46.

[11] For example, see the piece by Sarfatti published in 1934. For details, see Arminjon, Nolde and Wolff, *Traité de droit comparé* I (n 5) 46.

[12] ibid 42.

remarks may even be relevant for a better understanding of the general development of the scholarly ideas on the classification of legal orders. For instance, they point out that their approach does not try to reach such a level of objectivity and correctness as characterises the taxonomy of either languages or organisms, as their concept unquestionably reflects certain personal preferences.[13] With this, the authors raise a fundamental question for comparative law classification methodologies: what kind of accuracy or objectivity can be reached in legal taxonomy? They argue that comparatists cannot strive for a level of accuracy similar to that of the natural sciences, as the classification of legal orders can be achieved in various equally convincing ways too. In addition, the authors emphasise that the preparation of an objective classification was in no way one of the aims of their project, since they only wanted to draft a classification for practical goals.[14] The authors therefore tried hard to sharpen the focus of their classificatory attempt, compared to the previous scholarly understandings that aimed at a high level of general inclusivity.

They also make another relevant observation on the equal weighing of those legal orders that are included in a comparative law project with a taxonomical scope. This point will be echoed during the future development of this issue. It can easily be understood that if a comparatist were to grant each legal order of the world the same importance in a classificatory project, this would prevent the project from being carried out successfully, as a vast amount of information would need to be collected, processed and translated at a prohibitive cost. However, if one focuses on the specific centres of legal development and their influence on other, not only neighbouring legal orders, a world map of legal orders may be successfully drafted. Because of this insight, the authors made an important distinction between core and derived legal systems (*systèmes souches et systèmes dérivés*),[15] and they tried to draft the world map of legal orders based on the structure of 'key' legal orders and their areas of influence.

With the help of these methodological premises and with a strong focus on private law, the Armijon–Nolde–Wolff manual classified the legal orders of the modern age into seven large-scale units:[16]

1. French;
2. German;
3. Scandinavian;
4. English;
5. Russian;
6. Islamic; and
7. Hindu.

---

[13] ibid 52.
[14] ibid 53.
[15] ibid 47–49.
[16] ibid 49.

Although the deficiencies of such a taxonomy are apparent at the first glance – for instance, there is no place on this map for the legal orders of the Far East, or the legal systems of so-called popular democracies; the European and Asian satellite states of the Soviet Bloc and the Soviet Union are simply united under the rather questionable label of 'Russian law' – the scholarly relevance of this attempt is obvious, as it exerted a serious influence on other similar concepts in the coming decades. It can be argued that the Arminjon–Nolde–Wolff classification had swiftly become a starting point for the other taxonomical attempts in the third paradigm. For instance, Konrad Zweigert or Åke Malmström also cited it as a point of reference.

B. The Attraction of Ideology and Ideals – The Typology of René David

René David's *Traité élémentaire de droit civil comparé* was published in 1950, the year of the first publication of the Arminjon–Nolde–Wolff manual. Having published many course books on the major legal orders of the world,[17] this was David's first book to deal with the classification as well as the description of the legal orders worldwide.

Like the authors of the Arminjon–Nolde–Wolff manual, David rejected the earlier classificatory attempts. In his eyes, those were all the results of applying random and, therefore, unscholarly criteria, and these made them unfounded in a scholarly sense.[18] However, he did not subscribe to the approach of the Arminjon–Nolde–Wolff manual either, as he approached the problem of classification from a different angle. In fact, the real problem for David was not the precise identification of the criteria for classification but the question of how and to what extent it is possible to be familiar with a legal order when preparing the classification of legal systems.

If one can properly define the necessary level of familiarity with a legal order in comparative law, the applied criteria for taxonomy can also be easily determined. Interestingly, David argues that it is enough if only some general features of legal orders are learnt and known for classification by a comparatist, instead of the multiple varieties of specific national legal provisions. He explains this surprisingly modest claim with the fact that an average lawyer in a given country does not know much more about his or her legal order either. In line with this argument, the main criteria that should always be taken into account for classification could be the general features of a given legal order, including the

---

[17] David, from 1945, published many university course books on the major legal orders of the world: *Droit anglais* (1945); *Droits allemand, suisse et suédois* (1946–47); *Droit soviétique* (1947–48); *Droit du Portugal et du Brésil* (1948–49); and he continued this series in the 1950s and 1960s (*Droits de la Belgique, des Pays-Bas, de l'Espagne et de l'Italie* (1951–52); *Les traits fondamentaux du droit anglais* (1953–54); *Les droits du monde contemporains* (1961–62). See R David, *Le droit comparé, droits d'hier, droits de demain* (Paris, Economica, 1982) 87.

[18] David, *Traité élémentaire de droit civil comparé* (n 8) 223.

structure and spirit, and the sources of law. In addition, David also submits that the various pieces devoted to the general discussion of major legal orders will necessarily be unable to discuss and present very detailed problems – that needs a different perspective of legal scholarship – they can only offer a 'big picture' of these legal orders.[19]

If legal orders are to be classified at a higher level of abstraction, the comparatist will immediately face a crucial problem. How can one interpret the relationship between the technical and ideological elements of legal orders? In fact, in David's eyes, legal orders are generally composed of two main groups of components. On the one hand, various technical elements should be mentioned here – for instance procedures, legal terminology, legal concepts and legal classifications – that is, those components that are related to the ordinary or technical functioning of the law. On the other hand, however, ideological components also form an integral part of legal orders, David argues, as these represent the manifold religious, political, social and economic premises grounding a given legal order.[20]

Needless to say, it is relatively easy to differentiate between legal orders from a technical aspect. No one can deny that the technical provisions in a given field of law are very likely different in most countries to some extent. Therefore, the question whether the classification of legal orders – from this technical perspective – makes any sense can legitimately be raised due to this undeniable diversity. David's answer to this question is clear: of course the classification of legal systems can make sense; however, the ideological components should play a preeminent role in this endeavour instead of narrow technical points. From a different angle, David also argues that the technical differences between the legal orders compared must always be interpreted and assessed in the light of either the difference or the similarity of their ideological backgrounds.[21] Therefore, the crucial criterion in David's understanding of classification is the ideological grounding, in the broadest sense, of a given legal order, so his attempt at classification focuses prominently on the philosophical background of legal orders and their vision of justice as a social principle.[22]

It is clear that David's concept differs fundamentally from that of the Arminjon-Nolde-Wolff manual, which concentrated mainly on private law, since he approached the world's legal orders from an angle that is sensitive to problems of legal philosophy, thereby transcending the technical and formal understanding of legal provisions.[23] That is, it regards the law as an outcome of those ideas that characterise our common existence and thinking, and not

[19] ibid 215–16.
[20] ibid 223.
[21] ibid 224.
[22] ibid.
[23] cf R David, 'Existe-t-il un droit occidental?' in KH Nadelmann and AT von Meheren-J Hazard (eds), *XXth Century Comparative and Conflicts Law Legal Essays in Honor of Hessel E Yntema* (Leiden, AW Sythoff, 1961) 56–64.

simply as the mere sum of various legal provisions. It should also be stressed that David's familiarity with the social role of ideology opened up an opportunity for an empathetic understanding of Socialist legal orders, as these legal systems represented such a vision of law as differed from the Western one qualitatively. This insight strongly influenced David's approach in his further work.

In sum, the problem of the manifold technical differences between various legal orders may be avoided by the study of the ideological and philosophical groundings of legal orders. And consequently, the common points of different legal orders become easily identifiable. As a next step, those legal orders that are parts of a common tradition – David unites the above-mentioned ideological components under the term 'tradition' – can be classified into several more abstract legal systems or legal families.[24] David united the world's legal systems into five legal families in 1950:[25]

1.   the law of the Western World;
2.   the law of the Soviet World;
3.   the law of Islam;
4.   Hindu law;
5.   Chinese law.

The most appealing point of this scheme was certainly the unity of common law and Continental legal orders. David submitted that the use of the term Western Law (*droit occidental*) can be justified, as these two technically rather different groups of laws – the common law and the civil law – are strongly intertwined with certain ideological components. Western societies have for a long time been backed by the moral premises of Christianity, the social and political principles of liberal democracy, and the structure of capitalism; and these common ideological components justify merging these legal orders into one single, more comprehensive unit.[26]

This rather unusual approach gave rise to a lively debate among David's contemporaries; some of them accepted the validity of David's position while others vehemently opposed it.[27] The criticism inspired David to rethink and refine this concept, and he dedicated a later piece to the issue of Western Law especially.[28] At the beginning of this paper, David reminds the reader of his earlier differentiation between the technical and ideological components of legal orders, and he points out that the discussion of Western Law only makes sense with respect to the ideological level of legal orders. If the law is regarded as a social phenomenon, being something more than a pure set of formal rules

---

[24] It should be mentioned here that David makes no clear difference between the terms 'legal systems' and 'legal family'.

[25] David, *Traité élémentaire de droit civil comparé* (n 8) 224.

[26] ibid.

[27] For a detailed enumeration of the various positions in this debate, see David, 'Existe-t-il un droit occidental?' (n 23) 56, fnn 2 and 3.

[28] ibid.

and technical provisions, no one can deny the existence of Western Law. The law should be envisaged as 'an approach to the coordination of human relations', argues David.[29] The best example to illustrate the former is to contrast the ideology behind Western Law with the ideological grounding of Soviet law. This contrast makes the unbridgeable differences between the two kinds of legal orders immediately obvious.

When the idea of rule of law or *Rechtsstaat* is contrasted with the statements of Marxist ideology, emphasising the instrumental nature of law and the 'withering away' of state, as well as government, when reaching the phase of Communism in the future, the strong links between the otherwise manifold legal orders of the common law world and Continental law will become irrefutable, although these legal orders strongly differ at the level of technical components.[30] It should also be noted that by putting such a strong emphasis on the concept of rule of law in this study, David renounces his earlier approach that traced the unity of Western Law back to the triad of Christianity, liberalism and capitalism. In a critical vein, David accepts that his earlier concept cannot be justified either by a historical study, or by a contemporary discussion. In so arguing, David points out that both the ancient Roman law and the medieval common law lacked the earlier triad of values as an underlying common basis; moreover, some Western legal orders had already integrated certain solutions from Socialist law into their corpus, while some Asian or African countries had started to introduce institutions from the Western Law.[31] These facts thus invalidate his earlier points on the nature of Western Law.

David's best-known and most-cited book – translated into numerous European languages[32] – was originally published in the 1960s. Undoubtedly, this volume should be regarded as a seminal piece of the paradigm of post-World War II comparative law. David did not change his methodology in the book published almost 15 years later; the differentiation between the technical and ideological components of legal orders still remained a major premise and he also subscribed to the previous taxonomical conclusions. However, David refined his approach on the classification of legal orders at two points.

First, he gave up the category of Western Law as a legal unit on the world map of legal orders, and he devoted separate chapters to both the common law and Continental law (Romano-Germanic legal family), which were previously united under the label 'Western Law'.[33] Interestingly, he did not reject the idea of Western Law once and for all, as he mentioned it in his argumentation as a potential alternative, but he no longer used it for classification. Second, in this

---

[29] ibid 58.

[30] ibid 58–61.

[31] ibid 59.

[32] The international reputation of the author and the book is indicated by the fact that German, English, Spanish, Finnish, Hungarian, Italian and Russian editions were published in the coming years. See David, *Le droit comparé, droits d'hier, droits de demain* (n 17) 87.

[33] For details, R David, *Les grands systèmes de droit contemporains* (Paris, Dalloz, 1982).

manual, he no longer mentioned Chinese or Hindu law as individual entities on the world map of legal orders, but instead labelled any legal orders not being part of the three main, European-origin legal families – Romano-Germanic, common law, and Socialist – as 'Other legal systems'. This 'other systems' category covered all religious, tribal or traditional legal orders having a specific ideological background that differed from either the Western or the Socialist approach.[34] Taking into account these refinements, David drafted the world's legal map as follows:

1.   Romano-Germanic legal family;
2.   Common Law legal family;
3.   Socialist legal family;
4.   Other legal systems.

All in all, David's classificatory schemes and his methodological premises have certainly had a strong impact on both comparative law research and the teaching of comparative law in the Western world.[35] Retrospectively, they may even have been regarded as conventional wisdom or starting points for critical reflection in the paradigm of post-World War II comparative law.[36] This approach has definitely become a classic that can and should be questioned, but no one can disregard it if the issue of classification is at stake.

C.   The Style of Legal Families – The Taxonomy of Konrad Zweigert

Konrad Zweigert published a seminal article at the beginning of the 1960s, and this paper laid down the basis of his approach to the classification of legal orders[37] that appeared in the chapter devoted to the issue of classification in the world-famous Zweigert–Kötz comparative law manual, which is accessible in both the original German version[38] and in the subsequent English translations.[39] The aim of Zweigert's paper is twofold. First, it has a clear methodological scope, since Zweigert elaborated his methodological premises for the issue of classification here. Second, it is also dedicated to the presentation of Zweigert's own approach.

---

[34] ibid 31–33.

[35] For a good summary of David's European impact, see S Whittaker, 'Le rayonnement de René David' in *Hommage à René David* (Paris, Association Henri Capitant-Dalloz, 2012) 65–71.

[36] For instance, the French comparatist René Rodiére clearly built up his approach on the basis of David's idea three decades later. See R Rodiére, *Introduction au droit comparé* (Paris, 1979) 23 and 25–27; or see J Husa, *A New Introduction to Comparative Law* (Oxford, Hart Publishing, 2015) 13.

[37] K Zweigert, 'Zur Lehre von den Rechtskreisen' in KH Nadelmann and AT von Meheren-J Hazard (eds), *XXth Century Comparative and Conflicts Law Legal Essays in Honor of Hessel E Yntema* (n 23) 42–55.

[38] K Zweigert-H Kötz, *Einführung in die Rechtsvergleichung* (Tübingen, JCB Mohr, 1971) 67–80.

[39] K Zweigert and H Kötz, *An Introduction to Comparative Law* (Oxford, Oxford University Press, 1998) 63–73.

Further, it even has a historical relevance with respect to the development of comparative law, since Zweigert continuously reflects on his contemporaries' arguments, so it offers a panorama on the ongoing post-World War II comparative law discourse in the 1960s with respect to the issue of taxonomy.

Before going into detail, Zweigert declares two major premises. The antecedents of both could be found in previous scholarly works,[40] but a clear advantage of this study is that it connects them and clarifies their relationship. In general, in Zweigert's eyes, classification can only have a relative scope in each case, and this inherent relativity depends on two main factors. The first is the relativity embedded in the subject-matter of comparison (*materiebezongene Relativität*). This concept implies that classificatory attempts will necessary lead to divergent outcomes if they are based on different fields of law. The world's legal map will be different by nature if one tries to draft it from the viewpoint either of private law or of constitutional law; for example the Romanist legal orders, being in a close relationship from a private law perspective, unite countries with rather diverse constitutional backgrounds.[41]

Second, it should also be borne in mind, Zweigert points out, that each classificatory attempt is strongly linked to a given time period, that is, to a given age of legal history (*zeitliche Relativität*). Therefore, for instance, the world map of legal orders can qualitatively differ if one compares its pre-World War II version with its post-World War II setting. Here, the position of Chinese law is mentioned as an illustration. Zweigert submits that Chinese law, which was categorised as Communist law when he wrote this article, had also been a legal order characterised by many traditional features.[42] In conclusion, it has to be accepted that the attempts at taxonomy can only have a relative validity, as they are heavily dependent on their premises with special regard to the field of law selected and the age studied.

Zweigert's other important insight as to the method of classification is that each previous classificatory attempt had a common deficiency. This is the fact that they all tried to classify legal orders on the basis of one single criterion. These previous attempts can therefore be described as 'one-dimensional', in the words of Zweigert.[43] On the contrary, Zweigert suggests a different approach to the premises of classification, since he is devoted to a 'multi-dimensional' understanding. The key to this new approach is the concept of style,[44] which

---

[40] For instance, the authors of the Arminjon–Nolde–Wolff manual point out that the outcome of classification may differ according to the specific field of law studies (eg private law vs constitutional law). See Arminjon, Nolde and Wolff, *Traité de droit comparé I* (n 5) 47. René David explains that each classificatory attempt is arbitrary to a certain extent, as it always depends on the specific subject-matter. David, *Traité élémentaire de droit civil comparé* 222.

[41] Zweigert, 'Zur Lehre von den Rechtskreisen' (n 37) 44.

[42] ibid.

[43] ibid 45.

[44] For a critical reading of Zweigert's concept, see P Cserne, 'Conceptualizing "Style" in Legal Scholarship: the Curious Case of Zweigert's "Style Doctrine"' (2019) 15 *International Journal of Law in Context* 297–309.

has successfully been applied to the history of art and in economics. Further, this concept is also applied by Canon 20 of the 1917 *Corpus Iuris Canonici*. The essence of the concept of style, according to Zweigert, is that it is capable of uniting all characteristic features and other peculiarities of a given phenomenon; therefore, by having this cluster of decisive features, the phenomenon studied can be detached from 'other totalities' with different sets of characteristics.[45] Based on the concept of style, Zweigert argues that the groups of legal orders can also have their own styles. The task of comparatists is to comprehend the individual styles of legal orders and to identify those components that are able to define the style of a given legal order.

In conclusion, he proposes five 'style-elements', and he also argues that, by a proper weighting of these factors, the legal styles of the world can be summarised and could serve as a scholarly basis for the taxonomy of legal orders. These five 'elements', to be studied synoptically, are as follows:

1.   historical origin;
2.   specific mode of legal thought;
3.   distinctive legal institutions;
4.   legal sources and their interpretation; and
5.   ideological factors.[46]

In conclusion, by applying the concept of style, Zweigert identifies eight different 'legal families' (*Rechtskreis* in German).[47] Interestingly, and this shows how 'normal science' worked in this age of comparative law, he referred to the classification of the Arminjon–Nolde–Wolff manual as both an authority and a starting point, although he created a qualitatively new approach to this issue. Thus, the eight main legal families of the world are:

1.   The Romanistic.
2.   The Germanistic.
3.   The Nordic.
4.   The Anglo-American.
5.   The Communist.
6.   Law in the Far-East.
7.   The Islamic.
8.   The Hindu.

Beside these legal families, Zweigert also mentions so-called 'hybrid' legal orders; for instance, the legal orders of Greece, Louisiana and Scotland. Zweigert argues that these legal orders have to be studied according to their degree of proximity to the major 'legal styles'.[48]

---

[45] Zweigert, 'Zur Lehre von den Rechtskreisen' (n 37) 45.
[46] ibid 43–52.
[47] ibid 55.
[48] ibid 54–55.

A critic of Zweigert – Åke Malmström – submits, when providing an in-depth assessment of his concept of legal style as a cluster of major characteristics of legal orders, that, with the help of this idea, Zweigert in fact declared the main principle of modern classification. This principle is the claim that any kind of legal taxonomy has to be based on multiple factors, not on a single factor. However, as Malmström pointed out, the application of the concept of style is highly dubious from a scholarly viewpoint, since it may lead to simplification and overgeneralisation.[49] As such, this concept, although it has been well received by the worldwide comparatist community since the 1970s, has never been incontestable.

Zweigert's concept may also be doubted from a different angle. It can even be argued that historical origin as an independent factor of legal style may be dispensed with, as all the other four factors contain historical references, and they also have their own historical dimensions. Therefore, either the factor of historical origin may be disregarded altogether, or, at least, the order of these factors has to be modified, Malmström argues. He suggests that if historical origin is kept as an autonomous factor in legal style, the order of these factors for their scholarly relevance should look like this:

1. historical origin;
2. ideological factors;
3. the legal sources;
4. the specific mode of legal thought;
5. distinctive legal institutions.[50]

D. The Concept of the *Encyclopedia*

At the beginning of the 1970s, the international community of comparative law scholars addressed an ambitious task under the aegis of the International Association of Legal Science. Since comparative law, as a scholarly enterprise, had been improving considerably during the post-World War II period, the idea of summarising the current state of the art in the form of an encyclopaedia came up almost naturally.[51] Originally, Zweigert was offered the position of editor-in-chief. This idea was an unquestionably huge challenge, as it was planned to publish national reports for most of the countries of the world, and it was also intended to include detailed analyses on each specific field of law. A prestigious community of editors and authors was gathered in order to help the realisation

---

[49] Å Malmström, 'The System of Legal Systems. Notes on a Problem of Classification in Comparative Law' (1969) 13 *Scandinavian Studies in Law* 129–49, 143.

[50] ibid 144.

[51] For discussion of the preparatory phase of this project and the concept of the *Encylopedia*, see U Drobnig, 'The International Encyclopedia of Comparative Law: Efforts toward a Worldwide Comparison of Law' (1972) 5 *Cornell International Law Journal* 113–29.

of this all-encompassing task; almost all important comparatists of this era could be found among the editors, including David, Zweigert, Rheinstein, Lawson and Tunc.[52]

The second volume of the *Encyclopedia*, edited by David, was devoted to the issues of major legal systems of the world, as well as to the problems of legal sources and legal unification, and he was also the author of the chapter on these two problems. As for the issue of classification, the first two chapters of this volume are relevant, since the first one discusses those different concepts of law that animate the major legal families, while the second one is devoted to an in-depth discussion of the major legal families.

The chapter on the various concepts of law presents six different concepts in detail. This taxonomy reflects David's view, which has already been presented, as it is based on his insight that Western Law is a unitary legal phenomenon and the classification of legal orders has to take this communality into account. The authors of this chapter present these concepts of law as follows:

1. The Western one.
2. The Socialist one.
3. The Muslim one.
4. The Hindu one.
5. The Far Eastern one.
6. The African one.[53]

This list shows that the editor maintained the opportunity to present common law and Continental law in a common frame, and the other concepts of law, having a different philosophical background, were contrasted with it. However, the next chapter, focusing on the major legal families of the world, was apparently influenced by another, contrasting approach. As the authors focus on the legal families at a less abstract level as compared to the general scope of the so-called 'concepts of law', the taxonomy proposed in this chapter changes in a qualitative manner. Contrary to the previous approach, this part identifies six major legal families:

1. The civil law system.
2. The common law system.
3. The system of Socialist law.
4. Islamic law.
5. Hindu law.
6. African law.

Surprisingly, the discussion of the Far East legal systems is not included in this chapter. This deficiency is even more striking as the previous chapter included a

---

[52] For the list of the editors of all 17 volumes, see ibid 118–19.

[53] R David et al, *International Encyclopedia of Comparative Law. The Different Conceptions of Law* (Tübingen-Leiden, Mohr-Martinus Nijhoff, 1975).

longer piece on the Far East concept of law. It can be supposed that the lack of a competent author may explain this strange editorial solution.

These two chapters, edited by the same person, are seemingly based on different approaches to taxonomy, which may encumber the clarification of their internal relationship; further, this may also raise the issue of incoherence. The first chapter tended to reflect David's ideas from the 1950s, whereas the second one seemed to have a strong tie with his seminal work, *Les grands systems de droit contemporains*, from the mid-1960s. The parallel appearance of these two approaches in the same work suggests that David did not want to make a choice between them once and for all – either the one that recognises the existence of Western Law, or the other one that distinguishes between Continental law and common law – but he may have considered both of them plausible, depending on the perspective chosen.

E. The Perspectives of a Multi-level Classification

Åke Malmström's paper – *The System of Legal Systems* – was published in 1969,[54] and it made a considerable contribution to the evolution of comparative law theories on taxonomy. This polemic has an important place in the post-World War II story of comparative law, as it provides the reader with a critical and meticulous discussion of the various approaches to the classification of legal orders in the third paradigm. That is, the inner development of these taxonomical concepts can be learnt from Malmström's paper, and his critical view helps us better understand their problem horizons.

The professor from Uppsala gave a fruitful contribution to the scholarly discourse on the classification of the world's legal orders. In his view, the task of taxonomy can only be realised with the help of a multi-level approach, so a new, more refined vision of classification has to be established. In order to achieve this, a proper classification has to unite various classificatory units with qualitatively different characteristics.[55] The taxonomies submitted earlier relied solely on units at the same level of abstraction – a family, a legal family, *Rechtskreis*, etc – and this forced them to accept conceptual limits that made it impossible to provide a real legal map of the world. This happened since these units were inherently limited by the very nature of their scholarly scope. The idea of a Romano-Germanic legal family neglects the obvious differences between the Latin and German legal traditions, owing to the higher level of abstraction implied in the concept of a legal family. For instance, the concept of a legal family is unable to integrate the differences between legal development and the techniques of codification, in order to remain capable of providing a common framework based on factors other than the diverging legal orders. Malmström's

---

[54] Malmström, 'The System of Legal Systems' (n 49).
[55] ibid 146.

idea of a multi-level taxonomy, with special regard to the general relativity of any classifications, makes it possible to have a more refined discussion of the world's legal orders, as compared to those attempts that apply only one single unit of classification.

Malmström suggests making a distinction between two different levels of abstraction. On a more abstract level, the term 'legal group' has to be applied; however, on a less abstract level, the application of the concept 'legal family' is advised. The concept of a legal family, as it has a more restricted scope, seems to be able to refine the entire classificatory scheme by making it more sensitive towards essential but less general differences.[56] All in all, this approach enables comparative law taxonomy to better reflect the apparent differences stemming from the uniqueness of both the ideological and the technical elements of legal orders than the previous attempts, which relied on one single unit of classification.

With the help of this approach, based on two different levels of abstraction, legal groups and legal families, Malmström suggests that the world map of legal orders should be composed of the following units:[57]

I. The Occidental (Euro-American) group:
   1. The family of (European) Continental legal systems;
   2. The Latin-American family of legal systems;
   3. The Nordic (Scandinavian) family of legal systems;
   4. The Common-law family.

II. The Socialist (Communist) group:
   1. Soviet law;
   2. The legal systems of the People's Democracies;
   3. The law of the Chinese People's Democracies.

III. The Asian Non-Communist systems.
IV. The law of the African States.

Malmström also adds that the use of the term 'group' for Groups III and IV does not seem to be entirely proper, as one cannot talk about the same level of unity with regard to what characterises the groups of Occidental law and Communist law. In addition, it cannot be denied that traditional and Western components have been incorporated into the legal systems of these two groups, so they apparently have a mixed nature.[58] Due to these problems and because of the limited European knowledge of these legal orders, Malmström did not suggest any further subdivisions but simply mentioned that the historical influence of either English or French law may mean a relevant dividing line.[59]

---

[56] ibid.
[57] ibid 147.
[58] ibid 146.
[59] ibid 147.

In order to illustrate the scholarly value of his multi-level approach, Malmström argues that even the concept 'legal family' can be broken down into further components. For instance, the Continental legal family can be divided into German and Latin laws. This remark clearly shows that Malmström thought it was impossible to create a permanently closed and empirical valid approach to taxonomy, but his definite aim was to contribute to this discourse of the comparatist community and to indicate those points where this line of thought could be improved further. Malmström's efforts illustrate well how puzzle-solving research has been working in the third paradigm of comparative legal studies.[60]

F. Patterns and Dynamics in Law – the Innovation of Ugo Mattei

Due to the failure of the Soviet Bloc after 1989 and the disappearing of the bipolar ideological order, the world as such changed irreversibly. This, inter alia, led to the once-settled taxonomies of the world's legal orders being challenged, since their political and geographical premises, appropriate for the bipolar world order, could no longer be maintained.[61] In addition, the spread of the idea of a multi-level classification and the gradual discrediting of Euro-centrism (which was also implied in the previous conception of a Socialist and a 'free' world) in comparative law also made this revision unavoidable in order to maintain continuity in comparative law despite the largely changed circumstances.

A leading Italian comparatist developed a novel presentation of the taxonomy in comparative law that intentionally contradicted various former components of the conventional wisdom. However, although his thinking was clearly both innovative and revolutionary in some ways, Mattei did not dismantle the settled framework, as his conception also preserved many important tenets – with special regard to the vocabulary applied – elaborated by the scholars of the 1960s and 1970s. For example, he argued that the relativity of these classificatory attempts should be accepted, and this was also valid for his approach, because he also applied a multi-level approach to his classification. What was entirely new was his intention to break with the former Euro-American-centric mind-set in order to overstep Western biases, with special regard to their implied private law focus, and he also decided to integrate the dynamics of legal changes in his concept.[62] In sum, Mattei's approach to classification showed what kind of scholarly potential the issue of taxonomy might acquire in the dramatically changed circumstances of the 1990s. By doing so, he also demonstrated the relevance and vitality of comparative law as a research tradition.

The core of Mattei's approach is to make the focus of classification a single criterion: the conception of law, or, to put it differently, the 'pattern of law'.

---

[60] See ibid 146.
[61] U Mattei, 'Three Patterns of Law: Taxonomy and Change in the World's Legal Systems' (1997) 45 *The American Journal of Comparative Law* 5–44, 10–11.
[62] ibid 10–12.

In essence, Mattei argues that, in a Weberian sense, law is to be regarded 'as a tool of social organisation'.[63] However, as modern anthropology teaches us, not only professional law – law in the Western sense – can be a form of social organisation; politics and tradition are also equally relevant patterns of social organisation in other parts of the world. Thus, in conclusion, legal orders may be grounded in three different patterns of law – those of professional law, political law and traditional law. Obviously, these three patterns are all present in every legal order to some extent; however, as Mattei argues, legal orders can be classified on the basis of which one is in a hegemonic position and is thereby able to have a decisive influence over the character of a given legal order.[64] Following this line of thought, Mattei concludes that the world's legal orders are to be grouped into three main legal families: '1. rule of professional law, 2. rule of political law, 3. rule of tradition law'.[65]

With the use of multi-level classification, the legal map of the world can be drafted as follows.[66]

I. Rule of professional law:

    1. Common Law –

        a. English sphere;
        b. United States sphere;

    2. Civil Law –

        a. German-influenced area;
        b. French influenced area;
        c. Scandinavian laws;
        d. traditional mixed systems;

    3. Mixed systems.

II. Rule of political law:

    1. Law of transition (former Socialist law);
    2. Law of development –

        a. African law;
        b. Latin American laws.

III. Rule of traditional law:

    1. Far Eastern legal orders –

        a. Chinese pattern;
        b. Japanese pattern;

    2. Islamic legal orders.

---

[63] ibid 12.
[64] ibid 14.
[65] ibid 19.
[66] ibid 40–42.

In addition, Mattei emphasises that this taxonomy is by no means a definitive one, as legal transplants or other historical circumstances may contribute to such a structural transformation in legal orders that the legal order can shift from the aegis of one pattern to another one. He calls these 'macro comparative revolutions', and many historical examples justify this point; just think of the modern history of Central European legal orders, or that of Chinese law. Further, if the comparatist chooses one specific field of law to study, he or she may realise that different areas of law may belong to different patterns of law due to their specific characteristics; here the politicised nature of constitutional law or the traditional basis of family law can provide good examples.[67] Overall, Mattei's approach has a flexible nature that clearly facilitates tailoring the features of a comparative law research design to the specificities of the issue studied.

Mattei's classificatory scheme is certainly very impressive, as it corrects the deficiencies of the former attempts at many important points, such as their Western biases or their rather static nature. Further, it brings into play new and relevant insights; the anthropological concept of 'pattern of law' as applied in Mattei's work seems to be the most relevant improvement in the theory of comparative law in the second half of the 1990s, as it definitely opened up new perspectives. In sum, with this sophisticated approach, Mattei was certainly able to save the issue of classification for future comparative law activities, despite the risk that the fall of the bipolar world order would render it unfit for further use.

G. The Classification of Legal Orders in Post-World War II Comparative Law

The earlier discussion in this chapter did not aim to present a meticulous analysis of all classifications that were elaborated in the third paradigm of comparative law.[68] On the contrary, it simply wanted to show the internal evolution – again, we need to recall the Kuhnian idea of puzzle-solving research – of this major research issue by discussing some influential approaches. All in all, it is submitted that by analysing these classificatory attempts, the outcomes of this kind of research can be studied properly.

A major insight of the earlier discussion is that the community of comparatists has to accept that a fully comprehensive and generally valid taxonomy of the world's legal orders can never be prepared in a scholarly way. That is, no comparative research is capable of creating the so-called *theatrum legale mundi*, as it was imagined by Leibniz. The various attempts at classifying the legal orders are limited by the complexity of legal phenomena. Taxonomy is determined by relativity in general: the level of abstraction of a given piece of research, the field of law studied, the time period of the research and the potential audience

---

[67] ibid 16.

[68] For an almost complete list of these concepts and approaches, see Varga, '*Theatrum legale mundi*: On Legal Systems Classified' (n 5).

are all factors that determine the outcomes in taxonomy. This conclusion was pointed out by Zweigert, when he argued that classifications were relative by their nature.

Thus, each classificatory attempt in post-World War II comparative law has to have a precisely determined scope. It means that its aims, its level of abstraction, the field of law studied and the time period have to be unambiguously determined. Due to the internal coherence of this paradigm, the comparatists who wanted to contribute to the issue of classification generally narrowed their research to both private law and contemporary legal orders. In addition, this paradigm contained another limitation, which, however, was never explicitly mentioned. The puzzle-solving research was focused on Western and Socialist legal orders; that is, it attempted to study these legal orders with a similarly high intensity, but the other legal orders of the world – basically, all the legal orders beyond Europe and North America – had the role of merely decorative illustrations, if any. In conclusion, well-elaborated classifications were solely created with respect to Western and Socialist laws, as shown in the oeuvres of both David and Zweigert.

A major step in the evolution of this research issue was the rejection of the previously dominant methodological monism. This process implied two shifts in research methodology. On the one hand, some scholars recognised numerous criteria as bases for classification; on the other, the units of classification (legal type, legal group, legal family, etc) also multiplied. The pluralisation of classificatory methodologies led to a greater flexibility of those approaches that previously focused on one single criterion and had only a restricted scope. This shift enabled the new approaches to grasp the complex reality of legal orders in a more refined and subtle manner. In sum, the inner evolution of taxonomy as a distinct research issue post-World War II contributed to a considerable degree to a better understanding of the characteristics of the world's legal orders, and thereby led to the general enrichment of legal culture.

III. THE RENEWAL OF COMPARATIVE LAW METHODOLOGY: THE VICTORY OF FUNCTIONALISM

A. Conceptual Discussion

Functionalism as a research method became one of the crucial methodological approaches of social sciences in the nineteenth century. As a contemporary scholar argues, we can differentiate between several approaches in social sciences: we can talk about the neo-Aristotelian,[69]

---

[69] In Aristotle's work, the concept of *telos* or *causa finalis*, which is connected to the nature of things, has an important role. According to this belief, every existing thing thrives for perfection, and the right law can be deduced from the nature of things. R Michaels, 'The Functional Method of

the evolutionist,[70] the structural[71] or the neo-Kantian[72] traditions of functionalism. This rich and divergent application of functionalism makes it necessary to clarify its core meaning, the so-called *genus proximum*. Without this clarification, it would be hard to understand functionalism in comparative law, which obviously adopts many presumptions of the general social-science application of functionalism as well.[73]

The variations of functionalism, which are sometimes connected to very different areas of science, are in fact connected by a common hypothesis, namely that, in the course of research, one must never study the phenomenon examined on its own and exclusively; the main goal of study should rather be to identify and understand what kind of role or function this phenomenon has within a so-called 'bigger entity'. This 'bigger entity', depending on the area of science, may be society,[74] history[75] or even the legal order.[76] Thus, the essence of functionalist approaches is that they never focus on a phenomenon individually but approach phenomena as being embedded in the context of a 'bigger entity', and basically from the aspect of their goals and their tasks.

Naturally, functionalism in legal scholarship puts the theses described earlier into practice in the course of exploring legal issues. Legal research of a functionalist nature is never interested in a legal provision or institution alone; it is always interested in the roles and tasks it fulfils within the legal order in the broadest sense. As such, it is much less sensitive to the dogmatic details than to the contextual issues with respect to the functioning of law. Due to this approach, legal functionalism becomes, by its very nature, more open to the social aspects

---

Comparative Law' in M Reimann and R Zimmermann (eds), *The Oxford Handbook of Comparative Law* (Oxford, Oxford University Press, 2006) 339–82, 345–47.

[70] The beginnings of evolutionist functionalism can be connected to Darwin and Comte. According to Comte, society is one such complex organism, in which all elements serve a certain kind of function related to development. This understanding therefore connects the concept of function with evolution: ibid 347–49.

[71] Structural functionalism developed in opposition to the previous two schools and can be traced back to Durkheim's views. Durkheim understood function as the relationship between elements, and he set as the goal of sociology the research of real, objective functions that are independent of origins and goals: ibid 349–50.

[72] Functionalism is given a major role in Cassirer's epistemology, which can be considered a manifestation of neo-Kantian functionalism. According to Cassirer, unique phenomena can and should only be understood in their functional relationship with other phenomena: ibid 355–56.

[73] See also Frankenberg's argumentation: he submits that comparative legal functionalism is no more than the vulgar version of Luhmann's functionalism. G Frankenberg, 'Critical Comparisons: Re-Thinking Comparative Law' (1985) 2 *Harvard International Law Journal* 411–56, 434.

[74] This is the typical starting point of the structural understanding of sociology, as it always tries to interpret different phenomena from the perspective of their relations with society itself and with one another.

[75] Marxism frequently tried to examine the role of certain phenomena emerging throughout history from the perspective of the historical dialectics of class struggle.

[76] In relation to legal scholarship, there can also be found approaches that aim at examining a given legal phenomenon in the light of the legal order as a whole. An example of this is the principle of systemic interpretation, which finds the rule in question only to be interpreted in light of the legal order as a whole.

of law, so it may also get close to providing the sociology or anthropology of the law.

Because of all this, in the methodology of post-World War II comparative law, the idea of the function of law – that is, the relationship between legal provisions and their roles in the social reality – was able to take a key role in the evolution of comparative law methodology. The concept of function of law appeared capable of enabling comparatists to find a 'neutral' common denominator when comparing legal orders based on different terminological, conceptual or ideological traditions. In other words, research would discover the indispensable element of any kind of comparison, the *tertium comparationis*,[77] which could be identified irrespective of the specificities of individual legal orders, for instance when some provisions of Continental and Socialist laws were to be studied. Needless to say, this approach offered a much more relevant and logical methodological starting point for comparative law projects than the earlier, predominantly speculative approaches stemming from either evolutionist or universalist premises.

B. The Earliest Attempts to Apply the Idea of Functionalism in Comparative Law

i. Preliminaries

The transformation of the methodological frame of comparative law into functionalism with a distinct and solid methodology has been firmly attached to the name of Konrad Zweigert.[78] Zweigert's merits in this field are undeniable; however, it needs to be mentioned that even before his work, several authors dealt with the possibilities of applying functionalism to comparative law.

The first of these scholars was Rabel, whose methodological presumptions have already been analysed in detail as part of the second paradigm of modern comparative law. Rabel's methodological thinking was developed partly in connection with the issue of qualification, which was considered a basic problem in the study of international private law. The novelty of his approach was that Rabel redirected the focus of research from general questions to specific ones, and he called attention to the importance of examining the social context behind legal institutions. By doing so, Rabel made the 'Copernican turn'

---

[77] For detailed analysis of the *tertium comparationis* in the logical operation of comparison, see V Knapp, 'Quelques problèmes méthodologiques dans la science du droit comparé' in Zweigert and Puttfarken (eds), *Rechtsvergleichung* (n 2) 334–44.

[78] See, eg, Frankenberg, 'Critical Comparisons: Re-Thinking Comparative Law' (n 73) 80; J Husa, 'Farewell to Functionalism or Methodological Tolerance?' (2003) 3 *Rabels Zeitschrift für ausländisches und internationales Privatrecht* 419–47, 422; or M Graziadei, 'The Functionalist Heritage' in P Legrand and R Munday (eds), *Comparative Legal Studies – Traditions and Transitions* (Cambridge, Cambridge University Press, 2003) 100–27, 101–02.

regarding the scope of comparative law inquiries, which was indispensable to devising the methodology of comparative law functionalism.

The work of Philipp Heck, published in 1932 under the title *Begriffsbildung und Interessenjurisprudenz*, is most probably less relevant than Rabel's achievements, but it must not be neglected either. Heck, similarly to Jhering, placed the concept of interest at the centre of legal research too. The study of interests in a legal context might open up new perspectives for comparative law as well. Heck argued that through analysing interests that appear behind the strict wording of personal or social relationships with a legal dimension, one can create so-called case types, which no longer closely relate to the concrete phrasing of law but grasp the social situation hidden behind the black-letter text of the law. With the help of such constructions, the comparison of legal orders building on different conceptual tools in a scholarly way became possible.[79]

ii. Functionalism and Legal Principles

As suggested, there had already been some attempts to insert the functional approach into the toolkit of comparative law in the period between the two World Wars. However, the scholarly value of these incoherent attempts lies much more in the questions to which they gave rise than in their methodology and consistency, since a complete methodology regularly applicable through the course of research could not yet be built on them.

Josef Esser's work meant a step forward, as he examined the problems of fundamental principles and judge-made law with the help of the comparative method, and he also applied many functionalist premises in his research. It is clearly visible in light of the methodological development of the following decades that Esser's research, comparing certain national legal orders, also meant the first successful achievement of modern functionalist research.[80] This is why his methodology and results are worthy of attention, as that might help in defining the positions of later concepts.[81]

In essence, Esser sought answers to two questions. First, what kind of common building blocks can be found behind laws in legal orders? Second, how do they influence the development and functioning of the legal system as a whole?[82] It was also argued by Esser that the legal system consists not only

[79] H Ficker, 'L'état du droit comparé en Allemagne' (1958) 4 *Revue internationale du droit comparé* 701–18, 716–17; W Friedmann, *Legal Theory* (London, Stevens & Sons, 1949) 226–27.

[80] M Rheinstein, 'Book review' (1957) 24 *The University of Chicago Law Review* 597–606, 598.

[81] The evaluation of the various concepts of functionalism is far from being evident. Ralf Michaels, one of the most recent researchers of functionalist methodology, argues that Esser's approach is 'richer and more sophisticated' than that of Zweigert. See Michaels, 'The Functional Method of Comparative Law' (n 69) 346.

[82] J Esser, *Grundsatz und Norm in der richterlichen Fortbildung des Privatrechts: Rechtsvergleichende Beiträge zur Rechtsquellen- und Interpretationslehre* (Tübingen, JCB Mohr, 1956). English reviews were written about this volume by Max Rheinstein and Wolfgang R Friedmann. In the following sections, this study presents the main line of thought in the volume based on these works.

of laws, but also of other elements that are not at the same level as laws. The most relevant among these 'other elements' are the legal maxims, the general clauses, the concepts, the institutions, the doctrines and the principles of judicial activity *(leges artis judiciariae)*.[83] These elements of legal systems, which are to be found 'beyond' laws, can be called, in aggregate, principles. The main goal of Esser's research was to present in detail the functioning of these principles through analysing various types of national judicial case law.

One of his reviewers pointed out that Esser's research results could be seen as the most comprehensive comparative analyses of judicial activity of the period,[84] since he examined English, American, French, Italian, Spanish and German laws, decisions and scholarly literature. Moreover, he analysed international case law in detail as well. Based on meticulous research, Esser came to the conclusion that the difference between the understanding of judicial activity in the two great legal cultures – common law and Continental law – was slightly exaggerated. He submitted that the development of judicial practice was defined and determined by the same societal problems in both legal families in the previous century. Tracing back the development of judicial practice to similar societal problems was to be regarded as a typically functionalist orientation. Moreover, he also argued that dissimilarities between Continental and common law can only be found with respect to the diversity of legal techniques. As a joint feature of common law and Continental law, he also pointed out that they always improve the quality of the legal orders, regardless of the legal culture in which they operate, thus the tracks of context-independent development can also be revealed.[85]

It is worth mentioning two legal history examples here, which illustrate the above-mentioned theses and show exactly what Esser meant by them. The first is the development of the institution of unjustified enrichment, which occurred in a similar way in the two legal traditions despite their completely different institutional backgrounds. The *Code civil*, for instance, did not contain any rules on unjustified enrichment, but French courts nevertheless developed a regulatory system over half a century that did not differ in any important elements from the codifications of the *Bürgerliches Gesetzbuch* (BGB) at the turn of the nineteenth–twentieth century and the Swiss Civil Code. The common law legal culture also came up with similar regulations with the help of analogies and extensions, based on the institution of the *action in assumpsit* that was originally applied to claim for compensation in the event of a breach of contract.

The other example is the issue of objective responsibility, which all modern industrial societies had to face by the end of the nineteenth century. Esser does not deny that one can obviously find differences on the surface of various

---

[83] Rheinstein, 'Book review' (n 80) 599.
[84] W Friedmann, 'Book review' (1957) 57 *Columbia Law Review* 449–51, 449.
[85] ibid 449.

national legal orders. However, the French, German, English and American regulations are closely linked by the fact that, in the course of developing the system of objective responsibility, the earlier subjective approach of responsibility had to be adjusted to the challenges created by the new, proliferating situations of damage that appeared during the emergence of an industrial society and mass production. This line of thought is closed with a typically functionalist conclusion: due to the entirely similar problems that appeared in the same way in all Western societies, the legal provisions developed to answer these situations are identical at the level of fundamental principles.[86]

Esser's all-encompassing and meticulous research, which is relevant not only from the point of view of comparative law but also from the perspective of legal theory and practice,[87] drew the attention of the scholarly community to the importance of comparative law in the study of the judiciary. Moreover, the application of the functionalist approach stemmed directly from the object itself, because discovering the common principles and points hiding behind the considerably different common law and Continental judicial practice would not have been possible with another methodology. Thus, comparative law functionalism, as Esser understood it, proved to be perfectly capable of discovering similar societal problems hiding behind different legal provisions, and thus of analysing the principles to be found in the background of diverse national forms of regulation. This attitude had a fertilising effect on the later developments of functionalist methodology in comparative law (see Zweigert's ideas, for example), since it was endorsed by most of those scholars who were engaged in the methodological discourse.

C. The Fundamental Principles of Functionalist Methodology

Zweigert's achievements of are unquestionably authoritative as regards the further evolution of the functionalist methodology in comparative law. His work covered both the grounding of comparative law functionalism as a distinct methodology, applicable to precise research programmes, and the critical discussion of its historical roots. These two dimensions are worth examining together, because the integration of the historical aspect of functionalism as interpreted by Zweigert may provide us with a much deeper insight into Zweigert's approach than if we only examine the relevant part of the well-known Zweigert–Kötz handbook.

---

[86] ibid 450–51.

[87] For instance, when examining legal principles from a theoretical aspect, Jakab considers Esser's work the starting point. See A Jakab, 'Critical Remarks on Alexy's Theory of Principles' in P Cserne et al (eds), *Theatrum Legale Mundi* (Budapest, Societas Sancti Stephani, 2007) 203–20, 203–04.

i. Historical Roots of Functionalism: Jhering's Method as an Ideal and as a Programme

It tells us a lot about Zweigert's view that he sees his predecessor in this method of modern comparative law in Jhering's work.[88] From the perspective of the evolution of functionalist methodology, Zweigert unequivocally considers Jhering's work to be the turning point of modern legal thinking. More precisely, Zweigert points out that the moment when Jhering completely changed his previous understanding of the law, and explicitly turned against legal scholarship focusing on concepts, has to be considered a key point in the history of modern legal thinking. Jhering's new approach focused on the aim (*Zweck*) of legal provisions,[89] and he argued that the legal protection of interests has to be the main impetus behind legal development. Thereby, instead of concentrating on pure conceptual games, Jhering encouraged scholars to have much closer contact with the social reality.[90] The attitude of rejecting that form of legal scholarship that focuses on concepts radically confronted the conceptual-dogmatic approach that became dominant in nineteenth-century Germany and then culminated in the creation of the system and conceptual constructions of the BGB.[91]

By acknowledging and emphasising Jhering's historical importance from the viewpoint of the formation of modern legal thinking, Zweigert did not mean to suggest that Jhering's ideas directly affected the research methodology of comparative law, but instead tried to depict him as the 'great predecessor' of comparative law functionalism.[92] It is basically argued by Zweigert that Jhering's methodology paved the way for the method of post-World War II comparative law, and so the functional approach, as it was based on three methodological premises that play a crucial role in functionalism as well. Zweigert formulates these premises, based on Jhering's works, as being that the method of research in comparative law has to be critical, free of dogmatism and realist.

The critical attitude in this context means that the comparatists cannot deal with legal phenomena only from the viewpoint of facts but always have to look for the reason behind the given legal solution too. They must examine why the problems are solved with the help of the given legal institution, so a simple descriptive presentation of legal issues can never be satisfactory in a comparative law research project. Besides searching for the reasons behind legal

---

[88] K Zweigert and K Siehr, 'Jhering's Influence on the Development of Comparative Legal Method' (1971) 19 *The American Journal of Comparative Law* 215–31.

[89] Friedmann, *Legal Theory* (n 79) 213–16.

[90] K Zweigert and K Siehr, 'Jhering's Influence on the Development of Comparative Legal Method' (1971) 2 *The American Journal of Comparative Law* 215–31, 216–17.

[91] See also M Rheinstein, 'Comparative Law and Conflicts of Law in Germany' (1934–35) 2 *The University of Chicago Law Review* 232–39, 232–33.

[92] Zweigert and Siehr, 'Jhering's Influence on the Development of Comparative Legal Method' (n 90) 218.

solutions, the critical approach also entails evaluating the given legal institution from a utilitarian or political perspective, and Zweigert is convinced that the researcher needs to analyse these aspects as well. Thus, the critical approach as formulated by Jhering opens up the scope of research towards the social functioning of legal institutions, and it thereby exceeds those methods that limit research to simple theoretical reflection or data collection.

As for the claim of being free from dogmatism, the scepticism towards legal scholarship focusing solely on legal concepts and terminology can be detected. Research cannot be bounded by the infinitely abstracted legal dogmatism and its overt preference for legal concepts. It follows that comparatists should aim to ignore the language of their own legal culture and use concepts 'free from any judgement, and based on a sociological classification'[93] in the process of examining legal institutions in different legal cultures.

The last methodological criterion, the claim of realism, expects that comparatists, if possible, should not only deal with legal issues in the strict sense of the term. On the contrary, they must take into account all relevant circumstances that had an impact on their research findings or had any relation to them, from ethical factors to economic policy.[94]

It is worth noting that Zweigert does not argue that Jhering's method stems from the above factors, but he submits that it was Jhering's impact that was decisive in modern comparative law's methodology's becoming critical, free from dogmatism and realistic.[95] This leads to the conclusion that, in fact, Zweigert developed the premises of his individual understanding of methodology 'dressed in Jhering's prestige', and with his frequent references to Jhering, he tried to strengthen his own ideas. In this way, he wished to insert his theory into the continuity of traditional, society-orientated legal theory, which, at least in Zweigert's opinion, started with Jhering's work.

ii. The Research Programme of Comparative Law Functionalism

Before discussing Zweigert's methodology, it has to be pointed out that Zweigert did not first publish his ideas on a functionalist approach to comparative law methodology in the Zweigert–Kötz volume; they had actually been published in different forms and in different languages about one and a half decades earlier.[96] As a result, the theses of functionalism had become well known to the professional community by the end of the 1960s. In fact, in these papers, Zweigert translated the previously mentioned three abstract research criteria – critical

---

[93] ibid 221.
[94] ibid 220–22.
[95] ibid 220.
[96] See, eg, K Zweigert, 'Zur Methode der Rechtsvergleichung' (1960) 13 *Studium Generale* 193–200; K Zweigert, 'Methodological Problems in Comparative Law' (1972) 4 *Israel Law Review* 465–74.

approach, no dogmatism and realism – into the 'language' of comparative law research programmes applied in scholarly practice. In Kuhnian terms, through these previous publications, Zweigert set up the framework for future puzzle-solving research.

Zweigert introduces the analysis of the details of functionalist methodology with two closely connected statements. On the one hand, he suggests that a stable and coherent methodology of comparative law has not yet emerged, not even in the decades following World War II. It seems that, with this, Zweigert wanted to emphasise the lack of a proper methodological starting point that would have been generally accepted by the legal science community, and which would have been appropriate under the new conditions and circumstances of the post-World War II area. Moreover, he also makes it apparent that the previous traditions of comparative law, its earlier paradigms, mainly approached the issues of comparative law with an abstract and philosophical attitude, and in his opinion this mindset cannot be regarded as appropriate.[97]

Hence, as a starting point, Zweigert simultaneously states that there is a lack of an elaborated methodology and that previous concepts have to be considered to be inadequate. In sum, the conceptual background of comparative law is found unsatisfactory. By forging the theses of functionalism, he wants to address these precise deficiencies, hence he wants to create a new methodology, which is more relevant to the problems of the period and is much more detailed as well. Besides these inner problems, the methodological renewal of comparative law seemed also to be necessary, since social sciences underwent significant development in the 1960s – including the rise of empirical sociology – and this made the imperfections previously mentioned in the methodology of comparative law even more apparent.[98]

In other words, the entire approach of comparative law has to be rebuilt on a new ground, according to Zweigert, and this can be none other than 'the basic methodological principle' of functionalism.[99] The principle of functionalism implies two main insights, and these help to clarify Zweigert's understanding. The first thesis, which frequently arises in the history of comparative law, is acknowledging and accepting the fact that only comparable phenomena can be compared.[100] Emphasising this idea is relevant because the national legal cultures of Europe developed seemingly divergent systems of legal concepts and legal institutions during the nineteenth century, and their differences raised the awkward question of whether the various solutions of national legal orders, which are different in their wording and institutional backgrounds, can be compared at all. As such, the main methodological dilemma of modern comparative law is when different legal phenomena can nevertheless be considered comparable.

---

[97] Zweigert and Kötz, *An Introduction to Comparative Law* (n 39) 33.
[98] ibid 33–34.
[99] ibid 34.
[100] ibid 34.

Zweigert's other insight is the same as Esser's previous thesis, according to which modern societies have been facing fundamentally similar problems, to which they usually give converging but technically very different answers.[101] Due to this difference of legal provisions and institutions – as follows from the above thesis – the level of analysis, which is important from the perspective of comparative law, is not to be found at the levels of legal techniques or institutions but at the level of the social or other problems to be solved.

By putting these two ideas together, one gains an understanding of the theoretical core of the concept of functionalism as designed by Zweigert. If a comparatist really wants to make a meaningful comparison between different foreign legal systems, the research has to work with concrete social, economic or other problems in all cases.[102] The difference, or even accidental accordance, between legal techniques and legal institutions is in reality an irrelevant question for the research. Functionalism in comparative law turns the interest of comparative legal studies from the regular and technical appearances of the law to the background behind the law.

The further principles and other details of Zweigert's methodology logically derive from all those discussed above. Zweigert highlights that comparative law research can only start with a functional set of concepts, which are built on abstract social relations, not on dogmatic legal taxonomy. The best way for scholars is to define the problem studied without any reference to national legal concepts, thus they can avoid being constrained by a national set of concepts in comparative research.[103] In addition, if we find that the given problem is non-existent in a foreign legal system under review then, according to Zweigert, a mistake must have occurred when setting up the research design, because we have unwittingly chosen a familiar legal category. In such cases, the research question itself has to rephrased, this time clearly in functionlist terms.[104]

Another important claim is that, in the course of research, we have to refrain from further limiting or constraining the analysis from any other aspect, in order to find the real answer to the concrete problem. Zweigert demonstrates this with the example of sources of law: he draws attention to the fact that comparatists can never be satisfied with the so-called classical legal sources of law, but they have to take into account all phenomena that are considered to be legal sources in the examined country. These phenomena can sometimes be traced through a broad spectrum, starting from classical legal sources, through sample contracts and on to commercial practice. This requirement is completed by his belief that comparatists must aim to become as familiar with the given cultures as possible, as the legal systems under comparison can only be truly understood this way.[105]

[101] ibid 34.
[102] ibid 35. This position was explicitly welcomed by Socialist comparative law; see, eg, Z Péteri, 'Some Aspects of Sociological Approach in Comparative Law' in Z Péteri (ed), *Hungarian Law-Comparative Law/Droit hongrois-droit comparé* (Budapest, Akadémiai Kiadó, 1970) 75–94.
[103] ibid 34.
[104] ibid 35.
[105] ibid 36.

This functionalist research programme is not at all easy; many problems can be encountered. In order to avoid them, Zweigert has the following advice: 'Pay attention, be brave and be on guard!'[106] Hence, there is also a need for the personal intuition of the scholar, and for caution too. Comparative legal research can therefore never become a completely mechanical process. Even so, it should also be emphasised that Zweigert did not try to go further than the level of general principles in developing the methodology because, if he had done, he might have found that the details of the research and the precise research design always have to be clarified in light of the research questions and legal systems compared.[107]

Another important methodological insight coming from Zweigert is that when studying those legal institutions that are strongly influenced by ethical or evaluative considerations – such as public order, law of inheritance or family law – the comparatist cannot always carry out a successful research exercise. These meta-legal factors may differ from one another in the countries studied to such an extent that this divergence can even make the comparison of such provisions or institutions either impossible or unintelligible.[108] This is why comparative studies have to be focused on the so-called 'apolitical' areas of private law – therefore mostly on property law, contract law and tort law.

However, Zweigert argues that these areas of law are ruled by the 'presumption of similarity' (*presumptio similitudinis*). This presumption presupposes that 'the developed nations solve the arising regulatory needs in the same or in very similar ways'.[109] Interestingly enough, by suggesting the application of this presumption, Zweigert seriously restricts the leeway of comparative research, as he excludes not only the 'political' areas of private law from study, but constitutional law and criminal law as well.

In relation to the technical details of a comparative law research design, Zweigert also points out that, on the one hand, the determination of legal systems under study always depends on the scope of the given research[110] and, on the other hand, the first step of the research always has to be the preparation of a report that presents the relevant provisions of the national laws in the most neutral way possible.[111] Moreover, as much as possible, a system of applied concepts has to be developed for the research, one that is able to identify the functional common denominator(s), if any, that is the similar or even identical social constructions behind the different legal phenomena.[112] In reality, comparative law research means a comparison of the content of the national reports, presenting and discussing the domestic solutions to these functional concepts. This step is followed by the last phase of the research, a critical evaluation of the

---

[106] ibid.
[107] cf G Samuel, *An Introduction to Comparative Law Theory and Method* (Oxford, Hart Publishing, 2014) 25–44.
[108] Zweigert and Kötz, *An Introduction to Comparative Law* (n 39) 39–40.
[109] ibid 40.
[110] ibid. 41–42.
[111] ibid. 43.
[112] ibid. 44–45.

legal institutions examined.[113] In this phase, besides an evaluation and assessment in the strict sense, the comparatist may even envision a new legal solution or set of provisions, one with the ability to unite the best elements of the heterogeneous national models.

To conclude, Zweigert declares that the *raison d'être* of comparative law might be that, leaning on broad empirical research, it can lay the foundations of a universal jurisprudence, which is to be created in an inductive way, from one universal legal provision to another. The emergence of this comparative law-based universal legal scholarship may make it possible for legal scholars to deal with 'the Law' and not only with national legal orders, which only provide a narrow horizon, as Jhering had already argued a century ago.[114]

The preceding paragraphs have presented Zweigert's main theses on functionalist methodology. As for his sources, it is apparent that two authors, Jhering and Rabel, had an overwhelming impact on his work. It would be tempting to say that Zweigert's methodology is in fact an almost mechanical expansion of the line of thought of his two predecessors; however, we cannot form that conclusion.[115] As we have seen, Zweigert, inspired by Jhering's methodology, created premises for comparative law by using Jhering's heritage – critical approach, dogmatism-free attitude and realism – but adding real content to these premises and adapting them to the needs of post-World War II comparative law was Zweigert's merit alone. Zweigert considered Rabel as one of his most important predecessors and as an example to follow, in addition to Jhering; however, Zweigert had to develop Rabel's fragmented methodological hypotheses (which were never explained consistently) into a coherent scholarly system. This is why, even despite his two important predecessors, Zweigert's work is of a revelatory nature, and it should be regarded as much more than a simple improvement on some previous initiatives. In essence, Zweigert elaborated a methodology – based on some previous inspirations and fragments – of such coherence that it could easily become widely accepted by the professional audience, the scientific community, as a generally applicable methodological toolkit from the 1970s onwards.

D. The 'Case-oriented Factual Approach' – the North-American Approach to Functionalism

At the beginning of the 1960s, another understanding of comparative law methodology – similar to Zweigert's functionalism but different in its emphasis – began to emerge in the legal scholarship of the United States. This was the

---

[113] ibid. 46–47.

[114] In his book, *The Spirit of Roman Law*, Jhering writes: "It is a task for jurisprudence to cast its chains (particularity) off and to re-discover the quality of universality that has long been lost: and this will come into being in a new form of comparative law." ibid. 46.

[115] See also Frankenberg, 'Critical Comparisons: Re-Thinking Comparative Law' (n 73) 439. According to Frankenberg, Zweigert brought Rabel's approach 'back to Earth', so he made it suitable for real research.

so-called 'case-oriented factual approach', the name coined by the former German immigrant Rudolf B. Schlesinger. The elaboration of this methodology was connected to the famous *Cornell Common Core* project, in which Schlesinger, who was the head of this project, attempted to study and reveal the 'common core' of contract law.[116] In this comprehensive, and therefore very impressive, research project, the grounding of a firm and precise methodology seemed indispensable. Without this, a comparative research study that tried to map so many legal orders of the world with regard to their contract law provisions would have become an illusory endeavour.

Schlesinger's 'case-oriented factual approach' differs from Zweigert's functionalist method as it tries to get 'one more step closer' to reality. More precisely, it does not stop at recognising the concrete functional similarities with respect to legal provisions but aims at dissecting the examined phenomena at the level of facts.[117] That is, Schlesinger's approach does not seek to study the functional similarities of different legal institutions – as did Zweigert, through presenting the same functions of European real-estate registering and American Title Insurance Companies[118] – but separates specific sets of facts from one another and asks what kinds of legal provisions were developed for these facts by the legal systems compared. In this way, this method, through integrating a novel level of analysis into the structure of comparative law functionalism – that of facts – makes the ordinary situation found in reality the main unit of comparative research.

This different perspective, of focusing on situations and sets of facts, is a necessary addition to comparative law research, according to Schlesinger, because the specificity of the different cases can protect the researcher from the 'unreal soaring of functionalist imagination'.[119] It is not too difficult to reveal the critique of Zweigert's approach at this point, which – like all theoretical constructions – can easily be seduced and misled by the highly abstract, therefore broadly defined concept of function. By placing the examination of facts at the forefront, Schlesinger wanted to emphasise the close interconnectedness of law and reality, and to urge the researcher to start from the level of facts and not from the 'theoretical or functional heaven' created by theories.

The American professor also highlights that there is no real contradiction between these two approaches – functionalism versus the 'case-oriented factual approach' – as the research might often lead to the conclusion that the

---

[116] The 10-year-long research project was supported by the Ford Foundation, and eight private lawyers participated in it alongside Schlesinger: Bonassies (Paris), Gorla (Rome), Leyser (Melbourne), Lorenz (Munich), Macneil (Cornell), Neumayer (Lausanne), Saxena (Rajasthan) and Wagner (Indiana). See further RB Schlesinger (ed), *The Formation of Contracts: A Study of the Common Core of Legal Systems* (New York, Dobbs Ferry, 1968).

[117] RB Schlesinger, 'The Common Core of Legal Systems. An Emerging Subject of Comparative Study' in K Zweigert and H Puttfarken (eds), *Rechtsvergleichung* (Darmstadt, Wissenschaftliche Buchgesellschaft, 1978) 249–69, 259.

[118] Zweigert and Kötz, *An Introduction to Comparative Law* (n 39) 39.

[119] Schlesinger, 'The Common Core of Legal Systems' (n 117) 261.

specific problems examined and cases relate to each other due to some kind of functional coherence, and this can easily form the basis of developing further functional conclusions.[120] Consequently, he does not question the *raison d'être* of functionalism; he only wants to define the starting point in a more precise manner, closer to reality.

Schlesinger's understanding of the comparative method, based on a 'case-oriented factual approach', may be summarised as follows. First, the legal systems compared have to be defined, which can result in many problems on its own. It is a basic question whether only the so-called 'mother legal systems' should be examined or their 'children' as well. Another problem could be finding and employing competent researchers who possess the relevant professional knowledge regarding the examined legal systems, therefore human resource considerations can often limit the research too.[121] According to Schlesinger, there are no general answers to these questions, but each component depends on the scope of the given research. It is evident that even this first step might have hidden difficulties, the solution of which is not always an easy task. Having chosen the legal orders compared, the national reports on the relevant legal provisions have to be collected, since these can provide the necessary technical information. At this point, Schlesinger's and Zweigert's perspectives match, because both of them consider these reports on national law the starting point of any kind of comparative research.

The next step is to dissect the problems relevant from the perspective of the research into smaller units, into some sets of facts. The most precise facts possible have to be determined, and only the relevant rules of the given legal orders with respect to these facts should be compared. This approach prevents researchers from 'getting lost' in the maze of various dogmatic or textual interpretations of legal provisions, but it compels them to be able to handle the specific, sometimes differently named, national solutions, which may also have a different place from the perspective of social reality.

As for facts, in general, Schlesinger makes a distinction between so-called physical and institutional facts. The first group does not raise any difficulties in research, because these facts can always be discussed in an objective way. However, the second group can give rise to some problems with regard to their comparative study, as fundamental social issues may be embedded in them, and this can make their comparison rather difficult or even impossible. In the case of great differences between institutional facts, for instance in the case of polygamy versus monogamy, the existence of a 'common core' can certainly be excluded, but the comparison may still be fruitful.[122] Further, the lack of a common core may also reveal important conclusions as regards both specific legal issues and broader social and/or historical questions.

---

[120] ibid 259–60.
[121] ibid 251 and 255–56.
[122] ibid 261.

In addition, Schlesinger contrasts the 'case-oriented factual approach' with finding the lowest common denominator in mathematics. Although the similarities of these two different processes are apparent, he emphasises that, in comparative law, it is not enough to find the common core, the lowest common denominator of legal provisions with a different domestic background; what kind of general lessons can be learnt from the discovery of common-core provisions should also be examined.[123]

From the paragraphs above, one can get an almost complete picture of the general methodological frame suggested by Schlesinger for comparative law enterprises, but this should be amended with a few more points. In his manual on comparative law, Schlesinger devotes a separate chapter to the difficulties and risks of comparative law. He presents three groups of problems that might pose serious difficulties in comparative law. First, he points out the problem related to the multiplicity of languages. Schlesinger asserts, for example, that in the legal language of Continental Europe, there is a differentiation between the subjective and the objective meaning of law (right and law); however, European legal sources do not always make this distinction apparent when applying these terms, which can create a problem for an American lawyer trying to interpret a European legal text.[124] Further serious problems can arise from the way a given legal order labels (ie classifies) a legal phenomenon in its own legal language. For example, the difference between the institution of the German and English notary/solicitor is significant, even if the name refers to the same role.[125] The last dangerous circumstance is provided by the difference between black-letter law and everyday use of legal provisions. As the 'case-oriented factual approach' is strongly connected to social reality, it is understandable why Schlesinger emphasises the relevance of this point. His answer is clear: comparatists always have to aim at getting to know the 'law in action', so they have to be realistic, critical and healthily sceptical about the sources on which their research is based.[126]

Schlesinger's methodology is highly sophisticated and, as shown by the success of the Common Core project, also enables comprehensive, large-scale research programmes to be carried out effectively. Through emphasising the examination of facts, he starts from a different level of analysis than Zweigert, but in the end both approaches put the regulatory, problem-solving social role of laws at the centre of the research, and so one cannot talk about a new approach in qualitative terms. It is more fitting to describe Schlesinger's methodology as a distinct branch of comparative law functionalism. This approach differs from Zweigert's theory: it is sociologically highly sensitive, it claims to be concrete, and most probably it draws its unique characteristics from the specificities of the

---

[123] ibid 261–62.

[124] RB Schlesinger, *Comparative Law. Cases-Texts-Materials* (New York, Foundation Press, 1970) 619–22.

[125] ibid 622–28.

[126] ibid 629–36.

common law context that gave birth to it. It can be argued that the main reason behind the seeming difference between these two methodologies is that the one that emerged in the context of European jurisprudence proved more receptive to theoretical generalisations, while the other was born in the case-orientated world of American law. However, the functional approach to the law is common to both of them.

E. Criticism of Comparative Law Functionalism

As a result of the ground-breaking work of Zweigert and the American follow-up, it can be argued that functionalism became the dominant methodological basis of comparative law as from the 1970s. This was partly due to the active publication and other scholarly activities of the leading functionalist authors, and partly due to the obvious success of the Cornell project, which went beyond the strictly interpreted comparative law professional community. Naturally, alongside this methodological breakthrough, the first sceptical voices were heard as well, which contributed to the emergence of the first recent critique of comparative legal functionalism.[127]

In the evolution of this methodological critique, the post-modern critical approach, which became widespread by 1980 in the social sciences, played the key role. The first genuinely critical paper was published in 1985 by Günter Frankenberg.[128] Frankenberg's piece also has an important place from the perspective of the later, even more elaborate criticism, as this study revealed all those conceptual milestones that were debated and attacked in later, functionalism-sceptical papers. As such, in this sense, the subsequent studies focusing on the same issue were at least partially influenced by Frankenberg's seminal article.[129]

The uniqueness of Frankenberg's approach, as compared to the general scholarly attitude in the comparative law community, is that he provided a detailed discussion of comparative functionalism from the perspective of social sciences – at the time of writing the study he was a researcher at the Max Planck Institute, which dealt with research in the social sciences – so his view and understanding were obviously different from those of the conventional legal understanding. Due to his social sciences background, his discussion exceeded the sociology-orientated but still fundamentally legal-minded approach characterising the work of Zweigert and Schlesinger. Because of this, his critical remarks were able to enrich the discourse on the theory of functionalism with qualitatively new points.

---

[127] See also, eg, Husa, 'Farewell to Functionalism or Methodological Tolerance?' (n 78) 420–21; Graziadei, 'The Functionalist Heritage' (n 78) 108–13.
[128] Frankenberg, 'Critical Comparisons: Re-Thinking Comparative Law' (n 73) 66.
[129] ibid 434.

Frankenberg's conclusion is quite laconic. He declares that comparative law functionalism should be considered the vulgar version of sociological functionalism, as formulated by Niklas Luhmann. His main problem with this approach is that its representatives did not devote enough energy to satisfactory answers to the questions that are necessary if one wants to apply the method successfully. The main question, in his eyes, is what we mean by law and function. Instead of clarifying the basic problems, however, the comparative law understanding of functionalism is based on two unfounded assumptions. On the one hand, it relies on the concept of legal systems, and assumes that all legal systems actually face the same problems and solve them with similar results.[130] These observations lead to a transcendental, hence logically unfounded point, namely, that similar problems bring similar solutions into being, regardless of the technical details. This is the point where, according to Frankenberg, functionalism already confuses reality and theory, so it wanders into scholarly dubious areas.[131]

Such a transcendental assumption of similarity – Zweigert's *praesumptio similitudinis* – results in the tenet that this method can only be operationalised if all differences are consciously disregarded during research. Nevertheless, the decision on what we consider similar and what is different is not as easy to make as it would first seem. In order to defend the presumption of similarity, Zweigert does not recommend a simple examination of those areas of law that have a strong moral background or are manifestly politically grounded, and this is how he makes his method capable of preserving its 'general scope' in comparative law. Frankenberg concludes that comparative law functionalism, placing similarity at the centre, thus limits the concept of law too much, and it hence regards law as a formal technique for conflict resolution. Therefore, comparative law functionalism deprives law of essential dimensions, namely its political and moral aspects, and it is questionable in itself whether the law, as a phenomenon embedded in a socio-cultural context, can be understood at all without these.[132]

Besides seriously curbing and limiting the concept of the law, another problem of functionalism is that it is seemingly unable to handle the apparent societal fact that not every law and legal provision is related functionally to social relationships, simply because there are laws that go against the needs of a society or they are simply not connected to the social reality. While in social sciences, in such cases, we talk about dysfunctionality or social trivialism, functionalist comparatists simply deny the existence of this question, and thus they further limit the scope of their method, which is based on the rather weak presumption of similarity.[133]

---

[130] ibid 436.
[131] ibid.
[132] ibid 437.
[133] ibid 437–438.

Another problem of comparative law functionalism, in Frankenberg's eyes, is that it is intertwined with the nineteenth-century evolutionist understanding of legal development. Considering legal development as a history of evolution can really be questioned in light of the findings of contemporary social sciences. Needless to say, one can find both multi-directional and intersecting processes in legal development, in contrast to the previously dominant concept of linear evolution.[134]

The next problem in the dominant understanding of functionalism is that it exclusively connects law to institutions (courts, law making, etc), thus radically decreasing the role of ideologies, rites and interpretations. In other words, it only regards law as a system of rules or legal provisions operated by a given set of institutions, and therefore it completely disregards any other aspects of the law, such as societal or psychological dimensions. Frankenberg calls such an approach to law rule-orientated (logocentric) and argues that this theoretical background is insufficient to lay the foundations of a de facto social theory, which Zweigert's approach of functionalism would like to appear.[135]

Apparently, the focus of Frankenberg's critique is stating and proving that in reality the dominant functionalist theory is not *a de facto* social approach, as its main personalities led others to believe. So, functionalism stems from premises – the presumption of similarity, evolutionism and rule-orientation – that seem to be unfounded with respect to the general development of social sciences from the 1970s. Moreover, the false presumptions limit the concept of the law to the rules created by state organs to such an extent that this alone questions the contemporary relevance and social-scientific nature of this approach. In sum, Frankenberg argues, comparative law functionalism is nothing more than another appearance of legal formalism, which reigned for decades beforehand. Simply, it cannot be regarded as a methodology with any real innovation.[136]

This problem could be solved, according to Frankenberg, by a change in perspective. The comparatist has to find a position of participant observation, as known from anthropology, and this can be achieved by being critical, exceeding logocentrism, and being able to tolerate ambiguity and difference.[137] With this shift in perspective, researchers can rise above their cultural preconceptions and the often false evaluations that stem from them.

---

[134] ibid 438.

[135] ibid.

[136] Besides all of this, Frankenberg also points out a philosophical contradiction. Searching for and identifying functional similarities indicates the existence of an unspoken hypothesis too – that there is a neutral perspective, based on which the attributes of different legal solutions can be judged from the outside. According to Frankenberg, this resembles the Weberian value neutrality, but it is very anachronistic in the light of the difficulties stemming from hermeneutics and the complexity of perspectives. The need for a neutral perspective is in the end no more than the manifestation of the ethnocentric approach dominating European thinking for centuries.

[137] ibid 455.

F. Common Core and Ius Commune Casebooks Projects

Despite the often harsh critiques of functionalism in comparative law, some European comparative law research projects, based on a functionalist starting point, gained new momentum from the second half of the 1990s. The main reason for this might be that, in parallel with the advancement of European integration, the need to extend the unification of law to private law seemed to be evident, and this may even be regarded as a revival of the notion of the medieval *ius commune*.[138]

There have been two ongoing functionalist research projects based on the cooperation of European universities that show similarities in more than one respect. After a year-long preparatory period, the Trento Project,[139] in which Italian professors play a leading role, started in 1995. The aim of the two-phase programme is to discover the common core of European private law in the areas of contract, tort and property law. In the first phase, shorter pieces about certain sub-topics have been published as preparatory works,[140] and in the second phase the studies summarising and synthetising these findings are planned to be published. An interesting aspect of the project is that its leaders – Mauro Bussani and Ugo Mattei – declared at the very beginning that they wish to follow the path of Schlesinger and consider the Cornell project as a starting point.[141]

---

[138] The European Parliament, for example, had already called upon the European Commission in 1989 and 1994 to start preparing a European Civil Code.

[139] Its full name is The Trento Common Core of European Private Law Project.

[140] In this series the following volumes were published, according to the project website: R Zimmerman and S Whittaker, *Good Faith in European Contract Law* (Cambridge, Cambridge University Press, 2000); J Gordley, *The Enforceability of Promises in European Contract Law* (Cambridge, Cambridge University Press, 2001); M Bussani and VV Palmer, *Pure Economic Loss in Europe* (Cambridge, Cambridge University Press, 2003); F Werro and VV Palmer, *The Boundaries of Strict Liability in European Tort Law* (Durham, NC, Carolina Academic Press, 2004); EM Kieninger, *Security Rights in Movable. Property in European Private Law* (Cambridge, CUP, 2004); R Sefto-Green, *Mistake, Freud and Duties to Inform in European Contract Law* (Cambrdige, Cambridge University Press, 2005); M Gradizei, U Mattei and L Smith, *Commercial Trusts in European Private Law* (Cambridge, Cambridge University Press, 2005); P Bozzo, *Property and Environment* (Durham, NC, Carolina Academic Press, 2007); T Möllers and A Heinemann, *The Enforcement of Competition Law in Europe* (Cambridge, Cambridge University Press, 2007); M Hinteregger, *Environmental Liability and Ecological Damage in European Law* (Cambridge, Cambridge University Press, 2008); M Bussani and F Werro, *European Private Law: A Handbook* (Berne, Stämpfli, 2009); M Bussani and F Werro, *European Private Law: A Handbook*, vol II (Berne, Stämpfli, 2009); G Brüggemeier et al (eds), *Personality Rights in European Tort Law* (Cambridge, Cambridge University Press, 2010); J Cartwright and M Hesselink, *Precontractual Liability in European Private Law* (Cambridge, Cambridge University Press, 2011); E Hondius and HC Grigoleit (eds), *Unexpected Circumstances in European Law* (Cambridge, Cambridge University Press, 2011); and Cornelius Van Der Merwe and Alain-Laurent Verbeke (eds), *Time Limited Interests in Land in European Law* (Cambridge, Cambridge University Press, 2012).

[141] In their introduction to the programme, two leaders of the project framed its relation to the Common Core Project as follows: 'Schlesinger's methodological assumptions are the cultural heritage of all researchers engaged in comparative law and have probably been already imprinted in our cultural DNA.' M Bussani and U Mattei, 'The Common Core Approach to European Private Law' (1997–1998) *Columbia Journal of European Law* 339–56, 339.

They also admitted that their other main resource was the oeuvre of Rodolfo Sacco, a well-known Italian comparatist.[142]

The Trento Project basically set its aim as addressing the academic audience, and, through mapping and presenting different private law solutions, it envisions the establishment of a common European legal culture. On the other hand, the Ius Commune Casebooks Project[143] aims at taking one more step forward in another sector, namely in university legal education. Basically, the idea behind the casebooks project is to familiarise both students and law teachers with the idea of European *ius commune* as a source of common inspiration. This is not to suggest that uniformity exists in European national laws with respect to some fields of private law but to highlight 'the common solutions, concepts and principles'[144] that can bridge the borders between various national laws of the European Union. By providing high-quality material for European legal education, including both teaching and research, and with the support of the broad academic cooperation behind these volumes, the project envisages making a contribution to the formation of common European legal minds that are conscious of the existence of a high level of legal commonality, despite all apparent technical differences.

The purpose of this project is to write course-books[145] that present the material on certain subfields of private law with the help of cases and legal provisions systematised on a functional basis. In the course of presenting the methodology, the organisers highlighted the role of functionalism and a case-orientated approach, and they also hinted that they do not wish to concentrate solely on laws but also take into account those elements of legal systems that function on a different level – the level of fundamental principles. Practically, the materials of a casebook are composed of 'cases dealing with functionally comparable fact patterns arising out of "daily life" situations',[146] so

---

[142] For more details, see at www.common-core.org/. For an assessment of the set-up phase, see DJ Gerber, 'The Common Core of European Private Law' (2004) 52 *The American Journal of Comparative Law* 995–1001.

[143] Its full name is Ius Commune Casebooks for the Common Law of Europe.

[144] W Devroe and D Droshut, 'The Leuven Centre for a Common Law of Europe and the Ius Commune Casebook Project' (2003) 2 *ERA Forum: Scripta Iuris Europaei* 114–21.

[145] The following volumes were published in this series: W van Gerven et al (eds), *Tort Law – Scope of Protection* (Oxford, Hart Publishing, 1999); W van Gerven, P Larouche and J Lever (eds), *Cases, Materials and Text on National, International and Supranational Tort Law* (Oxford, Hart Publishing, 2000); H Beale et al (eds), *Cases, Materials and Text on Contract Law* (Oxford, Hart Publishing, 2002); J Beatson and EJH Schrage (eds), *Cases, Materials and Text on Unjustified Enrichment* (Oxford, Hart Publishing, 2003); D Schiek, L Waddington and M Bell (eds), *Cases, Materials and Text on National, Supranational and International Non-Discrimination Law* (Oxford, Hart Publishing, 2007); H-W Micklitz et al (eds), *Cases, Materials and Text on Consumer Law* (Oxford, Hart Publishing, 2010); H Beale et al (eds), *Cases, Materials and Text on Contract Law* (Oxford, Hart Publishing, 2010); S Van Erp and B Akkermans (eds), *Cases, Materials and Text on Property Law* (Oxford, Hart Publishing, 2012); A Hartkamp, C Sieburgh and W Devroe, *Cases, Materials and Text on European Law and Private Law* (Oxford, Hart Publishing, 2017).

[146] Devroe and Droshut, 'The Leuven Centre for a Common Law of Europe and the Ius Commune Casebook Project' (n 144).

Schlesinger's approach, putting the focus on factual situations in comparative law methodology, is endorsed in the very spirit of the casebooks project. However, the cases studied are not exclusively selected from national case laws; the supranational component is also present here, since EU law and European human rights law are also considered as an important source of these seminal cases. The casebooks therefore have a unique – European – character, as they consider national laws of the European Union and the European supranational legal regimes as a common frame of reference for finding the European *ius commune*. Clearly, this exceptional outlook seems to be capable of pointing out the common components of the European legal tradition clearly, concisely and persuasively.

The outlook of the *ius commune* casebooks may be well illustrated by the almost 1,000-page volume on non-discrimination law. This volume covers not only the substantive components of anti-discrimination law, but also deals with the issues of enforcement bodies in detail. As for each issue of non-discrimination law – grounds of discrimination, direct discrimination, indirect discrimination, harassment, victimisation, reasonable accommodation and positive action – the casebook provides readers with a detailed discussion of the relevant international law and European Union law sources, as well as discussion of various national cases focusing on specific and often technical issues.[147] This approach makes it possible to understand the general structure of the legal background and to get to know the specific points of a given legal issue through the lenses of supranational – predominantly ECJ case law – and national judgments coming from many member countries of the European Union. In sum, the generally 'bottom-up' approach is an efficient basis for the comparative conclusions that end each chapter, and also points out common points in the seemingly diverging European legal orders. Upon reading this impressive volume, the existence of a European *ius commune* with respect to anti-discrimination law is simply undeniable, although there are no uniform legal sources at a EU law level that might make it apparent at first sight.

The authority of the project is demonstrated by the fact that legal departments in the United Kingdom, Germany, France, Belgium, the Netherlands, Australia and Japan all use the already published volumes, and the UK's Supreme Court has referred to the volume dealing with tort law in two cases.[148] All in all, comparative law functionalism, as seen from the paragraphs above, has been a living tradition in the legal culture of unifying Europe. This also shows that it is still a key approach in many research initiatives that address problems in a comparative way.

---

[147] See Schiek, Waddington and Bell (eds), *Cases, Materials and Text on National, Supranational and International Non-Discrimination Law* (n 145) 33–870.
[148] For more details see at www.casebooks.eu/.

IV. THE THIRD PARADIGM

The foundations of the third paradigm of comparative law became solid in the two decades following World War II, and in the period thereafter, certain sub-topics developed further through systematic 'puzzle-solving research' carried out by the worldwide community of comparatists. Interestingly, the representatives of this paradigm have never deliberately turned against the hypotheses of the previous paradigm. One cannot find a personality like Lambert among them, who would have made it clear that he consciously abandons the framework of the previous paradigm. This could happen because the reasons for the emergence of the third paradigm include not only scholarly dissatisfaction with the previous paradigm, but also the crisis that developed in comparative law in the decades following World War II, due to the dramatically changed context of world politics. Because of the formation of the so-called Socialist legal orders (the Soviet Union, the satellite states in the Eastern Bloc, and some countries in Asia and Africa) and from the attempts to address the anomalies appearing in conventional comparative law, a new set of exemplars emerged, which served as a basis for a new paradigm, centred around structurally and qualitatively transformed problems (the classification of legal systems, comparative legal functionalism).

It was already apparent at the beginning of the study of Socialist legal orders that the toolkit of comparative law that was dominant in the first half of the century was insufficient for a thorough understanding of these laws. Within the framework of the previous paradigm, only very schematic statements could be made about Socialist legal orders, such as that, based on the comparison of the institutions of civil law, these systems are no more than degenerate, simplified versions of Western legal systems;[149] or that Western and Socialist laws cannot be compared due to their ideological differences, and thus Socialist legal orders simply do not exist for Western comparative legal scholarship.[150] These schematic, simplifying statements, which also reflected political preconceptions, were obviously not acceptable to any scientific community, especially not at a time when, due to the gradual easing of the Cold War situation (including the normalisation of the international situation, the great rise in global commerce, and the increasing interest of the Socialist Bloc in comparative law), Socialist legal systems became interesting and attractive to Western researchers as well.

Hence, during the examination of Socialist laws and legal provisions, the paradigm of *droit comparé* was not able, or was only barely able, to give real scholarly answers to the qualitatively new questions. In addition, parallel to

---

[149] It is less well-known that René David, besides his work in comparative law, also seriously dealt with the questions of the unification of law and harmonisation of law. For his writings on these topics, see in detail David, *Le droit comparé, droits d'hier, droit de demain* (n 17) 293–94.

[150] For a detailed exposition of this standpoint, see Osakwe, 'Introduction: The Greening of Socialist Law as an Academic Discipline' (n 2) 1259–60.

this deficiency, the inadequacy of the structural principles defining the second paradigm became even clearer.[151] This apparent crisis situation directed the researchers of the era towards new problem horizons, and urged them to rethink their methodology at a fundamental level. The theoretical foundations of the classification of legal systems made it possible to put the Socialist legal systems on the world map of legal orders, thus detailed research of their legal institutions could start as well. Due to the classificatory attempts, the unique character of Socialist legal systems gained ground in Western comparative law, and thus – even despite the ideological differences – they became comparable with the Western tradition. The taxonomy of legal orders as a scholarly issue, in reality, gave rise to the 'macro level' of the third paradigm, which examined the legal systems of the world in their entirety, compared to one another.

At the same time, the functionalist methodology, with its roots in Rabel's heritage, was further developed in both Germany and the United States, and as a result, some points of sociological understanding were integrated into the methodology of comparative law and fertilised it. This new methodological orientation, the functionalist methodology, created the 'micro level' of the paradigm, where research was conducted at the institutional level, embedded in the context of larger families of law. We cannot forget that behind both previous areas there stands the enlargement of the concept of law, combined with social and ideological elements, and also an approach to law that increasingly sees its subject as a legal system. From these new considerations emerged the new generalisations and exemplars of the paradigm of post-World War II comparative law, creating a firm basis for many research initiatives that tried to solve new puzzles when comparing legal orders and legal provisions.

These 'macro' and 'micro' levels above stand in close connection to one another, which ensures the cohesion of this paradigm. The classification of the legal systems drew attention to the significance of the social and ideological elements determining the nature of legal orders; comparative law functionalism brought the analysis of the social aspects of law to the forefront, and thus contributed to the widening of the concept of the law with sociological elements; while the functionalist view facilitated the taxonomy of legal systems by stating that if certain rules fulfil the same functions in different legal systems, the given legal systems might be put into the same group. These mutual correlations that assume one another and are built upon one another form the basis of the third paradigm itself, which provides the framework for the majority of comparative legal research projects nowadays.

---

[151] Ancel, 'Les grands étapes de la recherche comparative au XXe siècle' (n 2) 17.

5

New Trends in Contemporary Comparative Law: Towards a Paradigm Shift?

I. A CHANGING SCHOLARLY LANDSCAPE

N O ONE CAN doubt that comparative law, as a scholarly field, has been transforming continuously since the late 1990s. Many insightful publications devoted to the methodology,[1] the perspectives[2] or the future[3] of comparative law have appeared, and these all suggest that the new forms of critical reflection may even lead to a radical transformation of the discipline, as compared to the post-World War II paradigm. Two trends in this ongoing process can easily be identified. First, undeniably, the concept of legal culture has had a general impact on the last two decades' comparative law thinking; some even talk about the emergence of 'comparative legal cultures'[4] as a replacement for the 'orthodox' comparative law tradition. Second, the background of comparative law methodology has also started to change, as the presumption of methodological exclusivity, heavily dominating both functionalism and culturalism in comparative law, seems to be increasingly unacceptable to some comparative law scholars, and therefore a more tolerant and pluralist attitude has begun to take shape in the methodology. This chapter will discuss and assess these developments from the perspective of the Kuhnian approach. The final question asked by this chapter is whether this ongoing process may result in a paradigm shift, radically changing the established methodological frame of legal comparison, or if it is better to consider it as a sum of important steps in puzzle-solving research.

---

[1] See, eg, M van Hoecke and M Warrington, 'Legal Cultures, Legal Paradigms and Legal Doctrine: Towards a New Model for Comparative Law' (1998) 47 *ICLQ* 495–536; or J Husa, 'Methodology of Comparative Law Today: From Paradoxes to Flexibility?' (2006) 58 *Revue internationale de droit comparé* 1095–17.

[2] See, eg, M Reimann, 'The Progress and Failure of Comparative Law in the Second Half of the Twentieth Century' (2002) 50 *The American Journal of Comparative Law* 671–700.

[3] See, eg, K Boele-Woelki and DP Fernandez Arroyo (eds), *The Past, the Present and Future of Comparative Law. Le passé, le présent et le futur du droit comparé. Ceremony of 15 May 2017 in Honour of 5 Great Comparatists* (Paris, Springer, 2018).

[4] Cs Varga, 'Comparative Legal Cultures?' (2007) 48 *Acta Juridica Hungarica* 95–113.

II. A CULTURAL TURN IN COMPARATIVE LAW?

A. Cultural Claims in Comparative Law: The Example of Legrand

An unambiguous sign of the prospective changes may be the intensive campaign for the integration of the concept of legal culture, or various cultural insights, into the toolkit of comparative law. It is needless to explain in detail that legal culture – as it is interpreted in postmodern legal studies, putting a serious emphasis on uniqueness and difference[5] – can only play a very limited role within the classic functionalist tenets, as it is simply incompatible with an approach that predominantly focuses on rules and similarity. As such, the intensive advocacy of a cultural turn in comparative law may amount to such a qualitative change that it may be capable of leading to a radical change in the structure and exemplars of puzzle-solving comparative law research.

This 'revolutionary' process started in the 1990s, and one can find three scholars who played a prominent role in the promotion of cultural premises in comparative legal studies. They were Pierre Legrand, David Nelken and Csaba Varga. Legrand was appointed a professor of comparative legal cultures at Tilburg University in 1996;[6] Nelken, as professor of the sociology of law, has taught classes with the title 'comparative legal cultures';[7] and Varga also tried to integrate the so-called cultural approach into his legal theory,[8] thereby influencing theoretical legal scholarship in Central Europe.

The titles of their works firmly indicate that a process of renewal has started in the theory of comparative law. The question marks they include in some of those titles are also very telling, since they express the open-endedness of this debate, as well as its unfinished nature. Throughout the debate, various authors have made serious efforts to restructure the foundations of comparative law from a theoretical point of view, and they have also demonstrated that the concept of legal culture must play a key role in this renewal.

Before going into detail, it has to be mentioned that this wave of the cultural approach was obviously inspired by the achievements of the 1980s. First of all, one should mention the oeuvre of Lawrence Friedman, who devoted several decades of his professional life to researching legal culture, mainly in the context of the United States. He laid down such basic tenets as, for instance, that legal culture consists of different attitudes towards the law; that legal thinking is necessarily bound by its culture, and legal culture determines the limits within which legal thought can change; and that there must be a differentiation between 'internal' and 'external' legal culture. Internal legal culture is the

---

[5] For further detail, see P Legrand, 'Comparative Legal Studies and the Matter of Authenticity' (2006) 1 *Journal of Comparative Law* 374–93.

[6] See P Legrand, 'How to Compare Now' (1996) 16 *Legal Studies* 232–42.

[7] D Nelken (ed), *Comparing Legal Cultures* (London, Routledge, 1997).

[8] Varga, 'Comparative Legal Cultures?' (n 4).

culture of legal professionals, while external legal culture consists of attitudes to the law shared by those outside of the offcial sphere of law.[9] In short, many statements of today's cultural comparatists can be traced back, implicitly or explicitly, to the concepts of Friedman.

Since Legrand offered a comprehensive and theoretically elaborated approach, in order to integrate as many cultural insights as possible into the methodology of comparative law, a brief discussion of his ideas may perhaps illustrate the essence of that attitude, which sees the necessity for a 'cultural turn' in comparative legal thinking. Legrand's starting point here is his dissatisfaction with the recent state of affairs in legal comparison. Comparative law is a really fashionable subject, as Legrand had already asserted in the mid-1990s, but 'self-styled comparatists' normally do hardly anything more than simply put legal rules from different legal systems next to one another and try to find similarities and differences.[10] As Legrand aptly describes this phenomenon, 'they do not compare, they contrast'.[11] Maybe this is because they are unaware of even the most fundamental conceptual questions of legal comparison.

In order to change this unfavourable situation, correction had to start from the very basics, that is, from the theoretical foundations. First of all, when making comparisons, one must be committed to a theory. This means that, in order to find meaningful insights, fundamental questions focusing on the basic problems of law have to be discussed. For instance, where does law begin and where does it end in a given society? Where are the boundaries of law among the many normative phenomena? These questions – mainly related to the ontology of law – can lead us towards an empathic and in-depth understanding of legal cultures, and this is the point at which, for Legrand, real comparative work can start.[12]

Second, comparatists also have to be committed to interdisciplinarity.[13] They should accept this because, as Legrand argues, 'law does not exist in a vacuum'. Law is obviously part of a much broader context, and it can only be properly understood through interdisciplinary research. Legrand emphasises the importance of anthropology, linguistics and cognitive psychology,[14] while other authors add such traditional fields of study as economics, sociology, political science and history, since law can be found at the meeting points of the social phenomena studied by these disciplines.

Comparative legal studies must therefore turn towards the study of the foundations of legal cultures, which includes a plausible concept of law, as well as

---

[9] See LM Friedman, *The Legal System. A Social Science Perspective* (New York, Russell Sage Foundation, 1975).

[10] Legrand, 'How to Compare Now' (n 6) 234.

[11] ibid.

[12] ibid 235.

[13] This claim has already been raised by other comparatists from the 1990s; see, eg, R Sacco, 'One Hundred Years of Comparative Law' (2001) 75 *Tulane Law Review* 1159–76, 1174.

[14] Legrand, 'How to Compare Now' (n 6) 238.

the interdisciplinary dimensions of law in a given legal culture. That is why Legrand uses the example of a French painting – one by Jacques-Louis David – that depicts Napoleon drafting the *Code civil* by candlelight.[15] For Legrand, this painting properly illustrates 'the historically-conditioned relationship between legislative and judicial powers in France'. Hence, in this approach, French law is a cultural phenomenon with different cultural layers beyond the traditional view that it is simply the binding law of France.[16]

In conclusion, Legrand argues that comparative law should turn towards the different legal *mentalités* (cognitive orders) of legal systems, as the concept of *mentalité* is able to grasp and describe law as a cultural phenomenon.[17] For this reason, it is a real mistake to speak of 'legal families' in comparative law. Instead of the obsolete taxonomy of legal families, various legal *mentalités* must be studied, such as the civil law mentality, the common law mentality or even the Far Eastern mentality.

As an example of the capacity of this cultural approach, one might mention Legrand's discussion of the convergence between civil law and common law. There is a general opinion in Europe, shared by many leading comparatists, that a new legal order has been emerging since the establishment of the European Community of Coal and Steel, the *corpus iuris Europaeum* or *ius Europaeum*. Within the framework of this 'European law', the gradual convergence of civil and common law has also begun. This is the so-called 'convergence thesis' elaborated and defended by scholars such as Patrick Glenn and Basil Markesinis.[18]

However, as Legrand points out, if we approach the convergence thesis from a cultural point of view, fundamentally different conclusions can be reached. The common law *mentalité* is, according to Legrand, 'irreducibly' different from the civil law *mentalité*, and therefore it is impossible to speak of the convergence of these two *mentalités*.[19] This divergence is due to many factors, all of which are analysed by Legrand in detail.[20] Legrand's main conclusion is very

---

[15] See ibid 235.

[16] ibid 236.

[17] ibid 238; and see P Legrand, 'European Legal Systems are Not Converging' (1996) 45 *ICLQ* 52–81, 60–64.

[18] For a summary of these arguments, see B Markesinis, 'Learning from Europe and Learning in Europe' in B Markesinis (ed), *The Gradual Convergence: Foreign Ideas, Foreign Influences, and the English Law on the Eve of the 21st century* (Oxford, Clarendon Press, 1994) 30; and HP Glenn, 'La civilisation de la common law' (1993) 45 *Revue internationale de droit comparé* 559–75.

[19] Legrand, 'European Legal Systems are Not Converging' (n 17) 81.

[20] The main points are the following: (i) *The nature of legal reasoning.* Common law thinking is essentially inductive and empirical, while Continental law always prefers a deductive and theoretical approach. In Max Weber's terms, in the common law world, law is perceived 'as craft', whereas on the Continent it is mostly regarded 'as science'. (ii) *The role of systematisation.* The legal thinking of common law has little interest in theorising because it mostly finds this way of thinking useless. Modern civil law, in turn, is based on a rational systematisation of legal concepts, as it is perfectly expressed in several modern codes. (iii) *The character of rules.* In strict terms, one can find no abstract formulation of legal rules in common law, since law can only be inferred from cases, mostly on the basis of their *ratio decidendi*. In contrast, a civil lawyer always regards law as a set of precise rules having generalised meanings. (iv) *The role of facts.* Common law thinking is strongly

simple: due to these fundamental differences, it is simply unrealistic to speak of a convergence between common law and civil law at the level of *mentalités*. Moreover, this hypothetical convergence would also mean the reduction of the plurality of European legal thinking. This would obviously be undesirable, since these divergent *mentalités* mean different approaches to reality, by which they enrich our knowledge of the infinite reality. For these reasons, convergence would definitely make us poorer.[21]

B. The Proliferation of the Use of Legal Culture: Trends and Problems

Due to the impact of the intensive claiming of the application of cultural tenets and insights, an approach boosted by postmodern ideas[22] and the broadening of socio-legal studies as inspired by Friedman, the use of the concept of legal culture has proliferated in recent comparative legal studies. Therefore, in most of the cases, the existence of a generally shared understanding cannot be presumed, and thus the definition and delimitation of the main patterns of the interpretations of legal culture in contemporary comparative law are indispensable steps. In this section, three patterns will be specified in detail; however, this does not at all mean that others do not exist.[23] This section only tries to

---

related to the particularity of cases; that is, this tradition is convinced that legal knowledge emerges fundamentally from facts (*ex facto ius oritur*). Civil law mentality, however, is based on a different attitude, since it has made serious efforts to eliminate the factual dimensions of legal rules in order to create handy abstract concepts (*ex regula ius oritur*). (v) *The meaning of rights*. The formula 'no writ – no right' perfectly expresses that, in common law, rights are related to actions before courts. 'Rights' have no abstract meaning in this sense, as legal actions are based on a factual and concrete wrong rather than an abstract and independent right. Civil law follows an essentially different line of thinking; it acknowledges the 'existence' of subjective rights, independent of actions or other external factors. (vi) *The presence of the past*. Last, one should not forget that common law has a strong historical perspective, as it dates its origin back to 'time immemorial' (ie a time fixed by statute as prior to the reign of Richard I (1189)). This historical attitude has formed the customary and communitarian dimensions of English law. In contrast, Continental law is not historical in this sense, because it purports to organise the relationships of the present and close future independently of the influence and force of the past. See ibid 64–74.

[21] ibid 80–81.

[22] The definition of postmodernism is far from being settled due to the very nature of this attitude. But although no consensual definition has emerged yet, some key components can be more or less precisely identified. Therefore, when using the term 'postmodern', this books subscribes to the understanding of Gray, who argues that postmodernism 'can be described as a set of critical, strategic and rhetorical practices employing concepts such as difference, repetition, the trace, the simulacrum, and hyperreality to destabilize other concepts such as presence, identity, historical progress, epistemic certainty, and the univocity of meaning'. For further details, see A Gray, 'Postmodernism' in EN Zalta (ed), *The Stanford Encyclopedia of Philosophy* (Spring 2015 Edition) at https://plato.stanford.edu/archives/spr2015/entries/postmodernism/.

[23] For a different account of the application of legal culture in comparative research, see D Nelken, 'Comparative Legal Research and Legal Culture: Facts, Approaches and Values' (2016) 12 *Annual Review of Social Sciences* 45–62. Nelken argues that legal culture can be interpreted from the three qualitatively different perspectives. First, it may represent various mental, behavioural or factual patterns around the law (facts); second, alternatively, this term may also imply an approach looking

group the most typical ones that may be encountered when studying the recent scholarly discussion.

i. Legal Culture as Background of Law

A typical reference to legal culture aims at pointing out a certain constellation of extra-legal factors that may have a decisive – or at least a considerable – influence on law as such, or on a given legal institution or provision. These factors may come from manifold fields of study, mostly depending on either the social-science background of the scholar or the nature of the problem analysed. By these references to a set of extra-legal factors that form the cultural background of law or a legal provision, the research strives for a comprehensive or holistic approach, overstepping the pure, rule-orientated positivistic view of law. In essence, by abstracting a cultural context for a legal phenomenon and applying it in the formulation of the research insights, a legal research design can acquire a much broader scholarly scope, and this choice may seriously contribute to the scholarly value of the findings. Typically, references to or mentions of legal culture imply the inclusion of sociological, historical, political, socio-psychological or cultural studies research findings in legal research.

This approach can be illustrated by once again referring to Pierre Legrand's various articles. In essence, Legrand urges comparative legal studies to respect differences between legal orders instead of seeking the common and uniform points, and therefore advocates the study of the so-called *mentalités juridiques*, legal mentalities, that support the instrumental components of a legal order.[24] Legrand argues that these *mentalités juridiques*, having a decisive impact on the functioning of legal orders, may only be accessed through an interdisciplinary study based on the findings of social psychology, and linguistic and cultural studies, among others.[25] The in-depth study of European legal mentalities – those of Continental law and common law – through interdisciplinary lenses led Legrand to both insightful and provocative conclusions, such as the impossibility of a unified European civil code[26] and the denial of a real convergence between Continental law and common law.[27]

In sum, the concept of legal culture is widely used in order to provide a context for comparative legal research.[28] This approach is manifold, ranging from in-depth case studies to broad comparisons of various legal orders, but the fact that legal culture is used to contextualise a legal research effort is a

---

beyond the conventional rule- and institutional-focused legal inquiry (approaches); and, third, it may even become a basis for normative statements on the law (values).

[24] Legrand, 'European Legal Systems are Not Converging' (n 17) 56–61.

[25] For details, see Legrand, 'How to Compare Now' (n 6) 232–42, 236–38.

[26] P Legrand, 'Against a European Civil Code' (1997) 60 *MLR* 44–63.

[27] See Legrand, 'The European Legal Systems Are Not Converging' (n 17).

[28] For further examples of this approach, see V Gessner, A Hoeland and Cs Varga (eds), *European Legal Cultures* (Aldershot, Dartmouth, 1996).

common point. Moreover, attempts at such contextualisation without mentioning the term 'legal culture' had already been made in some classical works. For instance, René David argued that the ideology of the social role of law had a crucial part to play in the formation of legal families,[29] while Zweigert also put much emphasis on ideological factors and the role of history when elaborating his theory of the style of legal families (*Rechtskreis*).[30] In other words, a contextual understanding of law, whether broader or narrower, has always been a part of the methodology of modern comparative law. However, this approach has become rather popular in comparative legal studies during the last two decades – partly due to the proliferation of references to legal culture.[31]

ii. Legal Culture as Interactions Around Law

Legal culture may also be conceived of as a dynamic understanding of law in place of the static, black-letter rule or norm-focused approach. While positivist or descriptive legal studies can only analyse legal rules and their details, the findings of legal sociology, legal anthropology and cultural studies may help in understanding the interactions with respect to the usual functioning of a legal order. Evidently, these interactions may occur either at the macro-level, where different social and political forces compete and interact to determine the actual set-up of the legal order, or at the micro level, animated by citizens' everyday interactions having a legal purpose.[32] The analysis of these interactions may even help in the comprehension of how the ordinary meaning of law is construed by both macro- and micro-level interactions, that is, how the normative universe around law – nomos[33] – evolves by the everyday practice of normative commitments. In this way, this form of study may help to reveal how culture, as a social practice,[34] is capable of influencing the everyday perception of law.

From the various insights of legal anthropology, the concept of 'semi-autonomous social fields' offers a valuable contribution to conceptualising this complex and often contradictory process at the micro level of these interactions.

---

[29] David, *Traité élémentaire de droit comparé* (Paris, LGDJ, 1950) 223.

[30] See K Zweigert and H Kötz, *An Introduction to Comparative Law* (Oxford, Oxford University Press, 1998) 63–73.

[31] The oeuvre of David Nelken from this period may illustrate how an increasingly intensive interest was formed with regard to the comparative study of legal cultures. See, eg, D Nelken (ed), *Comparing Legal Cultures* (Aldershot, Dartmouth, 1997); or D Nelken, 'Using Legal Culture: Purposes and Problems' (2010) 5 *Journal of Comparative Law* 1–39.

[32] M Kurkchiyan, 'Comparing Legal Cultures: Three Models of Court for Small Civil Cases' (2010) 5 *Journal of Comparative Law* 169–94, 170.

[33] For details, see R Cover, 'The Supreme Court, 1982 Term – Foreword: Nomos and Narrative' (1983–1984) 97 *Harvard Law Review* 4–19.

[34] For the various methodological approaches of culture, see JW Mohr and CM Rawlings, 'Formal Models of Culture' in JR Hall, L Grindstaff and M-C Lo (eds), *Handbook of Cultural Sociology* (London, New York, Routledge, 2010) 119–29. From the aspect of the history of ideas, see AL Kroeber and C Kluckhohn, *Culture. A Critical Review of Concepts and Definitions* (Cambridge, MA, Peabody Museum of American Archeology and Ethnology, 1952).

Some studies have already used this approach in a comparative way to get a better picture of a given legal question.[35] This term, 'semi-autonomous social fields' (SASFs), was coined by Sally Falk Moore at the end of the 1970s.[36] Moore started from the conceptual framework of classical anthropological thinking and passionately argued that 'law and social context could not be separated'. As a further step, she also relied on the comparative lessons of two case studies: the dress industry in New York; and the Chagga tribe of Mount Kilimanjaro, where she personally carried out the field work.[37] Essentially, from this anthropological perspective, modern societies are based on the endless normative interactions of these semi-autonomous units of community organisation. As such, people's decisions are always influenced by the competition between divergent normative claims emanating from various SASFs. In addition, owing to this regulative potential, they are also able to resist, at least partially, external pressures, that is state law or claims set forth by other SASFs.[38]

A well-known model of macro-level interactions around the law was already established by Lawrence M Friedman. In his path-breaking volume that, among other achievements, revitalised the use of legal culture in Western legal scholarship, he described the 'legal system' as the continuous interaction between structure, substance and culture.[39] In this concept, 'structure' meant the institutional setting, while 'substance' referred to the legal provisions coordinating the behaviour of both citizens and institutions.[40] The third component, 'culture', was an umbrella term used by Friedman, as it summarised all those non-legal effects – social forces in the broadest sense – that were able to

---

[35] For example, PS Berman, 'Towards a Jurisprudence of Hybridity' (2010) 11 *Utah Law Review* 11–29, 20–24; M Hertogh, 'Crime and Custom in the Dutch Construction Industry' (2010) 4 *Legisprudence* 307–26; F Shariff, 'Power Relations and Legal Pluralism. An Examination of "Strategies of Struggles" Amongst the Santal Adivasi of Indian and Bangladesh' (2008) 57 *Journal of Legal Pluralism and Unofficial Law* 1–43.

[36] SF Moore, 'Law and Social Change: The Semi-Autonomous Social Field as an Appropriate Subject of Study' (1973) 7 *Law and Society Review* 719–46; and for an excellent contemporary discussion of this concept in the broader context of the social effects of legal norms, see J Griffiths, 'The Social Working of Legal Rules' (2003) 48 *Journal of Legal Pluralism* 1–84.

[37] Based on this comparative study, as a general point, Moore argued that the SASFs are to be regarded as the fundamental units of social control instead of official state law, even if the latter has the obvious monopoly of use of force. That is, society is comprised of many social fields that are able to apply effective coercion or inducement that can motivate the behaviour of their members. Basically, in Moore's eyes, SASFs 'bring forth and maintain behavioural rules' (Griffiths, 'The Social Working of Legal Rules' (n 36) 23), thus they successfully exercise social control over a specific segment of society. It is also important that the boundaries of SASFs – that is, their scope of influence – are not to be defined by their organisations but by the 'fact that (they) can generate rules and coerce and induce compliance to them' (Moore, 'Law and Social Change' (n 36) 722; Griffiths, 'The Social Working of Legal Rules' (n 36) 24). The decisive element is therefore the ability to exercise social control, even if it is limited or solely particular; the degree of social formalisation is simply irrelevant. At the same time, SASFs are only partially autonomous, because the members of a given SASF may also be members of other SASFs, so the regulatory autonomy of a given SASF always interferes with those of other SASFs (Griffiths, 'The Social Working of Legal Rules' (n 36) 24).

[38] Griffiths, 'The Social Working of Legal Rules' (n 36) 26.

[39] Friedman, *The Legal System. A Social Science Perspective* (n 9) 16.

[40] ibid 14.

give 'life and reality'[41] to the legal order. A special segment of these outside social influences on law was 'legal culture', as its function was to convert these external effects to relevant demands for the legal sphere of structure and substance.[42] That is, macro-level interactions around law – including political, social and other forces – should always amend the formal picture of the law if one wants to gain a realistic picture; and culture and legal culture may have a crucial role in their analysis and study.

If the analysed interactions, whether micro- or macro-level ones, are delimited precisely in a research project (as, for instance, based on social regulatory units or on a given legal body), they can be studied in comparative projects.[43] Obviously, these kind of comparative studies, interested in how interactions shape the perception of law in different contexts, do not necessarily refer to their precise methodological bases but to their intent to compare interactions of social, political or everyday life when construing a meaning of law, and thereby creating normative commitments that connect them to this way of analysis.[44] In sum, these studies may reveal important insights into the socio-cultural embeddedness of law from a comparative aspect. Therefore, they also point out the cultural determination of law, even without explicitly invoking 'legal culture' as a conceptual term in many cases.

iii. Legal Culture as a Sum of Attitudes Towards Law

The attitudinal interpretation of legal culture is also rooted in Lawrence M Friedman's concept of legal culture. In essence – as already mentioned – he interpreted legal culture as a medium of conversion, able to transform various interests, generated by diverse social forces, into relevant demands towards the legal system as such.[45] That is to say, the function of legal culture in Friedman's interpretation is the maintenance of the continuous conversion process between the colourful social reality, composed of regulatory claims and demands, and the legal system as a technical unit of regulation. As for the components of legal culture, Friedman points out that 'it refers to public knowledge of and attitudes and behavior patterns towards the legal system'.[46] Thereafter, he highlights that

[41] ibid 15.

[42] ibid 15–16.

[43] For example, see A Sajó, 'Pluralism in Post-Communist Law' (2003) 44 *Acta Juridica Hungarica* 1–20; for the presentation of the main comparative themes of legal anthropology, see FG Snyder, 'Anthropology, Dispute Processes and Law. A Critical Introduction' (1981) 8 *British Journal of Law and Society* 140–80, 144–51; for a recent summary of this way of studies, see F Pirie, 'Comparison in the Anthropology and History of Law' (2014) 9 *Journal of Comparative Law* 88–107.

[44] To illustrate this in a post-socialist context, see these two excellent case studies: M Mikus, 'Informal Networks and Interstitial Arenas of Power in the Making of Civil Society Law in Serbia' (2015) 57 *Sociologija* 571–92; D Vukoviff, 'The Hollowing Out of Institutions: Law- and Policymaking in Contemporary Serbia' in B Fekete and F Gárdos-Orosz (eds), *Central and Eastern European Socio-Political and Legal Transition Revisited* (Frankfurt, Peter Lang, 2017) 155–73.

[45] Friedman, *The Legal System. A Social Science Perspective* (n 9) 223.

[46] ibid 194.

these attitudes and patterns towards law may differ from group to group and from country to country, meaning that many different levels of abstraction of legal culture can be identified according to the intentions of the researchers.[47] For him, the most relevant among these different layers of legal culture is the differentiation between the so-called internal layer – the legal culture of the professionals – and the external layer – the legal culture of the people. Further, from a historical perspective, he also convincingly argues for the uniqueness of modern legal culture as a sociocultural entity.[48] That is, in this sense, legal culture may also be conceived of as a historical concept, in addition to its socio-legal meanings.

It is not necessary to explain why this understanding of legal culture stim-ulates comparative law scholarship. It certainly makes it possible to integrate insights from the sociology of law, or the role of social attitudes in general or those of specific target groups towards the law, into the research design of a comparative law research project. In this way, comparative research becomes capable of penetrating the social context of law by applying the statistical methods used by the sociology of law. This implies that, by integrating these statistical methods, the rather fuzzy and blurred social context of law can be translated into the 'language of numbers', which seems capable of enhancing the scholarly value of these studies in the marketing of legal studies and hence the chances of being published.[49] That is, if the applied concept of legal culture is defined properly in a research study, the use of these methods may be able to establish a handy framework for comparing two or more legal orders and their social context – mostly based on 'numbers' provided by the statistical analysis.

Among many excellent publications, a good example of this kind of compar-ative research is the well-known article by James L Gibson and Gregory A Caldeira that identifies various patterns of European legal cultures by cross-country comparison of survey data on attitudes towards law from the 13 members of the European Union in 1993.[50] This research was based on data from a Eurobarometer omnibus survey and individual, country-specific interviews, focusing on three legal values – rule of law, neutrality of law, and individual liberty. It analysed the survey data using statistical methods, and pointed out the existence of three different attitude sets – a rule-of-law-respecting one, a more sceptical one, and a mix of these two poles – at the level of public opinion on law in Western Europe.[51] Moreover, Gibson and Caldeira also argued that European attitudes towards law can be described using a factor analysis based on the three factor items that are correlated with the three legal values defined at the very

---

[47] ibid 198.

[48] ibid 204–07, 213–22.

[49] On the increasing importance of 'numbers' in legal comparison, see M Siems, *Comparative Law* (Cambridge, Cambridge University Press, 2014) 146–87 on 'numerical comparative law'.

[50] JL Gibson and GA Caldeira, 'The Legal Cultures of Europe' (1996) 30 *Law and Society Review* 55–85.

[51] ibid.70.

beginning of the research.[52] All in all, the comparative analysis of mass attitudes towards law has already proved to be a successful and inspiring subfield of comparative law, as it has enabled comparatists to integrate numerous methods of legal sociology into the tools of legal comparison.[53]

C. Three Typical Inconsistencies in the Application of Legal Culture in Comparative Law

Thus far, three possible uses of legal culture in comparative legal studies have been described. This section gives an overview of certain typical scholarly (mis) treatments of legal culture, and also characterises the contemporary use of this term in comparative law. These forms of inconsistent application will be typified, then examples will also be discussed in order to have a closer look at the problems arising. However, it must be stressed at this point that this section of the chapter does not claim that a given author is 'wrong' in terms of the conclusions of his or her article, but only argues that the application of legal culture in his or her argumentation might be questioned or criticised from a conceptual or methodological standpoint. This potential for methodological criticism seems to be inherent in the use of the term 'legal culture', as it has never had a well-defined and consensually shared working definition; instead, diverging approaches have been applied ever since the 1970s.[54]

i. Confusion of Different Understandings in the Same Study

A typical – and perhaps the most emblematic – example of the inconsistent use of the concept of legal culture is grounding the scholarly argumentation – slightly or deeply – in different understandings of legal culture in the same paper. For example, an author may start with the application of the holistic approach, pointing out the role of extra-legal factors in the modern development of a legal provision, and – a few pages later – may then try to broaden the methodological scope towards the discussion of certain attitudes, as they are expressed in statistical data, under the label 'cultural factors'. The main problem

---

[52] ibid 67.

[53] For further examples of this thread of research, see JL Gibson and RM Duch, 'Support for Rights in Western Europe and the Soviet Union. An Analysis of the Beliefs of Mass Publics' in FD Weil (ed), *Research on Democratisation and Society. Democratisation in Eastern and Western Europe* (Greenwich, JAI Press, 1993) 241–63; E Blankenburg, 'Patterns of Legal Culture: The Netherlands Compared to Neighboring Germany' (1998) 46 *The American Journal of Comparative Law* 1–41; M Kurkchiyan, 'Perceptions of Law and Social Order: A Cross-National Comparison of Collective Legal Consciousness' (2012) 26 *Wisconsin International Law Journal* 366–92.

[54] For details, see SS Silbey, 'Legal Culture and Cultures of Legality' in JR Hall, L Grindstaff and M-C Lo (eds), *Handbook of Cultural Sociology* 472–76. Silbey identifies four major lines within the discourse on legal culture: legal ideology; legal consciousness; legalities, cultures of legality, and counter-law; the structure of legality.

with this (mis)treatment is that it entails the parallel application of different methodological toolkits. In our hypothetical case, there is an interdisciplinary, multi-focused approach to the socio-historical background, and another one from the sociology of law, which relies heavily on statistical analysis. As these methods are partially irreconcilable, or can at best (by their very nature) only be bridged by hypotheses and anecdotal evidence, as they are rooted in different academic traditions and, therefore, imply different methodological premises, the scholarly value of this mixed solution may have rather questionable results. Further, due to the incompatibility of these methods, this inconsistency often leads to conceptual and terminological confusion. That is, this kind of inconsistent application of legal culture in a research design may seriously weaken the scholarly appropriateness of an otherwise well-established research effort from a narrow but relevant methodological aspect.

A good example of this conceptual inconsistency may be found in an otherwise very inspiring article, devoted to casting light on recent tendencies of internationalisation in Norwegian law. Although the analysis is aimed at one legal order, the comparative nature of the study cannot be denied, since the internationalisation of legal orders, as a general legal phenomenon, has already become a *sui generis* issue in comparative legal studies.[55] The discussion starts with making a distinction between legal culture as a phenomenon in its own right and as an instrument of legal analysis.[56] In general, the author broadly defines legal culture as a 'social phenomenon' and, in addition, argues that law is a product of legal culture.[57] Due to these general introductory remarks on the social embeddedness of law, one might suppose that the article subscribes to the holistic understanding of legal culture as a methodological starting point. That is, one expects the appearance of certain extra-legal factors that may explain, to various extents, the internationalisation of Norwegian law. However, a few pages later, the article makes a turn in a methodological sense, as it points out that the approach of van Hoecke and Warrington[58] is to be followed. This identifies legal culture as 'ideas and expectations of law made operational by institutional and institutional-like practices'.[59] As a closing methodological point, the author lists six criteria that may be able to provide a basis for legal cultural analysis: '(1) conflict resolution, (2) norm production, (3) idea of justice, (4) legal method, (5) professionalisation, and (6) internationalisation'.[60]

---

[55] cf Siems, *Comparative Law* (n 49) 249–59.
[56] J Øyrehagen Sunde, 'Live and Let Die. An Essay Concerning Legal-Cultural Understanding' in M Adams and D Heirbaut (eds), *The Method and Culture of Comparative Law* (Oxford, Hart Publishing, 2014) 221–34, 221.
[57] ibid 222.
[58] M van Hoecke and M Warrington, 'Legal Cultures, Legal Paradigms and Legal Doctrine: Towards a New Model for Comparative Law' (n 1).
[59] Øyrehagen Sunde, 'Live and Let Die. An Essay Concerning Legal-Cultural Understanding' (n 56) 231.
[60] ibid.

At this point, the inconsistent application becomes immediately apparent. It can be argued that although a holistic understanding of legal culture was defined as a starting point, the author slides partially into a dynamic, interaction-orientated interpretation of legal culture. The functioning of law – conflict resolution and norm production in the list quoted above – as such, is mentioned as a decisive point when defining the conceptual basis for the research. Needless to say, both conflict resolution and norm production are situated in the focus of either micro- or macro-level interactions, depending on the issue at hand. As such, their study needs research tools that manifestly differ from those if legal culture is applied as a background to the discussion. Unsurprisingly, the author's conclusion may be regarded as fairly narrow, since he advocates a 'practical approach to legal culture' instead of becoming a real insider within a given legal culture.[61] Moreover, no elaboration is offered regarding the practical implications of this turn. In fact, by the emphasis on the 'practical approach to legal culture', the article indirectly acknowledges the problems of applying such a concept of legal culture that may embrace practically everything that is in any way relevant to a given research.

ii. Under-theorisation of Legal Culture

A major threat for the application of legal culture is the problem of oversimplification. Some of the authors are willing to apply this term without any real scholarly reflection; that is, they do not ground their arguments for the cultural embeddedness of law in a solid methodological framework. Bearing in mind the various diverging meanings of 'legal culture', the problems of this mistreatment become apparent at the very beginning as, without consensus on its definition and categorisation, the term will easily lose its explanatory value. Therefore, it can be regarded as a nice ornament in the text, but not a real scholarly concept that contributes to the understanding of a given problem. In most of these cases, the authors simply mention 'legal culture' as the background to the question studied, or they refer to the cultural embeddedness of a legal rule but do so without either any serious methodological consideration or explanation. In these cases, the use of 'legal culture' as an idea serves no other purpose than to enrich the text of an article with a resonant scholarly buzzword that should connect a paper to this fashionable discourse. In sum, even simple references to the concept of legal culture may make a scholarly paper more attractive in the eyes of both readers and reviewers.

For instance, a recent paper on the cultural limits of the recent developments of European private law may be a good illustration of the nature of this kind of inconsistency when referring to legal culture.[62] This otherwise well-written

---

[61] ibid 234.
[62] S Law, 'From Multiple Legal Cultures to One Legal Culture? Thinking About Culture, Tradition and Identity in European Private Law Development' (2015) 31 *Utrecht Journal of International and European Law* 68–89.

and rather fascinating article pays noticeably little attention to the concept of 'legal culture' per se, even though this term is mentioned twice in its title. On the contrary, the concept of 'culture' is treated quite broadly, by relying on the work of many relevant authors. However, neither the relationship between general culture and legal culture, nor the specificities of legal culture are discussed. Only the threefold concept of Kaarlo Tuori – according to which legal culture is composed of three layers: surface level, middle level, and deep level – is specifically mentioned with regard to legal culture; and the author also invokes Duncan Kennedy's serious emphasis on the relevance of identity discourse in the functioning of law.[63] Unfortunately, the article does not endeavour to create an applicable working concept of legal culture. Although, certainly, when discussing the recent developments of European private law, under the aegis of the EU's harmonisation efforts, the variety of cultural settings and the lack of a common European culture may yet attain an important place,[64] all in all, this article may well illustrate why the choice of a working concept of legal culture as a first step in a research design is unavoidable, in the event that one intends to use this term as a real scholarly concept rather than simply as a textual decoration.[65]

iii. Over-theorisation of Legal Culture

Another danger in the application of legal culture is when scholars – keeping in mind the utmost complexity of the phenomenon – try to create such a comprehensive working concept of legal culture that it clearly becomes over-theorised. This problem means that those who intend to apply 'legal culture' in their studies merge too many kinds of specific knowledge into this single term. Certainly, this inconsistency is very understandable, and it also suggests that the authors have understood the conceptual weaknesses of legal culture as a term and its various methodological consequences; however, unfortunately, the answers given fail to resolve these dilemmas. Dilemmas that, in the application of legal culture, are illustrated well by a point made by van Hoecke and Warrington in their seminal article discussing the perspectives of comparative law at the end of the twentieth century. As a first step, they argue that 'law is not just a set of rules or concepts, nor is it an isolated social practice. Law and legal practice

---

[63] Ibid 83–84.

[64] The latest *Ius Commune Casebook* dedicated to the relationship between the European private laws and EU law offers an excellent illustration of this problem with special regard to the discussion of the various national case laws reacting to EU law instruments; see A Hartkamp, C Sieburgh and W Devroe (eds), *Cases, Materials, and Text on European Law and Private Law* (Oxford, Hart Publishing, 2017).

[65] See the discussion between Nelken and Cotterrell on the (im)possibility of operationalising the concept of (legal) culture. D Nelken, 'Disclosing/Invoking Legal Culture: An Introduction' (1995) 4 *Social and Legal Studies* 435–52; and R Cotterrell, 'The Concept of Legal Culture' in R Cotterrell, *Law, Culture and Society. Legal Ideas in the Mirror of Social Theory* (Burlington, Ashgate, 2006) 81–96.

are one aspect of the culture to which they belong. "Legal cultures" are part of more general cultures.'[66] Basically, they reveal that law cannot simply be studied in the conventional rule-focused way nowadays; socio-cultural contexts should also play a considerable role. However, if an approach centred on the cultural embeddedness of law is applied, this choice obviously gives rise to very complex methodological problems. The 'way out' from these methodological challenges may be the intensive use of various interdisciplinary approaches, as they might enable the scholar to handle this socio-cultural complexity.

As a second step, van Hoecke and Warrington list, in order to establish a concept of legal culture that is capable of meeting the requirements of the above-mentioned cultural complexity behind law, six different aspects of legal culture. This also implies that, in their eyes, legal culture should be understood as a synthesis of these six layers. These are as follows:

1.   the concept of law;
2.   a theory of valid legal sources, including both the structural and dynamic aspects;
3.   a methodology of law focusing on the interpretation of law and the internal relationships within adjudication;
4.   a theory of argumentation with special regard to extra-legal components;
5.   a theory of legitimation with respect to formal, historical, axiological and sociological dimensions; and
6.   a common basic ideology.[67]

It must also be mentioned that this approach to legal culture is specifically devoted to the lawyers' legal culture,[68] so it is focused on such points of legal culture as appear to be relevant from the legal viewpoint. In sum, van Hoecke and Warrington envisage the concept of legal culture in comparative law as a general 'umbrella' concept that is able to incorporate such 'soft' elements of the legal world as frequently remain invisible for conventional, rule-orientated legal research.

Although the comprehensive nature of this list, as compiled by these two authors, is certainly a clear advantage, it may also be argued that – from the perspective of undertaking legal research – it gives rise to some difficulties too. These difficulties result from the over-detailed nature of this conceptualisation of legal culture. Having analysed these six elements, one may conclude that they bring together, among other things, approaches from the following fields of study: legal theory, theory of adjudication, rhetoric, sociology of law, general

---

[66] van Hoecke and Warrington, 'Legal Cultures, Legal Paradigms and Legal Doctrine: Towards a New Model for Comparative Law' (n 1) 498.

[67] For details, see ibid 514–15.

[68] ibid 513–14.

and legal history, political science, political philosophy, sociology and cultural studies. Thus, a very – perhaps too – broad spectrum of different scholarly approaches is behind this impressive intellectual attempt to articulate a proper concept of legal culture for comparative law. However, realistically speaking, no conventional research plan can be realised with the help of this legal culture concept, as it would need the high-level application of so many fields of legal and cultural studies that would make it unsuitable for normal research activities. Alternatively, only extremely artificial and highly abstract points may be argued if starting with this legal culture concept. This danger is clearly seen by the authors too, as they suggest using various, but not all, elements from this list for either macro- or micro-level comparison, depending on the scope of the given study.[69] Thus, as the scope of a research project requires, the framework of the comparative study can be built up with the help of some elements of this concept of legal culture.

All in all, van Hoecke and Warrington made an impressive attempt to conceptualise legal culture in a comprehensive way, but their construction in its entirety may not be well suited to conventional research, due to its extremely complex interdisciplinary nature. Its real value may be that it reveals all the main components of legal culture as an ideal type – *Idealtypus* – and it facilitates the task of future researchers when selecting a given or some aspects of legal culture for a comparative study. Indeed, this criticism does not undermine the scholarly value of the fascinating study by van Hoecke and Warrington, as they also addressed this problem indirectly when separating the various elements for micro or macro comparison; moreover, it helps us understand the inherent limits of this inspiring concept.

III. THE DECLINE OF METHODOLOGICAL EXCLUSIVITY IN COMPARATIVE LAW THINKING

There is a popular interpretation of the contemporary evolution of comparative law as a scholarly field. Many authors argue that the last decades of theoretical comparative law thinking have been dominated by the 'fight' or the 'struggle' between orthodox functionalism and progressive culturalism.[70] The claim of this section is, however, more refined: some recent developments show that a new – qualitatively different – attitude toward methodology has begun to take shape in comparative law. This new mindset is not based on opposing 'methodological world views' but, on the contrary, looks for a new synthesis designed to replace the previously dominant methodological exclusivity. That is, after a

---

[69] ibid 515.

[70] cf Husa, 'Methodology of Comparative Law Today: From Paradoxes to Flexibility?' (n 1) esp 1097–99.

fierce competition between functionalism and culturalism, the phase of consolidation has already started.

A. The Functionalist-Culturalist Divide

In order to argue for this claim, this section must start with some partly retrospective explanation with respect to the post-World War II history of comparative law methodology.

As was discussed in the preceding chapter, the story of functionalist methodology starts in Germany, in the 1970s, with the methodological contributions of Konrad Zweigert, a well-known authority in general comparative law. Zweigert argued, in various publications, that comparing legal phenomena should have been based on new premises, as the methodology of comparative law had had a rather underdeveloped nature thus far. Stemming from Jhering's intellectual legacy, Zweigert suggested making the social function of legal provisions the basis of comparison (*tertium comparationis*). That is, comparison in law should be based neither on textual similarities nor on the specific legal techniques applied; it is the social functions they have that need to orientate comparative legal studies. Due to this change in perspective, civil law and common law legal orders became comparable, as codified legal provisions could be contrasted with case-law-based legal rules, even though they had a very different nature from a pure technical angle. In sum, the scope of legal comparison, in both a geographical and a substantive sense, had been considerably broadened by the functional approach established by Zweigert. This attitude paved the way for the broad success of comparative law from the 1980s.

It must also be stressed that, for functionalism, the law – as a phenomenon – has not been equal to a simple set of codified rules; both case law and settled business practices were also important subjects of study. Overall, by advocating and popularising 'functionalism' in comparative studies, Zweigert considerably broadened the scope of comparative legal inquiries and also established a rather firm methodological basis for future research. Unsurprisingly, many functionalist comparative projects started in the 1990s; the so-called Trento Project – under Italian leadership – and the Ius Commune Casebooks project started by Walter van Gerven, former Advocate General at the European Court of Justice, may be mentioned as flagships of this attitude. In addition, the European Union's efforts to harmonise and approximate certain segments of national laws have also been backed by a seemingly functional attitude, as has been illustrated by many preparatory works.

However, as one may learn from the study of the history of ideas, if there is development, an action, reaction must also occur. The obvious success of functionalism in comparative law gave rise to its criticism too. This criticism took shape under the label of culturalism, which has strong ties to both sociological and postmodern studies. That is, culturalism in comparative law could not be regarded as an autonomous and independent approach from the very beginning, but as a postmodern criticism of functional legal comparison. Later, from the mid-1980s, it developed into an independent understanding of legal comparison, as Frankenberg explained in his seminal article.[71]

In the mid-1980s, the German Günther Frankenberg exposed the tenets of a cultural understanding of comparative law in a rather systematic manner, as has already been discussed in the preceding chapter. Obviously, this approach has improved a lot since then, but Frankenberg's insights are still valid when conceptualising culturalism in comparative law. Thus, culturalism has a generally critical attitude toward outcomes of the 'functional revolution' of comparative law, led by such authorities as Zweigert and Schlesinger. First, Frankenberg pointed out that the social science bases of functionalism were quite weak, as these were strongly linked to the premises of social science positivism and evolutionism. Needless to say, these premises had already been heavily challenged by the results of postmodernism in the social sciences.[72] Furthermore, according to Frankenberg, intentional simplification and Euro-centrism also biased functionalism in comparative law. All in all, functionalism, as it had been conceived by Zweigert and his followers, was certainly not in line with the cutting-edge results of postmodernism at that time. It reflected the orthodox, therefore outdated, premises of general positivism that discredited it from a postmodern perspective.[73]

In essence, the main point of cultural comparatists, for instance Frankenberg and Pierre Legrand, has been the passionate claim of a shift from the attraction of similarity to the recognition of difference – and all the corollaries of this change in the scholarly mindset – in comparative legal studies. That is, comparative law must give up the goal of identifying similar or common components of legal orders – just remember the ideas of *droit commun législatif* or *droit commun de l'humanité* from the inter-war period – and it must focus on the understanding and explanation of differences that exist among legal orders in general and legal provisions in particular. Obviously, this impressive goal cannot be reached by the functional methodology, as it offered no tools for such an endeavour by its very nature. Thus, a new methodological attitude had to be developed, and this task was mainly carried out by Legrand. Legrand argued that hermeneutics has to become the main tool of cultural comparative law, as it enables the researcher to understand empathically the reasons behind the differences in various national laws.[74] In addition, the understanding of law as a phenomenon has to be fundamentally changed. Instead of the manifest rule-orientated approach of functionalism (logocentrism), the cultural comparatist should regard law as a historico-cultural phenomenon, and this implies that those – mostly cultural – features that make a given legal order unique will need

---

[71] See G Frankenberg, 'Critical Comparisons: Re-Thinking Comparative Law' (1985) 2 *Harvard International Law Journal* 411–56.

[72] See Gray, 'Postmodernism' (n 22).

[73] cf Frankenberg, 'Critical Comparisons: Re-Thinking Comparative Law' (n 71).

[74] For details, see Legrand, 'Comparative Legal Studies and the Matter of Authenticity' (n 5).

to become the real focus of studies. Due to all these factors, interdisciplinary research into the compared legal phenomena was strongly recommended by cultural comparatists, with special regard to the integration of the results of history, cultural studies, social psychology and political science into the framework of legal studies.

Thus, today's comparative law scholarly community seems to be divided along the axis of functionalism and culturalism. This opposition has been exposed by most of the latest literature; for instance, Siems[75] and Samuel[76] place great emphasis on this division when mapping the recent methodological landscape of comparative law. Pierre Legrand still advocates the superiority of the cultural understanding of legal comparison[77] over the previous, in his words, 'reigning orthodoxy' inspired by the functionalist tenets based on the 'desire for sameness'.[78] By and large, in the recent methodological discourse, boosted predominantly by 'culturalist' or postmodern ideas, the functionalist approach of comparative law – defined by authors such as Konrad Zweigert and Hein Kötz,[79] and by Rudolf Schlesinger[80] – has been regarded as an orthodox one, a remnant of the positivist and logocentric methodological past. In contrast, culturalism – based partly on the claims of grounding comparative law in postmodern philosophy, thereby including tolerance, empathy and difference in the conceptual framework[81] – is presented as the obvious and only way of conceptual progression.

B. The Rise of Methodological Tolerance: The Recognition of a Methodological Plurality

In sum, the methodological setting for comparative law seems to be strongly divided along contrasting and conflicting methodological premises: a fundamentally doctrinal and legal approach focusing on law as it is, on the one side,

---

[75] Siems, *Comparative Law* (n 49) 98–118 (discussing the criticism of 'traditional comparative law' under the umbrella term 'postmodern comparative law) and 119 (pointing out that the inclusion of the concept of legal culture into comparative legal studies may be regarded as a way to renew the earlier formal understanding).

[76] G Samuel, *An Introduction to Comparative Law Theory and Method* (Oxford, Hart Publishing, 2014) 108–20 (presenting the approach of Pierre Legrand as a scheme of intelligibility – the hermeneutical method – trying to contrast the tenets of functionalism).

[77] For a detailed summary of this approach, see P Legrand, 'The Same and the Different' in P Legrand and R Munday (eds), *Comparative Legal Studies. Traditions and Transitions* (Cambridge, Cambridge University Press, 2003) 240–311. For a recent discussion overtly criticising the 'reigning orthodoxy' due to the false epistemological bases, see P Legrand, 'Negative Comparative Law' (2015) 10 *Journal of Comparative Law* 405–53, esp 405–18 (praising the position of Frankenberg from 1985 as an antecedent of that of the author).

[78] Legrand, 'The Same and the Different' (n 77) 244–45.

[79] See Zweigert and Kötz, *An Introduction to Comparative Law* (n 30) 32–47.

[80] See RB Schlesinger, 'The Common Core of Legal Systems. An Emerging Subject of Comparative Study' in K Zweigert and HJ Puttfarken (eds), *Rechtsvergleichung* (Darmstadt, Wissenschaftliche Buchgesellschaft, 1978) 249–69.

[81] For a comprehensive account of the opportunities of culturalism in legal scholarship, see N Mezey, 'Law as Culture' (2001) 13 *Yale Journal of Law and Humanities* 35–67.

and a progressive, postmodern, critical and culturally-orientated attitude on the other. However, this section submits that this view is painfully simplistic, and the latest development of methodology shows the emergence of a qualitatively different mindset boosted by methodological tolerance.

As a starting observation, it should be pointed out that this diametric opposition between the two approaches is deficient, even from the perspective of these methodologies. For instance, there has never been a 'functionalist' author who has completely neglected or disregarded the relevance of cultural or contextual factors. The best example of this is Zweigert himself, who argued that when drafting the style – the sum of the distinctive features – of a given legal group (*Rechtskreis*), the history, the typical patterns of legal mind and the ideological components of these legal orders should always be taken into account. Another good example might be the work of René David, who shed light on the great importance of studying the ideological dimensions of law if one wants to acquire real results that reach beyond the technical surface of legal orders. Or, conversely, although cultural comparatists always stress the importance of a cultural and postmodern approach, they have never denied that their main goal is to provide a better understanding of a legal phenomenon. Even the articles by the leading figure in this approach illustrate this statement well. For instance, in a paper published at the end of the 1990s, Legrand focuses on the impossibility of a common European civil code. Although many cultural and interdisciplinary insights are provided in this study, the focus remains a purely legal problem, of whether or not a common European civil code would be favourable for plurijural Europe.[82] As such, even though the clear separation between these two methodologies is advocated in papers with a theoretical scope, it can never be perfectly discerned in the scholarly practice.

Second, in the last 10 years, a number of writings have been published that advocate a much more 'integrationist' and 'tolerant' approach to comparative law methodologies than previously. This is what one may identify as a qualitatively different methodological attitude. This new line of comparative law thinking, first reflected in Jaakko Husa's methodological works, seems now to have been taken over by Geoffrey Samuel and Mark van Hoecke.

Samuel, in his manual – mapping the main strategies of comparative law research from various perspectives – suggested that the plurality of comparative methods should be preserved and considered as sources with a strong potential. In essence, Samuel argues that comparative law methods represent different schemes of intelligibility, so they are not superior or inferior to one another but are simply different in their qualities and potentials. In addition, Samuel considers these schemes of intelligibility in the broader context of social sciences, which makes it possible to have a more distanced view on them. In this vein, Samuel

---

[82] Legrand, 'Against a European Civil Code'.

distinguishes three main schemes of intelligibility applied in recent comparative law methodology, namely functionalism, structuralism and the hermeneutical method rooted in Legrand's claim for an empathic approach targeting the 'deep structures' of the legal orders compared.[83]

Hence, depending on the research subject, the various – and diverging at many points – methods for legal comparison may be equally relevant. Thus, in Samuel's eyes, comparative law research should start with the study and discussion of the basic research questions, not by choosing a particular research method. The main points of a comparative law research agenda may be summarised in a list of ten methodological dichotomies:

1. comparison and law;
2. macro and micro comparisons;
3. similarity and difference;
4. genealogical and analogical comparison;
5. internal and external perspectives;
6. functional method and its alternatives;
7. the rule model and its alternatives;
8. nature and culture;
9. holism and individualism; and
10. actual and virtual facts.

In conclusion, Samuel stresses that the preparation of a comparative law research design must start with making decisions with respect to dichotomy no 1. That is, the comparatist always has to find adequate answers to two starting questions when drafting a research plan: 'what is meant by "comparison", and what is meant by "law"'.[84] The other methodological choices – for instance, setting up a specific methodological framework – are largely the consequences of these basic decisions. That is, methods with either a functionalist or a cultural character are equally important for comparative legal research, and they can even be combined if the subject studied requires it.

This idea was elaborated by van Hoecke, who advocates a so-called 'toolbox-approach' for comparative law research.[85] This idea may be considered the most promising methodological development in recent years. Basically, van Hoecke changes the scope of the heated methodological debates regarding the application of the comparative method, since he argues that the specific research method applied should always be adjusted to and shaped by the research subject. Hence, there is no need whatsoever for a methodological consensus among comparatists, since different problems may give rise to the application of diverse sets of

---

[83] Samuel, *An Introduction to Comparative Law Theory and Method* (n 76) 65–120.
[84] ibid 173.
[85] M van Hoecke, 'Methodology of Comparative Legal Research' (2015) 5 *Law and Method* 1–35.

research methods. According to van Hoecke, six different methods of comparative research should be delineated as follows.[86]

1. The functionalist method that represents the classic Zweigertian legacy, namely the comparison of laws on the basis of their social functions.
2. Structuralism, which tries to identify major blocks or units of national laws, not necessarily on a geographical basis, thereby creating a playground for macro comparison among legal families, legal traditions and so on.
3. The analytical method, concentrating on a conceptual analysis of legal orders. The basic concepts revealed by this method may become building blocks for a macro-level structural analysis too. The system of fundamental legal concepts as classified by Hohfeld may be an excellent illustration of the utility of this way of thought.[87]
4. The law-in-context approach that summarises the findings of cultural comparative law. Basically, no comparative law enterprise is possible without taking the context of the problem studied into account. That is, in comparative research, the context always has to be studied, whether it is the cultural background or the sociological embeddedness of a given norm. According to van Hoecke, the law-in-context approach is a mandatory tool in any comparative research project, as the context cannot be disregarded if one wants to reach valid outcomes.
5. The historical method, implying that most comparative studies cannot be carried out without setting out the historical background to the problems studied, at least regarding their major points.
6. The common core method. This fashionable term was coined by Schlesinger, who argued that main task of legal comparison was to find the common core behind the colourful surface of technical legal regulation. In fact, the premise that a common core exists may be a useful and inspiring starting point in research, and even the lack of such a common core can be a valid scholarly result.

In sum, van Hoecke encourages the comparatists to overstep the functionalist-culturalist dichotomy, and advocates applying the various methods in an open-minded – tolerant – way when carrying out comparative research programmes. Moreover, the emphasis must always be on the nature of the problem studied and the optimal selection of the methods, and therefore methodological identity as a cultural factor has only secondary relevance, if any, in the community of comparative law scholars. That is, there are neither 'good' nor 'bad' comparatists with respect to the standards of either functionalism or culturalism, but only those who are properly able to apply the various methods placed in their 'toolbox' and those who cannot.

---

[86] For details, see ibid 8–21.
[87] See WN Hohfeld, 'Fundamental Legal Conceptions as Applied in Judicial Reasoning' (1917) 26 *Yale Law Journal* 710–70.

IV. PARADIGM SHIFT IN CONTEMPORARY COMPARATIVE LAW?

Undeniably, these changes in the methodology of recent comparative law are rather impressive. At first glance, all the relevant methodological tenets of post-World War II comparative law seem to be heavily challenged. Functionalism has been regarded as an 'orthodox' and biased approach, and the replacement of conventional legal concepts with cultural and postmodern terms and insights has also been urged impatiently by many authors.[88] In addition, the methodological exclusivity of the competing approaches has been also questioned, and a new pluralistic, more tolerant understanding is also advised by some other authors. In sum, the methodological landscape of recent comparative law thinking is far from being settled in a strict scholarly way.

This may suggest that such a structural transformation has begun in comparative law as may amount to a paradigm shift. That is, the emergence of a new paradigm in comparative law is happening before our very eyes. However, if one takes seriously Kuhn's 'softened' vision on paradigm shift and its application to legal scholarship, as elaborated in chapter 1, grave doubts appear regarding this simple (and, therefore fascinating) conclusion. As such, the main point of this concluding section of this chapter is that although some signs of structural transformation can certainly be identified, many arguments can be raised against this conclusion, and these seriously reduce the scholarly validity of this position.

For Kuhn, a paradigm shift is a development in the history of a given scientific field when scientists or scholars start to approach their subject-matter from a different angle and in a new way. This implies that the members of the given scientific community no longer share the previously applied 'basic theory' – of principles and 'exemplars' – but begin to rely on new kinds of ideas on methods and generalisations.[89] In a very telling metaphor, Kuhn compares this transformation to a change in the way people view the world: the object remains the same but their understanding of it transforms radically, thereby providing a new perception of the same 'things'.[90] In addition, the main impetus behind such an essential transformation, as implied by a paradigm shift, is the effects of various anomalies' being able to challenge the application of settled and conventional methods and the 'exemplars' used.

Thus, through these Kuhnian lenses, the recent developments in comparative law thinking may be interpreted in a different way. First of all, it should be admitted that no anomalies emerged in the last two decades that cannot be explained in the settled frame of post-World War II comparative law. As for the

---

[88] cf Husa, 'Methodology of Comparative Law Today: From Paradoxes to Flexibility?' (n 1); for a detailed discussion, see Siems, *Comparative Law* (n 49) 97–118.

[89] TS Kuhn, *The Structure of Scientific Revolutions* (Chicago, IL, The University of Chicago Press, 1970) 198–204.

[90] ibid 111–14.

historical-evolutionist paradigm, the process of paradigm shift was triggered by the inability of this paradigm to answer the claims of those scholars who wanted to apply comparative law for such practical purposes as the unification of modern private law, or in order to contrast some private law provisions in both common law and Continental law.[91] Similarly, the birth of the post-World War II paradigm was boosted by the deficiencies in the paradigm of *droit comparé* when the scholarly understanding and study of Socialist law was a key issue for Western comparatists.[92] However, it is not possible to identify similarly challenging anomalies around recent comparative law, even though, undeniably, there are many challenges to the conventional setting of the third paradigm, such as post-modernity, globalisation, regionalisation and transnationalisation.[93] Hence, it may be argued that one condition for a paradigm shift is certainly lacking these days: the emergence of anomalies that would be able to direct the work of the comparatist community in qualitatively new directions.

In addition, it should be recognised that all the new contemporary initiatives for the renewal of comparative law – in general or regarding specific components – are organic refinements of already-existing theses. For instance, as has been argued, although they are conventionally considered prominent representatives of functionalism, the approaches of both Zweigert and David also implied a cultural understanding of law. David put strong emphasis on the necessary study of ideology behind the legal families; for him, ideology was a decisive factor in the formation of a legal family.[94] Meanwhile, Zweigert advocated the study of historical as well as ideological elements, besides conventional legal components, when drafting the style of a given *Rechtskreis*.[95] Given this, it cannot be argued that today's cultural approach would not have any antecedents in the work of 'classic' and 'orthodox' authors. Provocatively, it may even be submitted that these components, in their theories, made the formation of such extensive cultural claims possible with respect to comparative law. Conversely, although the advocates of the cultural turn formulate a sharp and – often proper and well-grounded – criticism of the recent state of the art in comparative law, they have never denied that the main subject-matter of comparative law is the law, although it is interpreted more broadly – mostly with the help of some tenets of either cultural studies or postmodernism – than in the 1960s or 1970s.[96] In sum, what is happening in comparative law nowadays can properly be described as a very intensive phase of puzzle-solving research (with special regard to the

---

[91] See ch 3.

[92] See ch 4.

[93] Siems, *Comparative Law* (n 49) 97–118 and 222–59.

[94] David, *Traité élémentaire de droit comparé* (n 29) 223–24.

[95] cf K Zweigert, 'Zur Lehre von den Rechtskreisen' in KH Nadelmann, AT von Meheren and J Hazard (eds), *XXth Century Comparative and Conflicts Law Legal Essays in Honor of Hessel E Yntema* (Leiden, AW Sythoff, 1961) 42–55.

[96] See, eg, Legrand, 'Negative Comparative Law' (n 77) 418–29 (Here, the author uses the example of the 2004 French statute prohibiting clothing showing an apparent religious allegiance in schools, to point out the hardships of conventional ways of doing comparative law.)

clarification of methodological issues), but it cannot be regarded with certainty as a paradigm shift, since some fundamental conditions for such a transformation still seem to be missing.

All in all, comparative law has been going through a very impressive phase of theory-building during these years. However, this does not equal a paradigm shift, although some kind of reconciliation between 'orthodox' and new ideas seems to be happening – as puzzle-solving research typically works. The possibility of this methodological reconciliation may be illustrated by the work of Jaakko Husa, who made serious efforts to save such classical components of comparative law as functionalism as a method or the theory of legal families for the aims of future research. Basically, by arguing for the application of a 'moderate version of functionalism', setting aside the presumption of similarity (*praesumptio similitudinis*) but preserving the frame,[97] or defending the concept of legal families as useful 'launch vehicles'[98] – a conceptual-theoretical tool – Husa carried out classic puzzle-solving research aiming at the continuous refinement of a set of exemplars in the light of new research insights. In addition, the methodologically pluralist attitude of both Samuel and Van Hoecke proved that older research methods, such as the historical or the functionalist approaches, should not be abandoned due to their heavy criticism but still remain useful tools in the complex toolbox of comparatists. Thus, criticism leads to the refinement and renewal of many classic tenets of post-World War II comparative law, rather than their dismantling and the subsequent introduction of a completely new comparative law mindset.

[97] J Husa, 'Farewell to Functionalism or Methodological Tolerance?' (2003) 3 *Rabels Zeitschrift für ausländisches und internationales Privatrecht* 419–47.
[98] J Husa, 'The Future of Legal Families' *Oxford Handbooks Online* (2016) at www.oxfordhandbooks.com/view/10.1093/oxfordhb/9780199935352.001.0001/oxfordhb-9780199935352-e-26, 8–9.

Concluding Thoughts

I. ON THE VALIDITY OF THIS RESEARCH, WITH SPECIAL REGARD TO THE RELEVANCE OF KUHN'S IDEAS

NEEDLESS TO SAY, the application of Kuhn's ideas in studying the history of legal scholarship is far from obvious. As was discussed in chapter 1, many doubts and issues may emerge with respect to this 'revolutionary' theory. Or, it is better to say, there are many more concerns than obvious points in its favour in the eyes of the academic community. In addition, a scholar should also always be concerned about the validity and relevance of his or her own work; self-reflection is therefore indispensable in scholarly activities. Hence, because of the presence of apparent doubts, it will be discussed here whether or not this unusual endeavour, taking Kuhn's oeuvre as a conceptual frame for the discussion of the modern European history of comparative law, was able to come up with such insights as may have any added value to the discourse on comparative law as such.

I am deeply convinced that the answer to the preceding question is affirmative. With the help of this conceptual framework, the veil of descriptive linearity can be pierced effectively, and this change of perspective has resulted in gaining a more structured and more refined version of the history of modern European comparative law, as compared to the earlier inquiries (sometimes otherwise very impressive and thoughtful, such as Constantinesco's seminal work). Basically, Kuhn's theory has offered a conceptual vocabulary to tame the complexity of scholarly development. With the 'disciplined' and 'empathic' application of some concepts coming from Kuhn's theory, this research could provide the readers with an extensive look into the development of modern comparative law in Europe. In place of a linear and cumulative process, simply leading to the recent state of the art, another story has been revealed: a story of different – sometimes subsequent, sometimes coexisting – shared understandings of how to carry out comparative legal enterprises that have competed for the attention of legal scholars throughout the various historical and intellectual periods in Europe.

One can also recognise the unity of those scholarly oeuvres that looked to be far from each other in either geographical or cultural terms at first glance, for instance those of Pollock and Kohler, or those of Lambert and Gutteridge. These otherwise seemingly diverging authors can be regarded as members of the same paradigm regarding their comparative law attitude, owing to their shared assumptions about the course of comparative law research. In other words, puzzle-solving, normal scholarly activity in the field of comparative law certainly did not take into account the various national and cultural borders that divided Europe during the nineteenth and twentieth centuries. In sum, this book's approach, relying on some conceptual innovations coming from Kuhn's theory, has presented a much more complex, much more interrelated and much more intriguing story of modern European comparative law than the linear approaches would ever have done, although their achievements undoubtedly cannot be denied.

Unsurprisingly, it can also be argued convincingly that the theory of paradigms, and especially the concept of paradigms shifts, can have no relevance at all for legal scholarship as such, since

> there never has been any common framework guiding legal research worldwide, which could have been replaced by a new paradigm, such as with the Copernican revolution that claimed that the Earth is turning around the sun and not the other way around.[1]

If one considers legal scholarship as a general study of legal phenomena, this statement cannot be doubted. However, if legal scholarship is understood as an umbrella term embracing all those scholarly approaches of the law that are based on various, sometimes centuries-old 'modern' research traditions, for instance natural law, positivist theories, sociological theories, law and economics and critical legal studies, one may reach a slightly different conclusion. These compartments of legal scholarship may have their own internal theoretical and conceptual development, and this specific and structured development – in contrast to the general development of legal scholarship as such – may be studied with the help of some Kuhnian terms, since the vision of these subparts sometimes changes radically, and this also implies a decisive transformation of their research premises. Just remember the rebirth of natural law following World War II in Europe,[2] or the expansion of the critical approach within socio-legal studies in North America.[3] Thus, with regard to these specific modern research traditions, such is modern comparative law too; it can be argued that some shared understandings of research issues always exist, and these certainly contribute to the formation of systematised scholarly activities carried out by groups of legal scholars. Furthermore, it is not excluded at all, as the intellectual history of legal scholarship shows, that these community-creating visions may change from time to time parallel to the emergence of qualitatively different understandings of the same issues.[4]

---

[1] Mark van Hoecke, email to the author, 12 October 2019.

[2] cf Z Péteri 'Gustav Radbruch und einige Fragen der relativistischen Rechtsphilosophie' (1960) 2 *Acta Iuridica Academiae Scientiarum Hungariae* 113–60.

[3] cf M Hertogh, *Nobody's Law. Legal Consciousness and Legal Alienation in Everyday Life* (London, Palgrave. Macmillan, 2018) 66–67.

[4] For instance, see the comparison between the so-called 'critical' and 'secular' approaches of socio-legal studies, Hertogh, *Nobody's Law* (n 3) 66–79; or the shift from positivism to antipositivism as argued by Dworkin when criticising Hart's conception of legal philosophy in R Dworkin, 'Hart's Postscript and the Character of Political Philosophy' (2004) 24 *Oxford Journal of Legal Philosophy* 1–37.

From a different angle, it can even be argued that these two approaches – arguing for the inapplicability of Kuhn's ideas to legal scholarship in general and the acceptance of a limited use of some Kuhnian concepts when studying elements of legal scholarship, especially modern legal research traditions – may be reconciled. Although none of the basic problems of legal scholarship have yet been resolved (just think of Kant's ironical remark on the incapacity of legal scholarship to find a suitable concept of law,[5] and therefore no insights of Kuhn are applicable to this general issue since there appears to be no progress with regard to the basic questions, such as the concept of law), the situation in these subsections of legal scholarship can be different. They do not strive for general answers, as was the case regarding the position of the Earth with respect to the Sun, but they try to improve and perfect their theories continuously for their specific research issues, as opticians tried to perfect their telescopes for astronomy. And if this is so, no one can deny that a 'disciplined' and 'conscious' use of some Kuhnian tenets may provide valuable contributions to the understanding of these specific courses of developments.

Obviously, the role of Kuhn's ideas should not be overestimated. They are simply conceptual tools for finding a better and more in-depth understanding of the evolution of scholarly thinking in specific fields of legal scholarship. Moreover, comparative law is a specific field that chases no general insights on the law as such but aims at understanding and explaining its own research issues better, from the nature of legal development to the taxonomy of the world's legal orders. Therefore, a restricted use of Kuhn's ideas can be justified, and the outcome of this research, as this book indicates, may also point out that this experiment made sense.

II. ON THE UTILITY OF HAVING A SINGLE BOOK ON THE HISTORY OF MODERN EUROPEAN COMPARATIVE LAW

Obviously, the outcome of this research has no definitive character. What has been written is certainly not done once and for all. What this book offers to the readers is an interpretation of the story of modern European comparative law – 'a history of comparative law' – and, needless to say, micro research can shade it further at any point. One can even find intriguing new findings in the latest relevant literature, for instance the narrative and critical analysis of the discussions at the 1900 Paris Congress,[6] or the conceptual deconstruction of Zweigert's concept of style.[7] These both definitely have an added value with respect to the vision of this book.

---

[5] 'Jurists are still searching for a definition of their concept of right.' See I Kant, *Critique of Pure Reason* (Cambridge, Cambridge University Press, 1998) 639.

[6] See M Fournier, *Comparative Law Gets Entitled: The 1900 Paris Congress in Contexts* (Victoria, University of Victoria, 2018).

[7] See P Cserne, 'Conceptualizing "Style" in Legal Scholarship: the Curious Case of Zweigert's "Style Doctrine"' (2019) 15 *International Journal of Law in Context* 297–309.

Some can also submit that these findings, coming from meticulous micro-perspective research, may question the general validity of an approach that has aimed at mapping the almost 200-year history of intellectual inquiry, that has endeavoured to provide a 'big picture' of modern comparative law, in a single book. Nonetheless, personally speaking, I am deeply convinced that a remark from the excellent British historian, Sir Steven Runciman, is particularly valid in this case too. Runciman argues in the introduction to his ground-breaking and world-famous *A History of the Crusades*, that 'a single author cannot speak with the high authority of a panel of experts, but he may succeed in giving to his work an integrated and even an epical quality that no composite volume can achieve'.[8] I think the case is somewhat similar here. This research aims at composing an integrated and conceptually coherent history of modern comparative law, though such an enterprise is of course threatened by many dangers. Nevertheless, it is also needed, simply because this 'history' is also a must for further research and discussion as a framework that can and needs to be refined.

III. ON THE RECENT PERSPECTIVES OF COMPARATIVE LAW

The use of comparative methods in legal scholarship is certainly no longer the privilege of comparatists. The application of a comparative outlook has definitely been proliferating in legal academia during the last decades, as is shown by many publications and the growing popularity of comparative courses in the curricula of law faculties. Therefore, it can be submitted, comparison has undeniably become a key component of legal studies in the broadest sense. Whether it concerns contemporaneous or substantive comparisons, the idea of relying on comparative methods has been broadly welcomed by many legal scholars.

This transformation is mostly due to the fact that there has never been such a favourable context for spreading the idea of legal comparison than the period following the fall of the bipolar world order. Our new world is marked by such terms as globalisation, supranationalisation, regionalisation or fragmentation. Obviously, these dynamics heavily touched the world's legal orders and, in addition, new legal phenomena – such as global law as a sum of heterogeneous quasi-legal orders[9] – have begun to take an increasingly characteristic shape. And, it can be convincingly argued, this new complexity of the world's legal affairs may only be understood properly with the help of a comparative outlook that is able to disregard domestic legal borders and to understand the interaction between various legal phenomena.

What can such a historical enquiry say when such a drastic transformation has been occurring right before our eyes? The proliferation of the use

---

[8] S Runciman, *A History of the Crusades*, vol I (Cambridge, Cambridge University Press, 1951) xiii.

[9] As a starting point of this discussion, see G Teubner (ed), *Global Law without a State* (Aldershot, Dartmouth, 1997).

of comparative methods in legal scholarship should surely be welcomed, but it must also be borne in mind that there is no single comparative law method that is applicable to any type of problem as some kind of panacea. This history teaches us that many traditions of comparative law have existed, and they cannot be termed simply as either good or bad, or as either orthodox or progressive. They were all born in a specific historical context, and their formation was also boosted by specific research aims – just think of the various ideas of *droit commun* in the paradigm of *droit comparé*, or of the need to compare legal orders having qualitatively different ideological backgrounds during the Cold War period. Thus, the reigning conception of comparative law is certainly always context-dependent to a large extent, and this should always be taken into account when looking for the one and only best way to make legal comparisons.

These different visions of comparative law cannot simply be juxtaposed and, thereby, contrasted with one another in order to decide which one is better, as they all have their own internal logic and rationale, strengthened by the systematic work of the scientific community behind them. However, this does not imply that they are incommensurable in the strict sense of this term.[10] If their uniqueness, stemming from their specific contexts and internal setting, is respected, they can be compared intelligibly with each other and their key points may be translated. Hence, this historical study suggests that future comparatists should always be aware of two points.

First, their methodology of carrying out comparative law research is definitely not the sole way of doing so, and other perspectives may also have some – or much – say on the subject studied. Methodological openness is thus certainly an important scholarly value in the field of comparative legal studies. Second, they should also keep in mind the inherent limits of the comparative law method applied with special regard to its premises on the concept of law and that of carrying out comparisons.[11] It can only be agreed with the remark these two starting choices decisively influence the design (and therefore the outcomes too) of a comparative law research project. Thus, this study of almost 200 years teaches the future that modesty and self-reflection is indispensable for comparative law work, while the obsession with methodological egoism and exclusivity has to be avoided. At least as much as is possible in legal scholarship.

---

[10] See TS Kuhn, 'Commensurability, Comparability, Communicability' (1982) *PSA: Proceedings of the Biennial Meeting of the Philosophy of Science Association* 669–88.
[11] cf G Samuel, *An Introduction to Comparative Law Theory and Method* (Oxford, Hart Publishing, 2014) 178.

Bibliography

Aarnio, A, 'Paradigms in Legal Dogmatics. Toward a Theory of Change and Progress in Legal Science' in A Peczenik, L Lindahl and B van Roermund (eds), *Theory of Legal Science* (Dordrecht, D Reidel Publishing Company, 1984) 24–38

Ancel, M, 'La confrontation des droits socialistes et des droits occidentaux' in Z Péteri (ed), *Legal Theory – Comparative Law. Studies in Honour of Professor Imre Szabó* (Budapest, Akadémiai Kiadó, 1984) 13–23

——, 'Le comparatiste devant les systèmes (ou "familles") de droit' in H Bernstein, U Drobnig and H Kötz (eds), *Festschrift für Konrad Zweigert* (Tübingen, JCB Mohr, 1981) 355–62

——, 'Les grands étapes de la recherche comparative au XXe siècle' in K Zweigert and HJ Puttfarken (eds), *Rechtsvergleichung* (Darmstadt, Wissenschaftliche Buchgesellschaft, 1978) 350–60

——, 'Cent ans de droit comparé en France' in *Livre centenaire de Société de législation comparée* (Paris, LGDJ, 1969) 3–21

——, 'La doctrine universaliste dans l'oeuvre de Lévy-Ullmann' in LFJ de la Morandière and M Ancel (eds), *L'oeuvre juridique de Lévy-Ullmann. Contribution á la doctrine moderne sur la science du Droit et le Droit comparé* (Paris, Centre français de droit comparé, 1952) 181–202

Arminjon, P, Nolde, B and Wolff, M, *Traité de droit comparé I* (Paris, LGDJ, 1950)

Armgardt, M, 'Leibniz as Legal Scholar' (2014) 20 *Fundamina* 27–38

Audren, F and Navet, G, 'Note sur la carrière d'Eugène Lerminier au Collège de France (1831–1849)' (2001) 4 *Revue d'histoire des sciences humaines* 57–67

Bachofen, JJ, *Das Mutterrecht: eine Untersuchung über die Gynaikokratie der alten Welt nach ihrer religiösen und rechtlichen Natur* (Stuttgart, Verlag von Krais & Hoffmann, 1861)

Bacon, Lord, *Novum Organum* (New York, PF Collier and Son, 1902)

Balogh, E, 'Lévy-Ullmann, Vice-Président de l'Académie Internationale de Droit Comparé' in LF Julliot de la Morandière and M Ancel (eds), *L'oeuvre juridique de Lévy-Ullmann. Contribution á la doctrine moderne sur la science du droit et le droit comparé* (Paris, Centre français de droit comparé, 1952) 119–35

Barnes, B, *TS Kuhn and Social Science* (London and Basingstoke, MacMillan, 1982)

Basdevant-Bastid, S, 'L'Institut de droit comparé de Lyon' in *Introduction à l'étude du droit comparé – Recueil d'Études en l'honneur d'Édouard Lambert* (Paris, Sirey-LGDJ, 1938) 11–15

Bergson, H, *L'évolution créatrice* (Paris, PUF, 1907)

Berman, PS, 'Towards a Jurisprudence of Hybridity' (2010) 11 *Utah Law Review* 11–29

Bird, A, 'Kuhn and the Historiography of Science' in WJ Devlin and A Bokulich (eds), *Kuhn's Structure of Scientific Revolutions. 50 Years On* (Heidelberg, Springer, 2015) 23–38

Blankenburg, E, 'Patterns of Legal Culture: The Netherlands Compared to Neighboring Germany' (1998) 46 *The American Journal of Comparative Law* 1–41

Boele-Woelki, K and Fernandez Arroyo, DP (eds), *The Past, the Present and Future of Comparative law. Le passé, le présent et le futur du droit comparé. Ceremony of 15 May 2017 in Honour of 5 Great Comparatists* (Paris, Springer, 2018)

Braudel, F, *L'identité de la France. Espace et histoire* (Paris, Flammarion, 1990)

——, 'La longue durée' (1958) 13 *Annales. Economies, Sociétés, Civilisations* 725–53

Breckman, W, 'Eduard Gans and the Crisis of Hegelianism' (2001) 62 *Journal of the History of Ideas* 543–64

Bryce, J, 'The Methods of Legal Science' in J Bryce, *Studies in History and Jurisprudence*, vol II (Oxford, Clarendon Press, 1901) 607–37

Bussani, M and Mattei, U, 'The Common Core Approach to European Private Law' (1997–1998) *Columbia Journal of European Law* 339–56

Caemmerer, E von and Zweigert, K, 'Évolution et état actuel de la méthode du droit comparé en Allemagne' in *Livre centenaire de Société de législation comparée II* (Paris, LGDJ, 1969) 267–81

Cairns, JW, 'The Development of Comparative Law in Great Britain' in M Reimann and R Zimmermann (eds), *The Oxford Handbook of Comparative Law* (Oxford, Oxford University Press, 2006) 131–73

Comte, A, *Discours sur l'esprit positif* (Paris, V Dalmon, 1844)

Constantinesco, L-J, *Traité de droit comparé III. La science de droits comparés* (Paris, Economica, 1983)

——, *Traité de droit comparé I. Introduction au droit comparé* (Paris, LGJD, 1972)

Cotterrell, R, 'The Concept of Legal Culture' in R Cotterrell, *Law, Culture and Society. Legal Ideas in the Mirror of Social Theory* (Burlington, Ashgate, 2006) 81–96

Courtney, CP, 'Montesquieu and Natural Law' in DW Carrithers, MA Mosher and PA Rahe (eds), *Montesquieu's Science of Politics. Essays on the Spirit of Laws* (Lanham, MD, Rowmand and Littlefield, 2001) 41–69

Cover, R, 'The Supreme Court, 1982 Term – Foreword: Nomos and Narrative' (1983–1984) 97 *Harvard Law Review* 4–68

Cserne, P, 'Conceptualizing "Style" in Legal Scholarship: the Curious Case of Zweigert's "Style Doctrine"' (2019) 15 *International Journal of Law in Context* 297–309

Dalberg-Larsen, J, 'Change or Progress in Legal Science' in *ARSP Beiheft 25* (Stuttgart, Franz Steiner Verlag, 1985)

David, R, *Le droit comparé, droits d'hier, droits de demain* (Paris, Economica, 1982)

——, *Les grands systèmes de droit contemporains* (Paris, Dalloz, 1982)

——, 'Rapport écrit' in M Ancel (ed), *Livre du centenaire de la Société de législation comparée* (Paris, LGDJ, 1975) 145–51

—— et al, *International Encyclopedia of Comparative Law. The Different Conceptions of Law* (Tübingen-Leiden, Mohr-Martinus Nijhoff, 1975)

——, 'Existe-t-il un droit occidental?' in KH Nadelmann, AT von Meheren and J Hazard (eds), *XXth Century Comparative and Conflicts Law Legal Essays in Honor of Hessel E Yntema* (Leiden, AW Sythoff, 1961) 56–64

——, 'Lévy-Ullmann et le droit comparé' in LF Julliot de la Morandière and M Ancel (eds), *L'oeuvre juridique de Lévy-Ullmann. Contribution á la doctrine moderne sur la science du droit et le droit comparé* (Paris, Centre français de droit comparé, 1952) 75–84

——, *Traité élémentaire de droit civil comparé* (Paris, LGDJ, 1950)

Davies, N, *Europe: A History* (New York, Harper, 1998)

Del Vecchio, G, 'L'unité de l'esprit humain comme base de la comparaison juridique' (1950) 2 *Revue internationale de droit comparé* 686–91

——, 'La communicabilité du droit et les doctrines de G-B Vico' in *Introduction á l'étude du droit comparé. Recueil d'Études en l'honneur d'Édouard Lambert* (Paris, Sirey-LGDJ, 1938) 591–601

——, L'idée d'une science du droit universel comparé' (1910) 39 *Revue critique de législation et jurisprudence* 487–505

Devroe, W and Droshut, D, 'The Leuven Centre for a Common Law of Europe and the Ius Commune Casebook Project' (2003) 2 *ERA Forum: Scripta Iuris Europaei* 114–21

Drobnig, U, 'The Comparability of Socialist and Non-Socialist Systems of Law' (1977) 3 *Tel Aviv University Studies in Law* 45–57

——, 'The International Encyclopedia of Comparative Law: Efforts toward a Worldwide Comparison of Law' (1972) 5 *Cornell International Law Journal* 113–29

Dworkin, R, 'Hart's Postscript and the Character of Political Philosophy' (2004) 24 *Oxford Journal of Legal Philosophy* 1–37

Ehrlich, E, 'Montesquieu and Sociological Jurisprudence' (1915–16) 29 *Harvard Law Review* 582–600

Elison, LM, 'Kohler's Philosophy of Law' (1961) 10 *Journal of Public Law* 409–25

Eörsi, G, *Összehasonlító polgári jog* (Budapest, Akadémiai Kiadó, 1975)

Esser, J, *Grundsatz und Norm in der richterlichen Fortbildung des Privatrechts: Rechtsvergleichende Beiträge zur Rechtsquellen- und Interpretationslehre* (Tübingen, JCB Mohr, 1956)

Ewald, W, 'Rats in Retrospect' in S Besson, L Heckendorn Urscheler and S Jubé (eds), *Comparing Comparative Law* (Geneva, Schulthess, 2017) 19–34

Felski, R, 'From Literary Theory to Critical Method' (2008) 1 *Profession* 108–16

Ficker, H, 'L'état du droit comparé en Allemagne' (1958) 4 *Revue internationale du droit comparé* 701–18

Flodin, M, 'The Possibility of Revolution in Legal Science' in Z Bankowski (ed), *Revolutions in Law and Legal Thought* (Aberdeen, Aberdeen University Press, 1991) 175–82

Foucault, M, *L'archéologie du savoir* (Paris, Gallimard, 1969)

Fournier, M, *Comparative Law Gets Entitled: The 1900 Paris Congress in Contexts* (Victoria, University of Victoria, 2018)

Frankenberg, G, *Comparative Law as Critique* (Cheltenham, Edward Elgar, 2016)

——, 'Critical Comparisons: Re-Thinking Comparative Law' (1985) 2 *Harvard International Law Journal* 411–56

Friedman, LM, *The Legal System. A Social Science Perspective* (New York, Russell Sage Foundation, 1975)

Friedmann, W, 'Book review' (1957) 57 *Columbia Law Review* 449–51

——, *Legal Theory* (London, Stevens and Sons, 1949)

Garraud, P, 'Preface' in *Introduction à l'étude du droit comparé. Recueil d'Études en l'honneur d'Édouard Lambert* (Paris, Sirey-LGDJ, 1938) xxi–xxv

——, 'Hommage à Édouard Lambert' in *Introduction à l'étude du droit comparé. Recueil d'Études en l'honneur d'Édouard Lambert* (Paris, Sirey-LGDJ, 1938) 3–5

Gerber, DJ, 'The Common Core of European Private Law' (2004) 52 *The American Journal of Comparative Law* 995–1001

——, 'Sculpting the Agenda of Comparative Law: Ernst Rabel and the Facade of Language' in A Riles (ed), *Rethinking the Masters of Comparative Law* (Oxford, Hart Publishing, 2001) 190–208

Gessner, V, Hoeland, A and Varga, C (eds), *European Legal Cultures* (Aldershot, Dartmouth, 1996)

Gibson, JL and Caldeira, GA, 'The Legal Cultures of Europe' (1996) 30 *Law and Society Review* 55–85

Gibson, JL and Duch, RM, 'Support for Rights in Western Europe and the Soviet Union. An Analysis of the Beliefs of Mass Publics' in FD Weil (ed), *Research on Democratisation and Society. Democratisation in Eastern and Western Europe* (Greenwich, JAI Press, 1993) 241–63

Gillispie, CC, 'Lamarck and Darwin in the History of Science' (1958) 46 *American Scientist* 388–409

Giuliani, A, 'What is Comparative Legal History? Legal Historiography and the Revolt Against Formalism, 1930–60' in A Masferrer, KÅ Modéer and O Moréteau (eds), *Comparative Legal History* (Cheltenham, Edward Elgar Publishing, 2019) 30–77

Glasson, E, *Le mariage civil et le divorce dans les principaux pays de l'Europe* (Paris, G Pedone-Lavrier, 1879)

Glenn, HP, 'La civilisation de la common law' (1993) 45 *Revue internationale de droit comparé* 559–75

Goulé, P, 'La Société de législation comparée (Paris)' in *Introduction à l'étude du droit comparé – Recueil d'Études en l'honneur d'Édouard Lambert* (Paris, Sirey-LGDJ, 1938) 696–701

Gray, A, 'Postmodernism' in EN Zalta (ed), *The Stanford Encyclopedia of Philosophy (Spring 2015 Edition)* at https://plato.stanford.edu/archives/spr2015/entries/postmodernism/

Graziadei, M, 'The Functionalist Heritage' in P Legrand and R Munday (eds) *Comparative Legal Studies – Traditions and Transitions* (Cambridge, Cambridge University Press, 2003) 100–27

Griffiths, J, 'The Social Working of Legal Rules' (2003) 48 *Journal of Legal Pluralism* 1–84

Gutteridge, HC, 'Lévy-Ullmann' in LJ de la Morandière and M Ancel (eds), *L'oeuvre juridique de Lévy-Ullmann. Contribution à la doctrine moderne sur la science du Droit et le Droit comparé* (Paris, Centre français de droit comparé, 1952) 17–18

——, *Comparative Law* (Cambridge, Cambridge University Press, 1949)

Hähnchen, S, *Rechtsgeschichte. Von der Römischen Antike bis zur Neuzeit* (Heidelberg, CF Müller, 2012)

Hamza, G, 'Elemér Balogh (1881–1955): The Forgotten Great Scholar of Roman Law and Comparative Law' (2008) 3 *Nordicum-Mediterraneum* 12–17

——, 'Sir Henry Maine et le droit comparé' (2005) 45 *Acta Antiqua* 193–206

——, 'Az összehasonlító jogtudomány kibontakozásának útjai Európában' (1996) 38 *Állam- és Jogtudomány* 275–78

Hansson, B, 'Recent Trends in the Philosophy of Science' in A Peczenik, L Lindahl and B van Roermund (eds), *Theory of Legal Science* (Dordrecht, D Reidel Publishing Company, 1984) 5–12

Hartkamp, A, Sieburgh, C and Devroe, W (eds), *Cases, Materials, and Text on European Law and Private Law* (Oxford, Hart Publishing, 2017)

Hayek, FA von, *The Counter-Revolution of Science: Studies on the Abuse of Reason* (Indianapolis, IN, Liberty Press, 1979)

Hegel, GWF, *The Philosophy of History* (Kitchener, Ont, Batoche Books, 2001)

Hertogh, M, *Nobody's Law. Legal Consciousness and Legal Alienation in Everyday Life* (London, Palgrave. Macmillan, 2018)

——, 'Crime and Custom in the Dutch Construction Industry' (2010) 4 *Legisprudence* 307–26

Hirschl, R, *Comparative Matters. The Renaissance of Comparative Constitutional Law* (Oxford, Oxford University Press, 2014)

Hoecke, M van, 'Methodology of Comparative Legal Research' (2015) 5 *Law and Method* 1–35

Hoecke, M van and Warrington, M, 'Legal Cultures, Legal Paradigms and Legal Doctrine: Towards a New Model for Comparative Law' (1998) 47 *ICLQ* 495–536

Hohfeld, WN, 'Fundamental Legal Conceptions as Applied in Judicial Reasoning' (1917) 26 *Yale Law Journal* 710–70

Holdsworth, WS, *The Historians of Anglo-American Law* (New York, Columbia University Press, 1928)

Hollinger, DA, 'TS Kuhn's Theory of Science and its Implications for History' (1973) 78 *The American Historical Review* 370–93

Houtte, H van, *The Law of International Trade* (London, Sweet & Maxwell, 2002)

Hug, W, 'The History of Comparative Law' (1932) 45 *Harvard Law Review* 1027–70

Husa, J, 'The Future of Legal Families' *Oxford Handbooks Online* (2016) at www.oxfordhandbooks.com/view/10.1093/oxfordhb/9780199935352.001.0001/oxfordhb-9780199935352-e-26

——, *A New Introduction to Comparative Law* (Oxford, Hart Publishing, 2015)

——, 'Methodology of Comparative Law Today: From Paradoxes to Flexibility?' (2006) 58 *Revue internationale de droit comparé* 1095–1117

——, 'Farewell to Functionalism or Methodological Tolerance?' (2003) 3 *Rabels Zeitschrift für ausländisches und internationales Privatrecht* 419–47

Jakab, A, 'Critical Remarks on Alexy's Theory of Principles' in P Cserne et al (eds), *Theatrum Legale Mundi* (Budapest, Societas Sancti Stephani, 2007) 203–20

Kant, I, *Critique of Pure Reason* (Cambridge, Cambridge University Press, 1998)

Kennedy, D, 'Three Globalizations of Law and Legal Thought: 1850–2000' in DM Trubek and A Santos (eds), *The New Law and Economic Development. A Critical Appraisal* (Cambridge, Cambridge University Press, 2010) 19–73

Kiesow, RM, 'Science naturelle et droit dans la deuxième moitié du XIXe siècle en Allemagne' in P Amselek (ed) *Théorie du droit et science* (Paris, PUF, 1994) 187–210

Knapp, V, 'Quelques problèmes méthodologiques dans la science du droit comparé' in K Zweigert and HJ Puttfarken (eds), *Rechtsvergleichung* (Darmstadt, Wissenschaftliche Buchgesellschaft, 1978) 334–44

Kohler, J, *Philosophy of Law* (Boston, MA, The Boston Book Company, 1914)

——, 'De la méthode du droit comparé' in *Congrès international de droit comparé. Tenu á Paris du 31 Juillet au 4 août 1900. Procés-verbaux et documents* (Paris, LGDJ, 1905) 227–30

Koschaker, P, 'L'histoire de droit et le droit comparé sourtout en Allemagne' in *Introduction á l'étude du droit comparé. Recueil d'Études en l'honneur d'Édouard Lambert* (Paris, Sirey-LGDJ, 1938) 274–83

Kroeber, AL and Kluckhohn, C, *Culture. A Critical Review of Concepts and Definitions* (Cambridge, MA, Peabody Museum of American Archeology and Ethnology, 1952)

Kuhn, TS, 'The Natural and the Human Sciences' in DR Hiley, JF Bohman and R Shusterman (eds), *The Interpretive Turn: Philosophy, Science, Culture* (Ithaca, NY, Cornell University Press, 1991) 17–24

——, 'The Road Since Structure' (1990) *PSA: Proceedings of the Biennial Meeting of the Philosophy of Science Association* 3–13

——, 'Commensurability, Comparability, Communicability' (1982) *PSA: Proceedings of the Biennial Meeting of the Philosophy of Science Association* 669–88

——, 'Postscript-1969' in TS Kuhn, *The Structure of Scientific Revolutions* (Chicago, IL, The University of Chicago Press, 1970) 174–210

——, *The Structure of Scientific Revolutions* (Chicago, IL, The University of Chicago Press, 1970)

Kurkchiyan, M, 'Perceptions of Law and Social Order: A Cross-National Comparison of Collective Legal Consciousness' (2012) 26 *Wisconsin International Law Journal* 366–92

——, 'Comparing Legal Cultures: Three Models of Court for Small Civil Cases' (2010) 5 *Journal of Comparative Law* 169–94

Lakatos, I, 'Falsification and the Methodology of Scientific Research Programmes' in I Lakatos and A Musgrave (eds), *Criticisim and the Growth of Knowledge* (Cambridge, Cambridge University Press, 1970) 91–132

Lakatos, I and Musgrave, A (eds), *Criticism and the Growth of Knowledge* (Cambridge, Cambridge University Press, 1970)

Laki, J, *A tudomány természete. Thomas Kuhn és a tudomáyfilozófia történeti fordulata* (Budapest, Gondolat, 2006)

Lambert, E, *Le rôle d'un congrès international de droit comparé en l'an 1931* (Paris, Giard, 1929)

——, 'Conception générale et définition de la science du droit comparé, sa méthode, son histoire: le droit comparé et l'enseignement du droit' in *Congrés international de droit comparé. Tenu á Paris du 31 Juillet au 4 août 1900. Procés-verbaux et documents* (Paris, LGDJ, 1905) 26–60

——, *La fonction du droit civil comparé* (Paris, V Giard et Brière, 1903)

——, *L'histoire traditionalle des XII Tables et les critéres d'inauthenticité des traditions en usage dans l'école de Mommsen* (Lyon, Rey, 1903)

Law, S, 'From Multiple Legal Cultures to One Legal Culture? Thinking About Culture, Tradition and Identity in European Private Law Development' (2015) 31 *Utrecht Journal of International and European Law* 68–89

Legrand, P, 'Negative Comparative Law' (2015) 10 *Journal of Comparative Law* 405–53

——, 'Comparative Legal Studies and the Matter of Authenticity' (2006) 1 *Journal of Comparative Law* 365–460

——, 'The Same and the Different' in P Legrand and R Munday (eds), *Comparative Legal Studies. Traditions and Transitions* (Cambridge, Cambridge University Press, 2003) 240–311

——, 'Against a European Civil Code' (1997) 60 *MLR* 44–63

——, 'European Legal Systems are Not Converging' (1996) 45 *ICLQ* 52–81

——, 'How to Compare Now' (1996) 16 *Legal Studies* 232–42

Leibniz, GW, *Nova methodus discendae docendaeque iurisprudentiae* (Francofurti, Zunnerus, 1667) available at https://digital.slub-dresden.de/werkansicht/dlf/60761/1/

Lepaulle, P, 'Henri Lévy-Ullmann et le droit mondial' in LFJ de la Morandière and M Ancel (eds), *L'oeuvre juridique de Lévy-Ullmann. Contribution á la doctrine moderne sur la science du Droit et le Droit comparé* (Paris, Centre français de droit comparé, 1952) 111–18

Lévy-Ullmann, H, 'The Teaching of Comparative Law: Its Various Objects and Present Tendencies at the University of Paris' (1925) 2 *Journal of the Society of Public Teachers of Law* 16–21

Look, BC, 'Gottfried Wilhelm Leibniz' in EN Zalta (ed), *The Stanford Encyclopedia of Philosophy* (Spring 2020 Edition) at https://plato.stanford.edu/archives/spr2020/entries/leibniz/

Lyall, A, 'Early German Legal Anthropology: Albert Hermann Post and his Questionnaire' (2008) 52 *Journal of African Law* 114–38

Maine, Sir Henry S, *Ancient Law. Its Connection with the Early History of Society and its Relation to Modern Ideas* (London, John Murray, 1908)

Malmström, Å, 'The System of Legal Systems. Notes on a Problem of Classification in Comparative Law' (1969) 13 *Scandinavian Studies in Law* 129–49

Marcum, JA, *Thomas Kuhn's Revolutions. A Historical and an Evolutionary Philosophy of Science?* (London, Bloomsbury, 2015)

——, 'The Evolving Notion and Role of Kuhn's Incommensurability Thesis' in WJ Devlin and A Bokulich (eds), *Kuhn's Structure of Scientific Revolutions. 50 Years On* (Heidelberg, Springer, 2015) 115–34

Markesinis, Sir Basil, 'Learning from Europe and Learning in Europe' in Sir Basil Markesinis (ed), *The Gradual Convergence: Foreign Ideas, Foreign Influences, and the English Law on the Eve of the 21st century* (Oxford, Clarendon Press, 1994) 1–32

Masterman, M, 'The Nature of Paradigm' in I Lakatos and A Musgrave (eds.), *Criticism and the Growth of Knowledge* (Cambridge, Cambridge University Press, 1970) 59–90

Mattei, U, 'The Cold War and Comparative Law: A Reflection on the Politics of Intellectual Discipline' (2017) 65 *The American Journal of Comparative Law* 567–608

——, 'Three Patterns of Law: Taxonomy and Change in the World's Legal Systems' (1997) 45 *The American Journal of Comparative Law* 5–44

Mezey, N, 'Law as Culture' (2001) 13 *Yale Journal of Law and Humanities* 35–67

Michaels, R, 'The Functional Method of Comparative Law' in M Reimann and R Zimmermann (eds), *The Oxford Handbook of Comparative Law* (Oxford, Oxford University Press, 2006) 339–82

Mikus, M, 'Informal Networks and Interstitial Arenas of Power in the Making of Civil Society Law in Serbia' (2015) 57 *Sociologija* 571–92

Mohr, JW and Rawlings, CM, 'Formal Models of Culture' in JR Hall, L Grindstaff and Ming-Cheng Lo (ed), *Handbook of Cultural Sociology* (London, New York, Routledge, 2010) 119–29

Montesquieu, C de S *L'esprit des lois* (1758)

Moore, SF, 'Law and Social Change: The Semi-Autonomous Social Field as an Appropriate Subject of Study' (1973) 7 *Law and Society Review* 719–46

Morandière, LFJ de la, 'Henri Lévy-Ullmann' in LFJ de la Morandiére and Marc Ancel (eds), *L'oeuvre juridique de Lévy-Ullmann. Contribution á la doctrine moderne sur la science du Droit et le Droit comparé* (Paris, Centre français de droit comparé, 1952) 11–15

Nelken, D, 'Comparative Legal Research and Legal Culture: Facts, Approaches and Values' (2016) 12 *Annual Review of Social Sciences* 45–62

——, 'Using Legal Culture: Purposes and Problems' (2010) 5 *Journal of Comparative Law* 1–39

—— (ed), *Comparing Legal Cultures* (London, Routledge, 1997)

——, 'Disclosing/Invoking Legal Culture: An Introduction' (1995) 4 *Social and Legal Studies* 435–52

Nietzsche, F, 'Philosophy During the Tragic Age of the Greeks' in F Nietzsche, *Early Greek Philosophy and Other Essays* (New York, Macmillan, 1911) 71–170

Ortega y Gasset, J, *Korunk feladata* (Budapest, ABC, 1944)

Osakwe, C, 'Introduction: The Greening of Socialist Law as an Academic Discipline' (1987) 61 *Tulane Law Review* 1257–78

Otetelisanu, A, 'Les conceptions de ME Lambert sur le droit comparé' in *Introduction à l'étude du droit comparé. Recueil d'Études en l'honneur d'Édouard Lambert* (Paris, Sirey-LGDJ, 1938) 39–46

Øyrehagen Sunde, J, 'Live and Let Die. An Essay Concerning Legal-Cultural Understanding' in M Adams and D Heirbaut (eds), *The Method and Culture of Comparative Law* (Oxford, Hart Publishing, 2014) 221–34

Peschka, V, 'A polgári jogelméleti gondolkodás a XX. század első felében' in C Varga (ed), *Jog és filozófia* (Budapest, Akadémia Kiadó, 1981) 9–53

Péteri, Z, 'A jogi kultúrák összehasonlításának előtörténetéhez' (2007) 48 *Állam- és Jogtudomány* 509–26

——, 'Paradigmaváltás a jogösszehasonlításban?' in K Raffai (ed), *Placet experiri. Ünnepi tanulmányok Bánrévy Gábor tiszteletére* (Budapest, Print Trade, 2004) 228–38

——, 'A jogösszehasonlítás kezdetei az angol jogtudományban' (1975) 18 *Állam- és Jogtudomány* 393–414

——, 'Goals and Methods of Legal Comparison' in Z Péteri (ed), *The Comparison of Law – La comparaison de droit* (Budapest, Akadémiai Kiadó, 1974) 45–58

——, 'Some Aspects of Sociological Approach in Comparative Law' in Z Péteri (ed), *Hungarian Law-Comparative Law/Droit hongrois-droit comparé* (Budapest, Akadémiai Kiadó, 1970) 75–94

——, 'Gustav Radbruch und einige Fragen der relativistischen Rechtsphilosophie' (1960) 2 *Acta Iuridica Academiae Scientiarum Hungariae* 113–60

Picot, G and Daguin, F, 'Circulaire' in *Congrès international de droit comparé. Procès-verbaux des scéances et document. Tome premier* (Paris, LGDJ, 1905) 7–9

Pirie, F, 'Comparison in the Anthropology and History of Law' (2014) 9 *Journal of Comparative Law* 88–107

Pollock, Sir Frederick, 'History of Comparative Jurisprudence' (1903) 5 *Journal of the Society of Comparative Jurisprudence* 74–89

——, 'English Opportunities in Historic and Comparative Jurisprudence' in Sir Frederick Pollock, *Oxford Lectures and Other Discourses* (London, Macmillan 1890) 37–64

——, 'Droit comparé: prolégomènes de son histoire' in *Congrés international de droit comparé. Tenu á Paris du 31 juillet au 4 août 1900. Procés-verbaux et documents* (Paris, LGDJ, 1905) 248–61

Pollock, Sir Frederick and Maitland, FW, *The History of English Law*, vols 1–2 (Cambridge, Cambridge University Press, 1968)

Popper, K, *The Logic of Scientific Discovery* (London, Unwin Hyman, 1990)

——, 'Normal Science and Its Dangers' in I Lakatos and A Musgrave (eds), *Criticism and the Growth of Knowledge* (Cambridge, Cambridge University Press, 1970) 51–58

Post, AH, 'Ethnological Jurisprudence' (1891) 2 *The Monist* 31–40

Pound, R, 'Scope and Purpose of Sociological Jurisprudence [continued]' (1911/12) 25 *Harvard Law Review* 140–68

Rabel, E, *Das Recht des Warenkaufs. Eine rechtsvergleichende Darstellung*, vol 1 (Berlin, Boston, de Gruyter, 2011)

—— 'On Institutes for Comparative Law' (1947) 47 *Columbia Law Review* 227–37

——, 'Aufgabe und Notwendigkeit der Rechtsvergleichung' (1924) *Rheinische Zeitschrift für Zivil- und Prozessrecht* 279–301

Radbruch, G, 'Anselme Feuerbach, precurseur du droit comparé' in *Introduction á l'étude du droit comparé. Recueil d'Études en l'honneur d'Édouard Lambert* (Paris, Sirey-LGDJ, 1938) 284–91

Reimann, M, 'The Progress and Failure of Comparative Law in the Second Half of the Twentieth Century' (2002) 50 *The American Journal of Comparative Law* 671–700

Rheinstein, M, 'Book review' (1957) 24 *The University of Chicago Law Review* 597–606

——, 'In Memory of Ernst Rabel' (1956) 5 *The American Journal of Comparative Law* 185–96

——, 'Comparative Law and Conflicts of Law in Germany' (1934–35) 2 *The University of Chicago Law Review* 232–69

Rezsohazy, R, *Sociologie des valeurs* (Paris, Armand Colin, 2006)

Rodiére, R, *Introduction au droit comparé* (Paris, 1979)

Runciman, S, *A History of the Crusades*, vol I (Cambridge, Cambridge University Press, 1951)

Sacco, R, 'One Hundred Years of Comparative Law" (2001) 75 *Tulane Law Review* 1159–76

Sajó, A, 'Pluralism in Post-Communist Law' (2003) 44 *Acta Juridica Hungarica* 1–20

Saleilles, R, 'Rapport sur l'utilité, le but et le programme du congrès' *Congrès international de droit comparé. Procès-verbaux des scéances et document. Tome premier* (Paris, LGDJ, 1905) 9–17

——, 'Conception et objet de la science du droit comparé' in *Congrés international de droit comparé. Tenu á Paris du 4 Juillet au 4 août 1900. Procés-verbaux et documents* (Paris, LGDJ, 1905) 167–89

Samuel, G, *An Introduction to Comparative Law Theory and Method* (Oxford, Hart Publishing, 2014)

Schiek, D, Waddington, L and Bell, M (eds), *Cases, Materials and Text on National, Supranational and International Non-Discrimination Law* (Oxford, Hart Publishing, 2007)

Schlesinger, RB, 'The Common Core of Legal Systems. An Emerging Subject of Comparative Study' in K Zweigert and HJ Puttfarken (eds), *Rechtsvergleichung* (Darmstadt, Wissenschaftliche Buchgesellschaft, 1978) 249–69

——, *Comparative Law. Cases-Texts-Materials* (New York, Foundation Press, 1970)

—— (ed), *The Formation of Contracts: A Study of the Common Core of Legal Systems* (New York, Dobbs Ferry, 1968)

Schnitzer, AF, *De la diversité et de l'unification du droit* (Bâle, Verlag für Recht und Gesellschaft AG, 1946)

Schorske, CE, 'Politics and the Psyche: Schnitzler and Hofmannsthal' in CE Schorske, *Fin-de-siécle Vienna* (New York, Vintage Books, 1981) 3–23

——, 'Gustav Klimt: Painting and the Crisis of the Liberal Ego' in CE Schorske, *Fin-de-siécle Vienna* (New York, Vintage Books, 1981) 208–78

Schott, R, 'Main Trends in German Ethnological Jurisprudence and Legal Ethnology' (1982) 14 *Journal of Legal Pluralism* 37–68

Schwenzer, I, 'Development of Comparative Law in Germany, Switzerland and Austria' in M Reimann and R Zimmermann (eds), *The Oxford Handbook of Comparative Law* (Oxford, Oxford University Press, 2006) 69–106

Shalakany, A, 'Sanhuri, and the historical origins of comparative law in the Arab World' in A Riles (ed), *Rethinking the Masters of Comparative Law* (Oxford, Hart Publishing, 2001) 152–88

Shapin, S, 'Kuhn's Structure: A Moment in Modern Naturalism' in WJ Devlin and A Bokulich (eds), *Kuhn's Structure of Scientific Revolutions. 50 Years On* (Heidelberg, Springer, 2015) 11–21

Shariff, F, 'Power Relations and Legal Pluralism. An Examination of "Strategies of Struggles" Amongst the Santal Adivasi of Indian and Bangladesh' (2008) 57 *Journal of Legal Pluralism and Unofficial Law* 1–43

Sharrock, W and Read, R, *Kuhn. Philosopher of Scientific Revolution* (Cambridge, Polity, 2002)

Siems, M *Comparative Law* (Cambridge, Cambridge University Press, 2014)

Silbey, SS, 'Legal Culture and Cultures of Legality' in JR Hall, L Grindstaff and Lo, MC (eds), *Handbook of Cultural Sociology* 472–76

Sintonen, M, 'Scientific and Conceptual Revolutions' in Z Bankowski (ed), *Revolutions in Law and Legal Thought* (Aberdeen, Aberdeen University Press, 1991) 11–21

——, 'Pragmatic Metatheory for Legal Science' in A Peczenik, L Lindahl and B van Roermund (eds), *Theory of Legal Science* (Dordrecht, D Reidel Publishing Company, 1984) 39–52

Snyder, FG, 'Anthropology, Dispute Processes and Law. A Critical Introduction' (1981) 8 *British Journal of Law and Society* 140–80

Stein, P, *Legal Evolution* (Cambridge, Cambridge University Press, 1988)

Sugiyama, N, 'Essai d'une conception synthètique du droit comparé' in *Introduction à l'étude du droit comparé. Recueil d'Études en l'honneur d'Édouard Lambert* (Paris, Sirey-LGDJ, 1938) 50–60

Szabó, I, 'Elemér Balogh et l'Académie internationale de droit comparé' in I Szabó and Z Péteri (eds), *Comparative Law – Droit comparé. Selected Essays for the 10th International Congress of Comparative Law* (Budapest, Akadémiai Kiadó, 1978) 11–22

Taylor, C, 'Interpretation and the Sciences of Man' (1971) 25 *The Review of Metaphysics* 3–51

Teubner, G (ed), *Global Law without a State* (Aldershot, Dartmouth, 1997)

Tushnet, M, *Advanced Introduction to Comparative Constitutional Law* (Cheltenham, Elgar, 2018)

—— (ed), *Comparative Constitutional Law* (Cheltenham, Elgar, 2017)

Uusitalo, J, 'Legal Dogmatics and the Concept of a Scientific Revolution' in Z Bankowski (ed), *Revolutions in Law and Legal Thought* (Aberdeen, Aberdeen University Press, 1991) 113–21

Varano, V and Barsotti, V, *La tradizione giuridica occidentale* (Torino, G Giappichelli, 2014)

Varga, Cs, '*Theatrum legale mundi*: On Legal Systems Classified' in C Varga, *Comparative Legal Cultures* (Budapest, Szent István Társulat, 2012) 49–76

——, 'Comparative Legal Cultures?' (2007) 48 *Acta Juridica Hungarica* 95–113

Villa, V, 'Theories of Natural Sciences and Theories of Legal Science. Models and Analogies' in *ARSP Beiheft 25* (Stuttgart, Franz Steiner Verlag, 1985) 110–15

Villey, M, *La formation de la pensée juridique moderne* (Paris, PUF, 2003)

Vinogradoff, Sir Paul, 'Methods of Jurisprudence' in Sir Paul Vinogradoff, *Custom and Right* (Union, NJ, The Lawbook Exchange, Ltd, 2000) 1–20

——, 'The Teaching of Sir Henry Sumner Maine' in *The Collected Papers of Paul Vinogradoff I* (New York, The Legal Classics Library, 1995) 173–89

——, 'Historical Types of International Law' in *The Collected Papers of Paul Vinogradoff II* (New York, The Legal Classics Library, 1995) 248–58

——, *Outlines of Historical Jurisprudence I–II* (London, Oxford University Press, 1920–22)

Von Zachariä, 'Ueber den Zweck dieser Zeitschrift' (1829) 1 *Kritische Zeitschrift für Rechtswissenschaft und Gesetzgebung des Auslandes* 1–27

Vuković, D, 'The Hollowing Out of Institutions: Law- and Policymaking in Contemporary Serbia' in B Fekete and F Gárdos-Orosz (eds), *Central and Eastern European Socio-Political and Legal Transition Revisited* (Frankfurt, Peter Lang, 2017) 155–73

Wahl, E, 'Le Kaiser-Wilhelm-Institut für Auslaendisches und Internationales Privatrecht à Berlin' in *Introduction à l'étude du droit comparé – Recueil d'Études en l'honneur d'Édouard Lambert* (Paris, Sirey-LGDJ, 1938) 673–80

Weber, M, *Staatssoziologie* (Berlin, Duncker und Humblot, 1956)

Wehberg, H, 'Internationale Vereinigung für Vergleichende Rechtswissenschaft und Volkwirtschaftslehre' in *Introduction á l'étude du droit comparé. Recueil d'Études en l'honneur d'Édouard Lambert* (Paris, Sirey-LGDJ, 1938) 664–68

Whittaker, S, 'Le rayonnement de René David' in *Hommage à René David* (Paris, Association Henri Capitant-Dalloz, 2012) 65–71

Wild, AH de, 'Progress in Legal Science' in *ARSP Beiheft 25* (Stuttgart, Franz Steiner Verlag, 1985) 119–21

Windelband, W, *An Introduction to Philosophy* (London, T Fisher Unwin, 1921)

Wolin, SS, 'Paradigms and Political Theories' in P King and BC Parekh (eds), *Politics and Experience. Essays Presented to Professor Michael Oakeshott on the Occasion of His Retirement* (Cambridge, Cambridge University Press, 1968) 125–52

Wróblewski, J, 'Paradigm of Legal Dogmatics and the Legal Sciences' in Z Ziembiński (ed), *Polish Contributions to the Theory and Philosophy of Law* (Amsterdam, Rodopi, 1987) 75–88

Zajtay, I, 'Réflexions sur l'évolution du droit comparé' in H Bernstein, U Drobnig and H Kötz (eds), *Festschrift für Konrad Zweigert* (Tübingen, JCB Mohr, 1981) 595–602

——, 'Henri Lévy-Ullmann professeur du droit comparé' in LJ de la Morandière and M Ancel (eds), *L'oeuvre juridique de Lévy-Ullmann. Contribution á la doctrine moderne sur la science du Droit et le Droit comparé* (Paris, Centre français de droit comparé, 1952) 105–10

Zuleta-Puceiro, E, 'Scientific Paradigms and the Growth of Legal Knowledge' in *ARSP Beiheft 25* (Stuttgart, Franz Steiner Verlag, 1985) 126–34

——, 'Legal Dogmatics as a Scientific Paradigm' in A Peczenik, L Lindahl and B van Roermund (eds), *Theory of Legal Science* (Dordrecht, D Reidel Publishing Company, 1984) 13–24

Zweigert, K, 'Methodological Problems in Comparative Law' (1972) 4 *Israel Law Review* 465–74

——, 'Zur Methode der Rechtsvergleichung' (1960) 13 *Studium Generale* 193–200

——, 'Zur Lehre von den Rechtskreisen' in KH Nadelmann, AT von Meheren and J Hazard (eds), *XXth Century Comparative and Conflicts Law Legal Essays in Honor of Hessel E Yntema* (Leiden, AW Sythoff, 1961) 42–55

Zweigert, K and Kötz, H, *An Introduction to Comparative Law* (Oxford, Oxford University Press, 1998)

—— and ——, *Einführung in die Rechtsvergleichung* (Tübingen, JCB Mohr, 1971)

Zweigert, K and Siehr, K, 'Jhering's Influence on the Development of Comparative Legal Method' (1971) 2 *The American Journal of Comparative Law* 215–31

Index

Note: Alphabetical arrangement is word-by-word, where a group of letters followed by a space is filed before the same group of letters followed by a letter, eg 'civil law will appear before 'civilised nations'. In determining alphabetical arrangement, initial articles and prepositions are ignored.

Lightning Source UK Ltd.
Milton Keynes UK
UKHW020618301122
413110UK00006B/158

9 781509 946969